THE POWER OF UNEARNED SUFFERING

Religion and Race

Series Editor:

Monica R. Miller, Lehigh University
Anthony B. Pinn, Rice University

The local/global connections between religion and race are complex, interrelated, ever changing, and undeniable. Religion and Race bridges these multifaceted dimensions within a context of cultural complexity and increasing socio-political realities of identity and difference in a multi-disciplinary manner that offers a strong platform for scholars to examine the relationship between religion and race. This series is committed to a range of social science and humanities approaches, including media studies, cultural studies, and feminist and queer methods, and welcomes books from a variety of global and cultural contexts from the modern period to projects considering the dynamics of the "postmodern" context. While the series will privilege monographs, it will also consider exceptional edited volumes. Religion and Race seeks to impact historical and contemporary cultural and socio-political conversations through comparative scholarly examinations that tap the similarities and distinctions of race across geographies within the context of a variety of religious traditions and practices.

Title in the Series

The Power of Unearned Suffering: The Roots and Implications of Martin Luther King, Jr.'s Theodicy, by Mika Edmondson

THE POWER OF UNEARNED SUFFERING

The Roots and Implications of Martin Luther King, Jr.'s Theodicy

Mika Edmondson

LEXINGTON BOOKS
Lanham • Boulder • New York • London

Published by Lexington Books
An imprint of The Rowman & Littlefield Publishing Group, Inc.
4501 Forbes Boulevard, Suite 200, Lanham, Maryland 20706
www.rowman.com

Unit A, Whitacre Mews, 26-34 Stannary Street, London SE11 4AB

Copyright © 2017 by Lexington Books

MLK quotations reprinted by arrangement with The Heirs to the Estate of Martin Luther King Jr., c/o Writers House as agent for the proprietor New York, NY. © Martin Luther King Jr. © Renewed Coretta Scott King.

All rights reserved. No part of this book may be reproduced in any form or by any electronic or mechanical means, including information storage and retrieval systems, without written permission from the publisher, except by a reviewer who may quote passages in a review.

British Library Cataloguing in Publication Information Available

Library of Congress Cataloging-in-Publication Data
The hardback edition of this book was previously cataloged by the Library of Congress as follows:

Names: Edmondson, Mika, author.
Title: The power of unearned suffering : the roots and implications of Martin Luther King, Jr.'s theodicy / Mika Edmondson.
Description: Lanham : Lexington Books, 2017. | Series: Religion and race | Includes bibliographical references and index.
Identifiers: LCCN 2016052513
Subjects: LCSH: King, Martin Luther, Jr., 1929-1968. | Theodicy. | Suffering--Religious aspects--Christianity.
Classification: LCC BX6455.K56 E36 2017 | DDC 231/.8092--dc23 LC record available at https://lccn.loc.gov/2016052513

ISBN 978-1-4985-3732-2 (cloth: alk. paper)
ISBN 978-1-4985-3734-6 (pbk.: alk. paper)
ISBN 978-1-4985-3733-9 (electronic)

∞™ The paper used in this publication meets the minimum requirements of American National Standard for Information Sciences Permanence of Paper for Printed Library Materials, ANSI/NISO Z39.48-1992.

Printed in the United States of America

To Michael and Shirley Edmondson

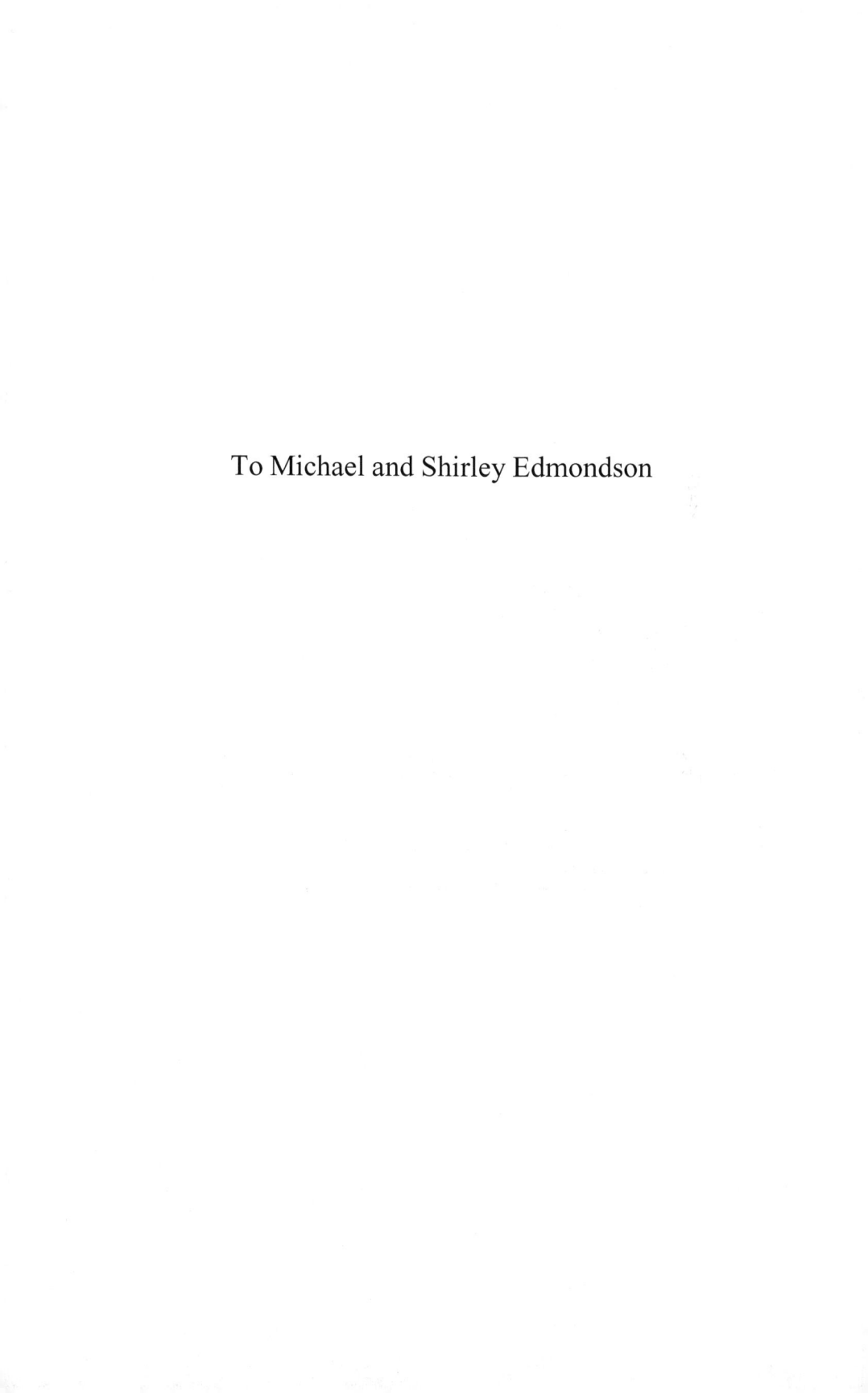

CONTENTS

Acknowledgments ix
Introduction xi

1: ROOTS AND DEVELOPMENT OF KING'S THEODICY

1 Family and Cultural Roots 3
2 Black Church Roots 25
3 Early Engagement with Protestant Liberalism 59
4 Later Engagement with Protestant Liberalism 93

2: CRITICS AND CONTEMPORARY RELEVANCE OF KING'S THEODICY

5 The Black Humanists 123
6 The Womanists 151

Conclusion: Contemporary Relevance 185
Bibliography 213
Index 225
About the Author 229

ACKNOWLEDGMENTS

I would like to thank my precious wife Christina and wonderful daughters Zoe and Shiloh, whom I love from the depth of my soul. To my mother, whose love and wisdom I will always cherish. To my brothers Vernon and Michael, my in-laws Mike and Brenda Barland, and extended family who have always offered words of encouragement at just the right times. To my New City Fellowship church family who have been more patient and gracious than I deserve. To Rufus Burrow, Jr. and Lewis Baldwin who are giants in the field of King Studies, yet always made time for a curious student. Dr. Burrow's amazing article "The Doctrine of Unearned Suffering" sowed the seeds that flowered into this project. To Dean Ronald Feenstra, the entire faculty of Calvin Theological Seminary, and countless other professors whose skill and knowledge have helped bring me to this point. To the countless other friends who offered hugs at just the right time and smiles at just the right time and most importantly prayers at just the right time, your contributions have meant more to me than you know. To my late grandmother Lucy Mae Sales, whose strength reminds me of Delia Lindsay King. You taught me how to trust Jesus with my tears. And finally, to my late father Michael Vernon Edmondson who never met a stranger. You taught me that the most important legacy is love.

INTRODUCTION

On January 10, 1958, a year after the famous Montgomery Bus Boycott, Karolyn L. Trimble wrote a letter to the young Martin Luther King, Jr. with a pressing concern. She asked, "Rev. King . . . Why is it that God has let Negroes suffer so? . . . We have been taught from very early ages that God loves everybody. But as I take inventory of the races I can see something strange."[1] This penetrating question has always stood at the heart of the black experience in America. Often without the benefit of formal theological training, enslaved and oppressed black believers have long wrestled with life's most painful contradictions. Their answers took the form of prayers, sermons, spirituals, humor, and activism and offer one of the most important theological legacies of the American church. Beneath the sweltering sun of southern cotton fields, they shouldered on with the hope that the omnipotent God could "make a way out of no way"—that, because of Christ, God would somehow bring good from the evils inflicted on them. This doesn't mean suffering itself is good. But in light of the cross of Jesus Christ, believers have held that God's omnipotent goodness will have the final say over every form of suffering, no matter how severe. This hope in God's redemptive purposes in suffering has sustained black Christians through historic brutalities like chattel slavery, Jim Crow, the lynching tree, and segregation.

King inherited this 250-year-old redemptive suffering tradition through family and church influences, developed it using resources from the academy, and applied it to the freedom struggle. For King, the cross of Christ represented the definitive proof of God's purpose to bring redemptive good out of suffering, and the guiding example of how to actively engage suffering towards a redemptive goal. In sermons, speeches, and articles he often noted that "unearned suffering is redemptive" and successfully deployed this cross-centered theodical vision throughout his participation in the Civil Rights Movement of the 1950s and 1960s. King arguably represents the apex of the redemptive suffering tradition, a cross-centered, clearly formulated, battle-tested theodical vision that the church needs today. In the face of the overwhelming pain caused by police brutality, mass incarceration, disparities in housing and healthcare and the many challenges the black community and church face, we are once again asking "Why Lord?" What is the meaning of black suffering and how are Christian believers called to respond in the face of it? That's precisely why a book-length study on King's theodicy is so vital today, not because King's theodicy offers all of the answers to the myriad of complex problems the black church and community faces. It definitely does not. But because it offers a hopeful articulation of God's purposes in black suffering and clear direction for how to engage it.

Although a number of works explore King's redemptive suffering formula as an atonement theology,[2] few deal with it according to this additional dimension, as an answer to the problem of evil.[3] King, who was no stranger to unearned suffering, considered the problem of evil to be "the most baffling problem facing the theist."[4] Though he was reluctant to speak of his personal trials, King and his family were the targets of daily death threats, two house bombings, numerous unjust imprisonments, multiple beatings, and a near fatal stabbing.[5] He frequently employed the redemptive goal of suffering as a positive explanation of God's intentions in allowing the great hardships faced by himself, his people, and the participants within the Civil Rights movement.[6] Therefore, the lack of focused attention on King's use of the redemptive suffering motif as a theodicy constitutes a notable gap within King scholarship.

The works that do mention King's theodicy tend to treat it in a peripheral and oversimplified way, not considering its central place in his thinking or the diverse streams of influences which converged to make King's approach unique.[7] Often scholars have stressed the impact of Protestant liberalism at the expense of King's black church heritage. For instance, Kenneth L. Smith and Ira Zepp Jr's *Search for the Beloved Community: The Thinking of Martin Luther King Jr.* ranks among the most significant works on King's theology. Furthering the effort to analyze King as a major theologian,[8] Smith and Zepp carefully trace King's intellectual development during his matriculation at Crozer Seminary and Boston University.[9] They focus on his early engagement with Protestant liberalism, the Social Gospel movement, the Christian Realism of Reinhold Niebuhr, and the theistic personalism of Edgar Brightman and Harold DeWolf. However, in an otherwise comprehensive treatment, Smith and Zepp almost entirely neglect the influence of the black church on King's thought.[10] Their research overemphasized King's published works which were tailored to the sensibilities of white sympathizers who would not have appreciated King's cultural roots. So Smith and Zepp mistook Protestant liberalism as King's fundamental theological and intellectual source.[11] In subsequent editions of their work, Ira Zepp himself readily acknowledges this crucial oversight. "There is no question that King's evangelical liberal Christianity was deeply affected by his black church heritage, which was the heart of the man . . . . And it is now our great good fortune that this 'heart' has been brilliantly delineated by several King scholars over the last decade and a half." [12]

Against the tide of voices that claim Protestant liberalism as King's primary theological influence, James Cone highlighted the faith of the black church as King's most important influence.[13] He argues that King's engagement with Protestant liberalism, the black integrationist tradition, Gandhi's method of nonviolent direct action, and Thoreau's philosophical justification of civil disobedience should all be interpreted in light of the black church tradition which he says, "decisively influenced the development and final shape of King's theology."[14] Cone rightfully views Protestant liberalism as a tool King critically employed to give broader and more acceptable expression to the black church spirituality he inherited through his upbringing.[15] However, in his several theological treatments on King, Cone gives little attention to King's redemptive suffering concept as a theodicy. In his most extensive work on King, *Martin & Malcolm & America: A Dream or A Nightmare,* Cone only briefly comments on the central role of the cross and black suffering in the formation of King's faith. He simply asserts that, for King, the cross of Christ is God's redemptive and paradigmatic revelation of unmerited suffering.[16] By contrast, in *The Cross and the Lynching Tree* Cone devotes an entire chapter to King's understanding of the cross and redemptive suffering[17] specifically mentioning King's formulation as a response to "the problem of evil which has haunted Christians throughout history."[18] However, neither of these otherwise extensive works specifically detail how King's cultural influences gave rise to his famous redemptive suffering formula.

Among writers that focus on King's theodicy, Lewis Baldwin devotes an entire chapter to the subject in his landmark work *There is a Balm in Gilead: the Cultural Roots of Martin Luther King Jr.* In a chapter entitled "King's Black Messianic Vision" Baldwin describes King's theodicy as a species of black messianism. According to Baldwin, King held that black American suffering has some grand divine purpose and unique redemptive significance for America and the world.[19] Baldwin notes the impact of diverse influences upon King's approach from the black church to Gandhi, Reinhold Niebuhr, and British Historian Arnold J. Toynbee—all of whom postulated that black Americans have a unique capacity to transform Western Civilization through the message of non-violence. Rufus Burrow Jr. advanced the discussion of King's theodicy even further with his brief but very important article "The Doctrine of Unearned Suffering." There, Burrow examined the complex and ambivalent relationship King had with theodical concepts like divine finitism. He argues that King's theodicy represents a careful blend of black cultural and formal academic influences. King's cultural influences provided the basic foundations and trajectory of his theodicy which he developed using liberal academic sources. Burrow also clarified a common misconception about King's theodicy, namely that King did not believe suffering itself was redemptive. Rather, King held that the right kind of engagement with suffering could be redemptive, a crucial point we will return to later.[20] Although Baldwin and Burrow's work have contributed much to our understanding of this idea, to date, there has been no book-length treatment of this central area of King's thought.

Among black humanist scholars, the late William R. Jones and Anthony Pinn offer the most comprehensive critiques of King's theodicy. Jones' *Is God a White Racist?* represents a landmark refutation of traditional redemptive suffering theodicies. There, he targets King through a detailed analysis of the black messianic theodicy of Joseph Washington.[21] Jones questions whether black suffering can be considered redemptive without the presence of a corresponding exaltation/liberation event which terminates the excessive suffering and vindicates the victim as innocent. Without the presence of an exaltation event, Jones suggests that redemptive suffering theodicies are left with undesirable possibility that black suffering is somehow deserved. Jones contends that Washington (and

INTRODUCTION

King) cannot rule out this possibility. Therefore, he concludes that King's theodicy unwittingly promotes a "slave soteriology," the inevitability and perpetuity of black suffering for the sake of white liberation.[22] Anthony Pinn continued the black humanist critique of King in his important monograph *I Wonder as I Wander*. There, Pinn traces African American responses to the problem of evil through the nineteenth and twentieth century, seeking to advance the black humanist cause by demonstrating the weaknesses in traditional black theodicies. For Pinn, redemptive suffering ranks among the most philosophically and morally unappealing approaches to theodicy. He alleges that King's theodicy undermines black resistance to oppression by calling blacks to wait passively for God to deliver them rather than actively strive for their own social liberation. He laments the black community's longstanding refusal to question the existence of God as a possible answer to the problem of black suffering.[23]

Among womanist theologians, Delores Williams follows Joanne Carlson Brown and Rebecca Parker's feminist critique of King's theodicy.[24] Brown and Parker suggest that King's theodicy reflects a moral influence type theory which moves the hearts of perpetrators through their victims' willing acceptance of violence. They characterize redemptive suffering theodicies as "martyr theology" which views suffering as essential to change oppressors and downplays their responsibility to choose non-violence.[25] Williams also assumes that redemptive suffering theodicies make unjust suffering inevitable and prioritizes the transformation of evildoers at the expense of their victims. She suggests that this teaching invariably acculturates black women "passively to accept their own oppression and suffering."[26] Fellow womanist Jacquelyn Grant concedes that King's redemptive suffering theodicy was useful as a survival strategy that helped blacks make sense out of seemingly hopeless life situations. However, she alleges that it is unable to provide sufficient substance for liberation.[27] As it stands, there have been almost no direct responses to the powerful critiques leveled by black humanist and womanist theologians. These important critiques need to be sufficiently addressed before King's theodicy can be responsibly applied to the contemporary social situation.

This book traces the roots of Martin Luther King Jr.'s redemptive suffering theodicy, reconsidering its relevance to contemporary discussions about theodicy among black theologians and within the black church. I argue that King's redemptive suffering theodicy successfully answers the challenges raised by its recent humanist and womanist critics.

Through its emphasis on the moral responsibility of God's free agents and the matchless power of God, King's version of the concept provides powerful motivation, guidance, and hope for liberative social action. King's theodicy addresses the concerns raised by womanist critics by emphasizing a moral influence approach to the cross which calls black women to resist oppression as empowered moral agents. By identifying their suffering with the suffering of Christ, King's theodicy also protects the dignity of black women who have suffered while resisting oppression, describing them as empowered witnesses rather than as mere victims. Finally, King's theodicy provides a powerful and practical resource to help guide the black church and community in its redemptive engagement with contemporary forms of suffering.

The book is divided into two main sections. Part 1 explores King's theodicy in its own historical context in order to gain a more accurate understanding of its roots and development. Chapters 1 and 2 examine the black experience and the black church as formative influences on King's theodicy. They intend to situate King's theodicy within the black church tradition. Special emphasis will be given to the black Baptist pastoral, music, and prayer traditions which informed his personalist conceptions of God and theodicy. Chapters 3 and 4 examine King's critical engagement and appropriation of Protestant liberal concepts to his theodicy. Special focus will be placed on the personalist philosophies of Edgar Brightman and Harold DeWolf, especially as it relates to concepts such as divine goodness, omnipotence, and infinity. These chapters mean to show that King's critically engaged (rather than uncritically adopted) the categories of Protestant liberalism in order to develop the basic theodicy he inherited from his traditional black Baptist roots. Although he drew deeply from the wells of liberalism, King consistently reformulated or rejected ideas that were unhelpful to liberation and out of step with his traditional black Baptist sensibilities. Overall, these chapters help establish that King's theodicy has the cultural resources to address the black communal context through which the black humanist and womanist theologians approach their work. King's redemptive suffering theodicy was forged amidst the proving ground of black suffering and therefore has the cultural capital to address the contemporary black social situation.

Having gained an understanding of King's theodicy in its own context, Part 2 applies it to the modern black social situation. Chapters 5–6 consider whether King's theodicy answers the modern humanist and womanist critics who accuse it of inculcating passivity and glorifying violence. Sensitive to my own limitations around fully understanding the suffering experiences of black women in America, I draw on insights from Joanne Marie Terrell, Karen Baker-Fletcher, and Katie Cannon to make the case that King's theodicy promotes liberation for black women. The final chapter considers how King's theodicy might be applied today. Overall, I hope this project will offer a more detailed understanding of this core aspect of King's thought and contribute to the ever growing field of King cultural studies. But even more than that, I hope it will remind the weak, weary, and downtrodden of the age-old hope that God still uses the cross Christ bore and the crosses we bear to bring freedom and liberation.

NOTES

1. Karolyn Trimble, "A Letter from Karolyn Trimble to Martin Luther King, Jr.," January 10, 1958, King Papers, Boston University, Boston Mass.; Lewis V. Baldwin, *There Is a Balm in Gilead: The Cultural Roots of Martin Luther King, Jr* (Minneapolis: Fortress Press, 1991), 230.

2. See especially Brian Brandt. *The Theology of the Cross and Ethic of Redemptive Suffering in the Life and Work of Martin Luther King, Jr.* Thesis (PhD)—Loyola University of Chicago, 2002. Brandt's helpful work focuses on King's formulation as a modern reworking of Abelardian atonement theory distinct from the standard Abelardian appropriations of early twentieth-century Protestant liberalism.

3. See Helen J. Losse, *Making All Things New The Redemptive Value of Unmerited Suffering in the Life and Works of Martin Luther King, Jr.* Thesis (M.A.) Wake Forest University. Dept. of Liberal Studies, 2000. Losse's insightful and detailed treatment is mostly biographical in nature. Although she acknowledges the various streams of influence on King's thought she does not undertake a serious scholarly consideration of them. Rather she chronicles the final turbulent years of King's life proving that, through it all, he maintained his hope unearned suffering is redemptive. See also William Prosser, *The Practical Theodicies of Dietrich Bonhoeffer and Martin Luther King Jr.: the Minority Struggle against the Majority*. Spartanburg, S.C.: Wofford College, 2010.

4. Martin Luther King Jr., "Religion's Answer to the Problem of Evil," in Martin Luther King, *The Papers of Martin Luther King, Jr.: Volume I: Called to Serve, January 1929–June 1951*, ed. Clayborne Carson, Ralph E. Luker, and Penny A. Russell, 1st ed. (University of California Press, 1992). In general, theodicies have sought to offer a positive account of why the omnipotent and

perfectly good God might allow the kinds of suffering that we see and experience in this world—especially the unmerited suffering incurred by the innocent.

5. In the spring of 1960 the editors of the *Christian Century*, aware of the constant threats against King's life, urged him for a submission on suffering and faith. His comments are brief so as to avoid the appearance of having a "martyr's complex." However, he reluctantly admits, "I have been arrested five times and put in Alabama jails. My home has been bombed twice. A day seldom passes that my family and I are not the recipients of threats of death. I have been the victim of a near fatal stabbing. So in a real sense I have been battered by the storms of persecution." Martin Luther King Jr., "Suffering and faith," *Christian Century* 101, no. 22 (July 4, 1984) in Martin Luther King Jr., *A Testament of Hope: The Essential Writings and Speeches of Martin Luther King Jr.*, ed. James M. Washington, (San Francisco: HarperCollins, 1991), 42.

6. King often described his approach to the problem of evil using the mantra "unmerited suffering is redemptive," a hopeful response that stresses humans as free and cooperative agents of God in social redemption and takes Christ's passion as the paradigmatic event that transforms the consciences of both individuals and collectives.

7. Rufus Burrow Jr's helpful article "The Doctrine of Unearned Suffering," is a notable exception to this trend. Burrow briefly treats King's redemptive suffering formula as a theodicy which synthesizes black church and Protestant liberal influences. Rufus Burrow, "The Doctrine of Unearned Suffering," *Encounter* 63, no. 1–2 (Wint–Spr 2002): 65–76.

8. Joseph Washington famously argued that that King was not a theologian, but merely an advocate of Gandhi's philosophical nonviolence. Joseph Washington, *Black Religion: the Negro and Christianity in the United States*, (Boston: Beacon Press, 1964).

9. Kenneth Smith and Ira Zepp Jr. *Search for the Beloved Community: The Thinking of Martin Luther King Jr.* (Valley Forge, PA: Judson, 1998) 2, Preston Williams was among the first within the Black community to call for a serious consideration of King's theology in the academy. See Lewis Baldwin, *To Make the Wounded Whole: the Cultural Legacy of Martin Luther King, Jr.* (Minneapolis: Fortress, 1992) 118. See also Preston N. Williams, "The Black Experience and Black Religion," in *New Theology*, No. 8, eds. Martin E. Marty and Dean G. Peerman (New York: the Macmillan Company, 1971), 227.

10. Brian Kane followed Smith and Zepp in their analysis, positing that King's theodicy was derived almost entirely from the thinking of Harold DeWolf. See Brian M. Kane, "The Influence of Boston Personalism on the Thought of Dr. Martin Luther King, Jr." (Thesis (M.T.S.), Boston University, 1985), 57.

11. Smith and Zepp, *Search for the Beloved Community*, 2.

12. Smith and Zepp, Preface to *Search for the Beloved Community*, xvii–xviii.

13. James Cone, "The Theology of Martin Luther King Jr," *Union Seminary Quarterly Review*, 40 no. 4, (1986): 21, 36 See Also James Cone, *Martin and Malcolm: A Dream or A Nightmare*, (Maryknoll, NY, Orbis, 1991) 121.

14. Cone, "The Theology of Martin Luther King Jr." 26

15. Cone readily admits some of the ways King rejected some traditional fundamentalist beliefs held by Daddy King, including the inerrancy of Scripture and Jesus' virgin birth and bodily resurrection. Despite such radical shifts, Cone insists that King saw "no major conflicts between liberal theology and Black faith." Cone, *A Dream or A Nightmare*, 132.

16. Cone, *A Dream or A Nightmare*, 127–128.

17. James Cone, *The Cross and the Lynching Tree*, (Maryknoll, NY: Orbis, 2012) 65–92.

18. Cone, *The Cross and the Lynching Tree*, 92.

19. Lewis Baldwin, *There is a Balm in Gilead: the Cultural roots of Martin Luther King, Jr.* (Minneapolis: Fortess, 1991) 231.

20. Burrow, Jr., "Unearned Suffering," 66, 75.

21. William R. Jones, *Is God A White Racist?: A Preamble to Black Theology* (Beacon Press, 1997), 80.

22. William Jones, *Is God a White Racist?* 80, 84, 95–97.

23. Anthony Pinn, *I Wonder As I Wander: An Examination of the Problem of Evil in African-American Religious Thought*. Thesis (Ph. D.)—Harvard University, 1994. See also Anthony Pinn, *Why Lord?: Suffering and Evil in Black Theology*, (New York: Continuum, 1995), 71–78.

24. Williams, *Sisters in the Wilderness*, 199–200. Brown and Bohn, *Christianity, Patriarchy, and Abuse*, 19–20.

25. Brown and Bohn, *Christianity, Patriarchy, and Abuse*, 20.

26. Williams, *Sisters in the Wilderness*, 199–200.

27. Jacquelyn Grant, "The Sin of Servanthood," in *A Troubling in My Soul: Womanist Perspectives on Evil and Suffering*, ed. Emilie Townes, (Orbis Books, 1993), 214.

I

Roots and Development of King's Theodicy

1
FAMILY AND CULTURAL ROOTS

INTRODUCTION

Years before King famously encountered Rauschenbusch's Social Gospel or Edgar Brightman's personalist philosophy, his parents and grandparents helped instill his basic approach to suffering. Within the wholesome household at 501 Auburn Avenue, King gradually adopted many of the theodical rudiments which would mature in the classrooms of Morehouse College, Crozer Seminary, and Boston University, and eventually come to full bloom in the turmoil of the Civil Rights Movement. King always understood himself to be a product of his parents' "home training"[1] and his early childhood experiences. Despite his middle class upbringing in the prosperous Sweet Auburn district of Atlanta, King was not immune to painful experiences of racism and personal loss. These early episodes had a formative impact on his growing personality and theological development. King was also a product of the black cultural environment of the segregated South, and an heir to a considerable legacy of black redemptive suffering-type theodicies extending from some of the earliest Negro spirituals to the works of Du Bois. Contrary to what some contemporary King scholarship might suggest, King's theodicy simply cannot be fully understood without properly considering this formative context.[2]

Although King arguably represents the apex of the black redemptive suffering tradition, some of the basic principles of his scheme were already deeply rooted both within the black community and his own family.

As early as 1931, King's father already believed that blacks had been especially called by God to bear a special burden of suffering in order to bring America to its destiny.[3] King Jr. would encounter this popular idea again while studying the writings of Du Bois at Morehouse College. Informed by the insights of his father, paternal grandmother, and traditional black theodicies, King held that suffering experiences presented unique opportunities redemptive engagement and for transformation. By 1951, he formally articulated a basic form of this view in paper written at Crozer Seminary. He wrote,

> Who can deny that many apparent evils turn out in the end to be goods in disguise? Character often develops out of hardship. Unfortunate hereditary and environmental conditions often make for great and noble souls. Suffering teaches sympathy.[4]

By 1959, King had developed the theme into a ready tool in the burgeoning Civil Rights movement. Redemptive suffering featured prominently in his speeches where it helped participants make sense of the fierce resistance they faced and the virtue of their cause.[5] It also reinforced their commitment to the central motif of the movement, non-violent resistance. In fact, King's belief in the positive possibilities for suffering kept him from responding to numerous personal attacks with bitterness. To his mind, unmerited suffering could be creatively engaged for the transformation of oppressors and their victims.[6] In 1961, King described redemptive suffering as a powerful force foundational to the entire non-violent campaign. He explains,

> The nonviolent say that suffering becomes a powerful social force when you willingly accept that violence on yourself, so that self-suffering stands at the center of the non-violent movement and the individuals involved are able to suffer in a creative manner, feeling that unearned suffering is redemptive, and that suffering may serve to transform the social situation.[7]

This statement reflects most of the essentials of King's theodicy. According to King, suffering is willingly borne and engaged in a creative manner for the transformation of the victim and the sufferer. He believed blacks could creatively engage their suffering to help redeem American society from injustice and move it toward the eschatological norm he called "the beloved community."[8] This core principle helped give young freedom fighters the courage to place themselves before unforgiving fire hoses and vicious police dogs. However, King's most mature theodicy would also emphasize the special capacity of African Americans to help the nation reach its destiny through suffering—the very idea articulated by his father and which he discovered in the works of Du Bois years earlier. In 1967, King wrote,

> Let us [American Negros] be those creative dissenters who will call our nation to a higher destiny, to a new plateau of compassion, to a more noble expression of humanness. We are superbly equipped to do this. We have been seared in the flames of suffering. We have known the agony of being the underdog. We have learned from our have-not status that it profits a nation little to gain the whole world of means and lose the end, its own soul. We must have a passion for peace born out of wretchedness and the misery of war . . . . So in dealing with our particular dilemma, we will challenge the nation to deal with its dilemma.[9]

At its core, King's theodicy represents a deep and sustained reflection on the history and meaning of the black experience in America. This reflection began in early childhood and continued throughout his life. Even as the Civil Rights Movement gained global recognition, King's theodicy never lost its black cultural moorings or the fundamental trajectory instilled in his childhood. King's engagement, synthesis, and reinterpretation of protestant liberal sources must be viewed through the lens of his family and culture.

KING DESCRIBES HIS ROOTS

Throughout his life, King remained deeply aware of the central significance of culture and family life in the formation of his own theological perspective.[10] In a seminary paper entitled "An Autobiography of Religious Development," he detailed how early experiences helped shape his religious outlook. There, King described his early home life and upbringing as "highly significant" in shaping his hopeful perspective on God and the redemptive nature of suffering. He also noted that it would be impossible to understand his religious development apart from considering his family and cultural influences.[11] Since no one knew King better than he knew himself, his strong attestation of the influence of his cultural and family environment on his own thought offers valuable support to our thesis.

King's conversion experience also illustrates the centrality of family and culture on his theology. He readily admits that his decision to join the church didn't precipitate from any moment of crisis or deep sense of conviction. At five years old, he walked the aisle out of a boyish desire to keep pace with his older sister who also joined that day.[12] According to King, religion was simply part of the warp and woof of his upbringing. He never had a dramatic moment of crisis or a sudden transformation. Rather, he describes being converted through gradually (and largely unconsciously) absorbing the religious values passed in his immediate family and community.[13] King understood himself as being especially indebted to his family and cultural roots for his basic Christian perspective and he maintained a deep appreciation of these influences throughout his theological career.[14]

It is worth noting that King's professor, George Washington Davis, enthusiastically agreed with King's self-assessment about the determining influence of his own culture and upbringing. Davis specifically noted "Correct!" and "Right!" in the margin alongside these sentences in King's otherwise mostly unmarked essay.[15] Besides serving as King's academic advisor and close friend during his years as Crozer, Davis taught nearly a third of King's 110 credit hours at Crozer.[16] There, King was first introduced to Rauschenbusch's social gospel and Brightman's personalism.[17] Though it began at Morehouse, King's transition from fundamentalism to evangelical liberalism came into full flower under Davis' careful tutelage at Crozer seminary.[18] But King's early exposure to evangelical liberalism came with the explicit caveat that his family and cultural influences continued to be foundational factors in his theological outlook. Under Davis' mentorship, King would have never been advised to shed himself of his cultural or family heritage in the theological task. Rather, Davis offered King new categories with which he could further analyze, synthesize, hone, and articulate the theological perspective he absorbed from his earliest experiences in the King family and as an African American in the segregated South.

THE FAMILY ROOTS OF KING'S THEODICY

King's first serious reflection on the problem of evil involved the sudden death of his beloved maternal grandmother, Jennie Celeste Parks Williams. As with many black families,[19] the Kings greatly benefited from the nurturing presence of a saintly grandmother. In a home dominated by the stern personality of King Sr., Jennie provided her sensitive oldest grandson (King Jr. or M.L. as the family called him) with a much-needed source of concern, comfort, and reassurance.[20] Two incidents illustrate how King's close relationship with his maternal grandmother helped shape his approach to suffering. The first involved an accident with his younger brother Alfred Daniel (A.D.). Stephen Oates recounts the story.

> One day when the King boys were playing upstairs, A.D. slid down the banister and accidently knocked Grandmother down. She did not move. M.L. stood there in shock, certain that Mama was dead—that he and A.D. had killed her. M.L. was so distraught that he ran upstairs and hurled himself out a window, falling twelve feet to the ground. He lay there motionless as his relatives screamed his name. When he heard that mama was all right, though, he got up and walked away as if nothing had happened. But his parents and family friends were incredulous: the boy had apparently tried to kill himself.[21]

Devastated by the thought of harming Jennie, the young King was racked with guilt, driven to the point of despair. This foreshadows how crushed he would be when his grandmother did die a few years later. While enjoying a parade his father warned him not to attend, a twelve year old King received terrible news from home about his grandmother.[22] She had been scheduled to speak at a Woman's Day function at the Mt. Olive Baptist Church, but never made it to the podium. M.L. raced home only to find a concerned crowd already gathered. They informed him that Jennie had suffered a serious heart attack and died on the way to the hospital. Stunned, King, Jr. couldn't shake the feeling that he failed Mama by not being there and that he was somehow responsible. Stephen Oates describes his reaction.

> Why had God taken Mama from him? Was God punishing his family because he had sinned, because he had left the house without telling

anyone, because he had run off to watch a parade? Grief-stricken, racked with guilt, the boy raced upstairs and leaped out the window after his Mama trying to follow her from this world. He struck the ground in a painful heap. Again shouting people ran up to him. He was still alive: bruised and shaken, but still in this world. Afterward, in his bedroom, he shook with sobs unable to bear the hurt he felt inside.[23]

Anxious about God's purpose in this painful event, King, Jr. had convinced himself that Jennie's death must be divine retribution for him sneaking to the parade. The idea that his "sin" was responsible for Jennie's loss was simply too much for his young mind to bear. This was now the second time he had attempted to take his own life under the strain of personal guilt. King Sr. remembers sitting with his son for nearly an entire afternoon explaining that God wasn't that angry with him for going to the parade.[24]

King Jr.'s breakthrough only came after his father trotted out a simple theodicy. King Sr. patiently reassured him "Don't blame what has happened to your grandmother or anything you've done . . . God has His own plan and His own way, and we cannot change or interfere with the time he chooses to call any of us back to Him."[25]

Although he didn't attempt to resolve the problem by tracing out God's exact purposes, King Sr. helped his son understand that all suffering was not the result of personal guilt. Moreover, he pointed out that God has some mysterious yet benevolent purpose even in painful events. This was a pivotal moment for King, Jr. which transformed him personally and helped establish the fundamental orientation of his theodicy.[26] Informed by this early experience, King Jr. eventually rejected the idea that physical evils are God's way of punishing moral evils. In a seminary paper entitled "Religion's Answer to the Problem of Evil," King describes this approach to suffering as "repugnant to the ethical sense of modern idealist[s]" and a "crude theory" founded on the "principle of retribution."[27] With this, King strongly denounced the very theodicy he initially held as a child, revealing how far his position had shifted. King concluded the essay with the idea that the problem of evil is ultimately mysterious—a point he also received from his father. He argues that every proposed "intellectual solution" to the problem of evil comes to an inevitable impasse, a point beyond which humanity cannot go and that the ultimate solution rests in the realm of faith.[28] Before King was ever exposed to the finer points of Edgar Brightman's philosophy of religion,

King Sr.'s pithy phrase about God having "his own plan and his own way" conveyed the mystery of suffering quite well to King Jr.'s twelve-year-old mind.[29]

It is no surprise that King Sr. sowed a formative seed that may well have blossomed into King Jr.'s redemptive suffering theodicy. Having grown up the son of struggling sharecroppers in racist Stockbridge Georgia, King Sr. (known as Mike King at the time) was all-too-familiar with suffering. His theodicy was shaped in large part by studying the lives of his parents—especially his godly mother, Delia Lindsay King. She met and married King Sr.'s father, James Albert King shortly after he lost part of his hand in a rock quarry accident. Embittered by constant hardships, and the dehumanizing realties and economic hopelessness of sharecropping in the Jim Crow south, James eventually sought solace in whiskey bottles.[30] Delia had her own share of adversity. Besides the daily brutalities and indignities of sharecropping, Delia's husband James was occasionally abusive, and the couple lost the third of their ten children Lucius at only a few days old.[31] Delia's faith kept her grounded and ever hopeful in the face of life's tragedies.[32] But as he watched his mother endure near constant hardships, King Sr. grew increasingly perplexed and embittered, especially as he realized that Delia's reward for her faithfulness to God would never come in her lifetime. He recalled, "Something was wrong, I knew, when someone who tried so hard, who kept her faith, and who provided so much sense of a righteous path for her children, came away, finally, with so little for herself."[33] Despite King Sr.'s deep struggles with his mother's suffering, he was inspired by her enduring faith which kept her from descending into the same spiral of bitterness as her husband. King Sr. recalls his mother's response to her own suffering. ". . . even in times of great suffering, which came so many times in her life," he said, "she never lost sight of the Lord. No tears could blind her to His presence, and she could not close her eyes so tight in sorrow or in rage that she did not see God's hand reaching out to her."[34] Delia King somehow recognized God's benevolent mysterious purposes even in the worst circumstances.

As he grew older, King Sr. came to appreciate Delia's remarkable outlook even more,[35] eventually appropriating it the social circumstances of blacks in America. As early as 1931, King Sr. suggested that God has a socially redemptive purpose for the suffering of black Americans. King Sr.'s comments convey many of the hallmarks of the redemptive suffering theodicy his son would later espouse. For this reason, they are worth quoting at length. King Sr. wrote,

> We [black Americans] had been asked by Him [God] to bear a great burden in our time . . . So many of us had come from places where Negroes were not regarded as part of the human race. We knew better. And we knew in time everyone else would understand our struggle, our patience, our anger, and our spiritual power to change not only our own condition but that of the rest of this nation. Nothing would ever overwhelm us. We could be set back, knocked down, and kicked around. But we'd live. And in our living, America would discover its future.[36]

Here, in the thought of King Sr., we see some rudiments of the redemptive suffering theodicy King Jr. (only two years old at the time) would later inherit and develop in conversation with protestant liberalism. First, King Sr. clearly conveys a sense of what Baldwin calls "black messianism," the idea of God's special calling upon and equipping of African Americans to bear a particular burden of oppression for the sake of transforming the nation.[37] According to King Sr., God had especially chosen African Americans to endure hardships as a pedagogical tool to help racist America realize its higher destiny. This core concept helped King Sr. (and many other African Americans) make sense of God's relation to the brutal history of black suffering in America. King Sr. labored over the years to help resolve the question of racism for his inquisitive son.[38] As a youngster, King Jr. struggled intensely to understand segregation[39] and he often asked his parents "urgent and pointed" questions about it.[40] King would attribute his early abhorrence of segregation to King Sr.'s influence and example.[41] It would be difficult to imagine that he wouldn't have also absorbed his father's basic understanding of God's purpose in black suffering.

As he grew theologically, King Jr. would engage this black messianic perspective so frequently that it represents a central component of his thought.[42] In 1955, he articulated the idea in a speech at the initial mass meeting of the Montgomery Improvement Association, a series of meetings which would later become the famous Montgomery Bus Boycott. There, at the Holt Street Baptist Church, King predicted,

FAMILY AND CULTURAL ROOTS

> Right here in Montgomery when the history books are written in the future, somebody will have to say: "There lived a race of people, fleecy locks and black complexion, of people who had the moral courage to stand up for their rights, and thereby injected a new meaning into the veins of history and civilization." And we're gonna do that. God grant that we will do it before it's too late.[43]

This powerful rhetoric helped move the beleaguered black citizens of Montgomery to action. Three years later, he concluded his famous memoir of the Montgomery Bus boycott *Stride toward Freedom* with the same theme.

> This is a great hour for the Negro. The challenge is here. To become instruments of a great idea [i.e., nonviolent resistance] is a privilege that history gives only occasionally. . . . The spiritual power that the Negro can radiate to the world comes from love, understanding, goodwill, and nonviolence. It may even be possible for the Negro, through adherence to non-violence, so to challenge the nations of the world that they will seriously seek an alternative to war and destruction . . . The Negro may be God's appeal to this age—an age drifting rapidly to its doom.[44]

Although King Jr. nuanced the idea and expressed it more frequently than his father, the essential components and their uses are the same. Both Kings viewed African Americans as having a divine calling and equipping to help transform America. Both Kings used the idea to counteract prevailing racist ideologies. For King Sr., the idea that blacks had a special spiritual power to transform the nation counterbalanced the prevalent dogma that blacks were inferior, to lift their self-image and so inspire them to action. King Jr.'s comments are intended to do the same thing. His talk of the Negro as "God's appeal to this age" is meant to instill a sense of worth, dignity, purpose, and calling into a people thoroughly denigrated and infected with the poison of self-hate. Moreover, both of them avoided turning black messianism into black supremacy. Both Kings rejected hatred toward whites as a morally satisfactory response to the problem of black suffering. Their view of blacks as a special providentially prepared people also included a thoroughgoing love ethic that sought the transformation (rather than domination or degradation) of whites. King Sr.'s statement from 1931 suggests that blacks would teach the nation through patiently enduring suffering, rather than taking up arms against their oppressors. King Jr. would echo this sentiment, insisting that blacks could not fulfill God's calling on them by "substituting one tyranny for another . . . by making a doctrine of black supremacy a substitute for white supremacy."[45] King consistently held to this view, even late in his career amidst increasing criticism and pressure to conform to the black nationalist ideals propounded most famously by Malcolm X.[46] Like his father before him, King Jr.'s black messianism was infused with an ethic of love aimed at the uplifting of all races.

Additionally, King Sr.'s comments from 1931 identify voluntary engagement with suffering as a kind of "spiritual power." King Sr. carefully noted that God "asks" (rather than demands) blacks to bear the burden of redemptive suffering. King Jr. would also pick this up and later identify non-violent, creative, and free engagement with suffering with *agape* love, a kind of spiritual power able to transform the moral conscience of oppressors and bring an end to racism.[47] Finally, King Sr.'s comment carefully distinguished between the mere suffering of victims and their redemptive engagement with suffering. It is in blacks' overcoming, what he calls our "living" through suffering, that the nation would "discover its future." Years later, King Jr. would also make a careful distinction between suffering itself, and the potential redemptive benefits. He denied any redemptive aspect to suffering itself. Instead, he maintained that social redemption could be experienced through the creative engagement with suffering.[48]

Some of the foundational components of King's redemptive suffering theodicy were already present in his familial environment by way of his father and paternal grandmother. We might even say that his family influence helped determine the fundamental orientation of King's theodicy. From a very early age King was already exposed to theodical rudiments such God's mysterious and redemptive purpose in black suffering, black messianism, voluntary suffering as a spiritual force, and the distinction between suffering and its socially redemptive consequences. It is likely that these concepts were basic to his thought well before he had any contact with protestant liberalism or Boston personalism. Delia King, Jennie Williams, and Martin King Sr, may have been just as influential on King's theodical thought as Edgar Brightman or Harold DeWolf. King's failure to cite his father or paternal grandmother explicitly does not undermine this claim because he freely admitted that the religious inheritance he received from his family environment was "largely unconscious."[49] However, the basic similarities between his father and paternal grandmother's approach to suffering and his own indicate that redemptive suffering was almost certainly among the religious ideals King Jr. absorbed from his upbringing in the King household.

THE CULTURAL ROOTS OF KING'S THEODICY

In the remaining space, I will demonstrate that redemptive suffering was not unique to the King family lineage; the concept was already deeply rooted in the black cultural identity. Black American theodical reflection traces back as far as the earliest Negro spirituals.[50] Despite their oppressors' claims, African Americans could not easily accept that slavery was God's intention for their lives.[51] Slaves struggled to grasp some ultimate meaning behind their dehumanizing condition in light of God's goodness and power. Spirituals like "Didn't My Lord Deliver Daniel" reflect this early tension.[52] In it, the author wonders "Didn't my Lord Deliver Daniel? And why not every man?"[53] Despite such tensions, blacks remained staunchly optimistic about God's purposes in suffering.[54]

As early as 1829, African Americans were articulating the view that God would use black suffering to prepare them as chosen instruments to bring Christianity to the world. Abolitionist David Walker summarized this early position in his famous *Appeal* as a way to undermine racist ideologies and to encourage resistance to oppression. "It is my solemn belief," he wrote, "that if ever the world becomes Christianized, (which must certainly take place before long) it will be through the means, under God of the blacks, who are now held in wretchedness, and degradation, by the white Christians of the world . . ."[55] Walker combined this messianic outlook with a strong sense of black self-determination which refused to view enslaved blacks merely as victims, but empowered witnesses who possess the key to their own liberation. As God's image bearers, blacks had an inherent responsibility and power to resist oppression in order to affirm their divinely endowed dignity and worth.[56] (As we will see, the dignity and responsibility of blacks to engage oppression would become prominent features of King's theodical vision over a century later.) The black messianic theme would continue within the Ethiopianist conceptions of Rev. Alexander Crummell. Crummell's parents exposed him to Walker's "chosen people" rhetoric as a child.[57] Crummell further popularized the idea that black Americans had a special role to play in the conversion of Africa.[58] He maintained that slavery was an evil that God providentially used to refine black Americans to be better messengers of the gospel, not only to America but to Africa as well.[59] Crummell understood black suffering in America as a process of refinement by way of ordeals toward the special destiny of Christianizing Africa. He noted, "The fact that black people in the United States had not been destroyed by slavery demonstrated that the sufferings of the 'captive exiles from Africa' were meant not as a judgment but as a discipline. Their tribulations were not intended to punish or destroy but to prepare the black for a glorious destiny."[60] The "glorious destiny" Crummell intended involved African Americans bringing the gospel to Africa and eventually establishing a new ideal Christian civilization. (One hundred years later, King would hold a similar teleological goal for redemptive suffering, namely in the establishment of the beloved community.) In 1861 Crummell spoke to the New Hampshire Colonization society about the "benefit of affliction, which humbles a people and brings them where God can safely honor them and make them great."[61] Disillusioned by his struggles on the mission field, Crummell eventually returned to the United States all but abandoning the idea of redeeming Africa. However, he held on to his core belief that black American suffering was redemptive.[62]

Among black women, abolitionist and early women's rights activist Maria Stewart provides a notable example of a redemptive suffering theodicy. A friend of David Walker's and parishioner of Alexander Crummell's,[63] Stewart's own conceptions were generally in-step with the theodical ideas they advanced. She maintained that black suffering could awaken the consciences of white America to its oppression of blacks. She also held that through hardships, God endowed black women with a special fortitude able to lift the entire African American race.[64] The redemptive purpose of black suffering was already widely held among blacks more than a century and a half before King's Southern Christian Leadership Conference (SCLC) ever adopted the motto "To save the soul of America" and before he ever described the Negro as entrusted by God to "teach the world to love"[65] or as "God's appeal to this age."[66]

The mid-nineteenth and early twentieth century brought new hardships which African Americans sought to explain. In the wake of the Civil War, newly freed blacks found themselves as scapegoats for scattered groups of embittered and disempowered whites in the South. Vigilante groups like the Ku Klux Klan were formed in order to "redeem" the South. And, with the withdrawal of federal troops from the South in 1877, the era of the lynching tree began. New forms of domestic terrorism proliferated in order to keep blacks subservient, unable to fully realize their citizenship.[67] Without much economic or political footing, African Americans were easy targets of constant intimidation, brutal attacks, and the oppressive socio-political systems which sprang up around racist ideologies. Propaganda pieces like *The Leopard's Spots* (1902), *The Clansman* (1905), and the wildly popular *Birth of a Nation* (1915) enshrined the South's perspective on race and Reconstruction.[68]

Against this backdrop of cultural denigration, W.E.B. Du Bois sharpened the black messianic vision with works like *The Conservation of Race, The Souls of Black Folk, The Gift of Black Folk,* and *Black Reconstruction in America.* Du Bois was highly influenced by Crummell's pan-Africanism and Ethiopianism and serves as a link between the mid-late nineteenth century articulations of black messianism and their early twentieth century expressions.[69] With its penetrating poetic expression and sociological analysis, Du Bois' formulation represents one of the most sophisticated expressions of the redemptive suffering tradition prior to King's own formulation.[70] Despite strongly critiquing the black church and jettisoning many of the religious tones associated with the theme, Du Bois maintained hope in the civilizing power of blacks.

Informed by Crummell, Du Bois argued that the beleaguered people of African descent had a unique spiritual capacity to help civilize humanity—indeed that they are the greatest hope for reason and goodwill to prevail in the world.[71] In order to achieve this destiny, Du Bois insisted that African Americans needed to resist the pressure to assimilate to the predominate culture. Rather they need to embrace and appreciate their distinctive culture and use their history of oppression to as a powerful witness to the help reach the ideal of human brotherhood. At the initial meeting of the American Negro Academy (with Crummell seated in the audience) Du Bois suggested the following two points be adopted as the very first parts of the Academy's creed. "1. We believe that the Negro people, as a race, have a contribution to make to civilization and to humanity which no other race can make. 2. We believe it the duty of Americans of Negro descent, as a body, to maintain their race identity until this mission of the Negro people is accomplished, and the ideal of human brotherhood has become a practical possibility."[72] Du Bois leaves little doubt about his vision for the Negro race. Through their humanizing and civilizing efforts, African Americans will help establish a global community. Indeed, according to Du Bois, blacks have a unique capacity to accomplish this.

Despite Du Bois' black nationalist inclinations, this view of the "mission of the Negro" deeply resonated with King. King also held that blacks were uniquely fit to help establish a "beloved community," a society which reflects the eschatological ideal, the ethical norm by which all other ethics are judged. Baldwin explains that Du Bois and King both "tended to view the messianic role of their people in a historical context, taking into account how blacks had always challenged America with a prophetic vision of freedom, justice and community."[73] Moreover, they also agreed about the significant role of black suffering in achieving this vision. In *The Souls of Black Folk*, Du Bois claims that "Negro blood has a message for the world."[74] This sounds remarkably similar to King's subsequent theodical assertion that "the Negro may be God's appeal to this age."[75]

Ultimately, King would offer a more sustained and robust treatment of non-violent redemptive suffering than Du Bois. However, King's theodicy was profoundly impacted by Du Bois' piercing analyses of the black condition. King probably seriously engaged Du Bois' thought for the first time in Walter Chivers' sociology classes at Morehouse College. Du Bois' works were commonly used in the curriculum at Morehouse during King's matriculation there. Du Bois taught at Atlanta University for several years where he completed some of his most famous publications. Throughout his career King poured over Du Bois' works, especially *The Philadelphia Negro*, *The Souls of Black Folk*, and *Black Reconstruction in America*.[76] In what would ultimately be his last major public speech, King helped commemorate Du Bois' 100th birthday calling him "one of the most remarkable men of our time" and "an intellectual giant."[77]

CONCLUSION

With this, we have traced a line of redemptive suffering themes from David Walker through W.E.B. Du Bois, demonstrating how some of the essential components of King's theodicy have deep roots within the black communal understanding of its history and purpose in the world—particularly the widely accepted idea that African Americans have been especially chosen and equipped by God to help bring about an ideal community and (more directly to our point) that this mission may be achieved by way of suffering. Additionally, we have shown the specific family and black cultural channels by which some of these theodical ideas came to King. Alongside simply being "in the air" of the early twentieth century black cultural self-understanding, there was a direct line of family influences extending from Delia King through Martin King Sr., and cultural influences proceeding from David Walker to Alexander Crummell, from Crummell to Du Bois, and finally from Du Bois to King. Therefore, we have established our claim that black cultural and family experiences were a significant source in the formulation of King's redemptive suffering theodicy.

Moreover, we have noted that proponents of redemptive suffering theodicies used the idea to inspire active resistance to oppression rather than acculturated victimization. Against the backdrop of predominant of racist ideologies and the brutal history of black suffering in America, redemptive suffering theodicies included black messianic themes in order to give a sense of self-worth, mission, and purpose to the downtrodden black masses. We will revisit this topic in more depth when we directly address King's contemporary Womanist and Feminist critics.

Though this chapter has mostly avoided directly dealing with the black church, it has never been too far away from the discussion. No treatment of King's thought would be complete without a thorough treatment of his black Baptist church context. As a son of several generations of Baptist ministers, King was fundamentally shaped within this environment. Additionally, he always carried out his public service from the capacity of Baptist pastor. So in the next chapter we turn our attention specifically to the black church roots of King's theodicy.

NOTES

1. Christine King Farris, *Through It All: Reflections on My Life, My Family, and My Faith*, First edition (New York: Atria Books, 2010), 3.
2. Lewis V. Baldwin, *There Is a Balm in Gilead: The Cultural Roots of Martin Luther King, Jr* (Minneapolis: Fortress Press, 1991), 92. Baldwin laments the common tendency to overlook King's early home life remains evident even among works devoted to King's cultural roots. According to Baldwin, some

noteworthy examples include William D. Watley, *Roots of Resistance: The Nonviolent Ethic of Martin Luther King, Jr* (Valley Forge: Judson Press, 1985), 17–45.; See also James H. Cone, "Martin Luther King : The Source for His Courage to Face Death," in *Martyrdom Today* (New York, NY: Seabury Press, 1983), 74–79. For serious studies of the impact of King's home environment see Walter E. Fluker, *They Looked for a City* (University Press of America, 1989), 191–192; Lewis V. Baldwin, "Understanding Martin Luther King, Jr Within the Context of Southern Black Religious History," *Journal of Religious Studies* 13, no. 2 (1987): 9–10; Lewis V. Baldwin, "Family, Church, and the Black Experience: The Shaping of Martin Luther King, Jr," *AME Zion Quarterly Review*, January 1978, 1, 3, 7, 9, 12. More recently, Rufus Burrow Jr. reasserted the importance of the black cultural studies genre for King scholarship suggesting that more work needs to be done in this area if King's theological contributions are to be correctly understood. He warns that neglecting either King's less formal black cultural stream of influence or his formal protestant liberal influences "leaves one with a truncated understanding of the life, work and contributions of King." Rufus Burrow, Jr., "The Beloved Community: Martin Luther King, Jr., and Josiah Royce," *Encounter* 73, no. 1 (Fall 2012): 40. Highlighting the work of Lewis Baldwin and James Cone as exemplary in this regard and the more recent works of Stewart Burns, Peter Ling, and Dwayne Tunstall as somewhat lacking, Burrow challenges King scholars to engage seriously with black cultural and family studies in order to gain a better appreciation of these central influences on King's thought. Ibid., 40–41; Stewart Burns, *To the Mountaintop: Martin Luther King Jr.'s Mission to Save America: 1955–1968*, Reprint (HarperOne, 2005); Peter J. Ling, *Martin Luther King Jr*, First Edition (Routledge, 2002). For a concise yet thorough of King's family and cultural roots see also Lewis V. Baldwin, "Martin Luther King, Jr, the Black Church, and the Black Messianic Vision," *Journal of the Interdenominational Theological Center* 12, no. 1–2 (1985): 93–108.

3. Martin Luther King, Sr., *Daddy King: An Autobiography*, 1st ed. (New York: William Morrow & Co, 1980), 94.

4. Martin Luther King, Jr., "Religion's Answer to the Problem of Evil," in *The Papers of Martin Luther King, Jr.: Volume I: Called to Serve, January 1929–June 1951*, First, vol. 1, The Papers of Martin Luther King, Jr. (Berkeley: University of California Press, 1992), 419. See also Edgar S. Brightman, *A Philosophy of Religion*, Reprint (Westport: Greenwood Press, 1940), 262.

5. Martin Luther King, Jr., "Untitled Montgomery Improvement Association Address" (Boston University, 1959), Box 2, I–XI, Folder 2, King Collection.

6. Martin Luther King, Jr., "Suffering and Faith," *Christian Century* 101, no. 22 (July 11, 1984; Original in April 26, 1960): 687.

7. Martin Luther King, Jr., "Love, Law, and Civil Disobedience," in *A Testament of Hope: The Essential Writings and Speeches of Martin Luther King, Jr.*, ed. James M. Washington (San Francisco: Harper and Row, 1986), 48.

8. Fluker, *They Looked for a City*, 130.

9. Martin Luther King, Jr., *Where Do We Go from Here: Chaos or Community?* (Boston: Beacon Press, 1968), 133–34.

10. Martin Luther King, Jr., "Pilgrimage to Nonviolence," in *Stride Toward Freedom: The Montgomery Story* (San Francisco: HarperCollins, 1987), 90.

11. Martin Luther King, Jr., "An Autobiography of Religious Development," in *The Papers of Martin Luther King, Jr.: Volume I: Called to Serve, January 1929–June 1951*, First Edition, vol. 1, The Papers of Martin Luther King, Jr. (Berkeley: University of California Press, 1992), 360.

12. Ibid., 361.

13. Ibid.

14. King, Jr., "Pilgrimage to Nonviolence," 19–20; "Face to Face: John Freeman of B.B.C. Interviews Martin Luther King, Jr." (UK, London: BBC, October 29, 1961), 4, The Archives of Martin Luther King, Jr., Center for Nonviolent Social Change, Inc., Atlanta, GA. Cited in Baldwin, *Balm in Gilead*, 20–21.

15. King, Jr., "Autobiography of Religious Development," 360–361.

16. Watley, *Roots of Resistance*, 19.

17. Clayborne Carson, Tenisha H. Armstrong, and Susan Englander, *The Martin Luther King, Jr., Encyclopedia*, ed. Susan A. Carson and Erin K. Cook (London: Greenwood Press, 2008), 75.

18. Watley, *Roots of Resistance*, 19–20; Baldwin, *Balm in Gilead*, 326.

19. E. Franklin Frazier, *The Negro Family in the United States* (Chicago: The University of Chicago Press, 1968), 114–116.

20. The nurturance of Alberta "Bunch" King (King's mother) also offered an important contrast to the rough edges of King Sr.'s abrasive personality. See King, Sr., *Daddy King*, 131.

21. Oates, *Let the Trumpet Sound*, 8–9. Most likely, Oates got his account from King biographer and family friend Lawrence Reddick. Though Reddick doesn't cite the source, he probably got the story either directly from King himself or his immediate family. Lawrence Dunbar Reddick, *Crusader Without Violence: A Biography of Martin Luther King, Jr*, 1st ed. (New York: Harper and Brothers Publishers, 1959), 60–61.

22. King, Sr., *Daddy King*, 109.

23. Oates, *Let the Trumpet Sound*, 12–13.

24. King, Sr., *Daddy King*, 109.

25. Ibid.

26. King, Jr., "Autobiography of Religious Development," 362.

27. King, Jr., "Religion's Answer to the Problem of Evil," 418.

28. Ibid., 432–433.

29. King may have drawn on his father's method of consolation as he preached over three of the four young victims of the infamous 16th Street Baptist church bombing. His 1963 sermon "Eulogy for the Martyred Children" climaxes with God's mysterious redemptive purpose in the death of the innocent and the hope of immortality—two lessons his father taught him when Grandma Jennie died. Martin Luther King, Jr., "Eulogy for the Martyred Children," in *I Have a Dream: Writings and Speeches That Changed the World, Special 75th Anniversary Edition*, 1st ed. (San Francisco: HarperOne, 1992).

30. King, Sr., *Daddy King*, 24–25.

31. Ibid., 25.

32. Ibid., 26, 74. Delia Lindsay repeatedly taught King Sr. never to hate whites in return for mistreatment. Years after she died, King Sr. passed Delia's lesson on to his young son M.L. at a number of crucial times in his life when he was tempted to hate whites in return for their hatred of him. See Baldwin, *Balm in Gilead*, 100–101.

33. King, Sr., *Daddy King*, 26.

34. Ibid., 25. Even though she died five years before his birth, Delia's hope in God's presence during times of suffering came to be shared by her grandson Martin King Jr. He would often remind members of the Montgomery Bus Boycott of God's presence in their struggle for justice. See Martin Luther King, Jr., "Remaining Awake Through a Great Revolution," in *A Testament of Hope: The Essential Writings and Speeches of Martin Luther King, Jr.*, ed. James M. Washington, Reprint (HarperOne, 1990), 270; Martin Luther King, Jr., "Our God Is Able," in *Strength to Love* (New York: Harper and Row, 1963). See Anthony B. Pinn, "I Wonder as I Wander: An Examination of the Problem of Evil in African American Religious Thought." (Ph.D. Dissertation, 1994), 121–122.

35. King, Sr., *Daddy King*, 25.

36. Ibid., 94.

37. Baldwin, *Balm in Gilead*, 8–9, 243–272.

38. King, Sr., *Daddy King*, 108–109.

39. Ibid., 108; King, Jr., "Autobiography of Religious Development," 362–363; Oates, *Let the Trumpet Sound*, 8–10.

40. King, Jr., "Pilgrimage to Nonviolence," 18–19.

41. Ibid., 20.

42. Baldwin, *Balm in Gilead*, 230.

43. Martin Luther King, Jr., "Address to the Initial Mass Meeting of the Montgomery Improvement Association," at the Holt Street Baptist church, Montgomery AL, (The King Center Archives, December 5, 1955), 4. Cited in Baldwin, *Balm in Gilead*, 233.

44. King, Jr., "Pilgrimage to Nonviolence," 224; Baldwin, *Balm in Gilead*, 236. Cornel West considers King an exemplar of what he styles "the exceptionalist tradition" of blacks who, through historical hardships, have been endowed with a peculiar capacity to love their enemies and patiently endure oppression in order to teach whites how to love. See *Cornel West, Prophesy Deliverance: An Afro-American Revolutionary Christianity* (Philadelphia: Westminster Press, 1982), 72, 74–75.

45. Martin Luther King, Jr., "Interview on World Peace," *Redbook Magazine*, November 1964, 3, 6–7.

46. James H. Cone, *Martin & Malcolm & America: A Dream or a Nightmare* (Maryknoll: Orbis, 2001), 107–8. Malcolm X thought the idea of loving an enemy was completely incompatible with loving oneself, especially when that love took the form of suffering. He mockingly called King's redemptive suffering concept a "wait-until-you-change-your-mind-and-then-let-me-up philosophy." Malcolm X, *Untitled Speech Delivered at Boston University* (Boston, 1960). Cited in Cone, *Martin & Malcolm & America*, 107.

47. Pinn, "I Wonder as I Wander," 1994, 122.

48. Martin King, Jr., "Shattered Dreams," Boston University, King Collection, Box 119a. XVI. 16, 10; Anthony B. Pinn, "I Wonder as I Wander: An Examination of the Problem of Evil in African American Religious Thought." (Ph.D. Dissertation, 1994), 123; Anthony B. Pinn, *Why, Lord?: Suffering and Evil in Black Theology*, First edition. (Continuum Intl Pub Group, 1995), 76.

49. King, Jr., "Autobiography of Religious Development," 361.

50. Pinn, "I Wonder as I Wander," 1994, 41–42. In this section, I am particularly indebted to Lewis Baldwin's work on King's cultural roots and Anthony Pinn's work on the history of black theodicies.

51. James H. Cone, *The Spirituals and the Blues: An Interpretation*, 2nd ed. (Maryknoll: Seabury Press, 1972), 113.

52. Dr. Benjamin Mays, president of Morehouse College during King's matriculation, held a deep appreciation for the role of the spirituals as reflections of the black communal consciousness. He suggests that spirituals which did not resonate with commonly held ideas within the community would have lost their audience and their place in the oral tradition. Benjamin E. Mays, *The Negro's God as Reflected in His Literature*, 3rd ed. (Boston: Chapman and Grimes, 1938; New York: Antheneum, 1973), 19–30. Cited in Pinn, *Why, Lord?*, 24.

53. James Weldon Johnson and J. Rosamond Johnson, eds., *The Books of the American Negro Spirituals* (New York: Da Capo Press, 2002), 148. Cited in Pinn, "I Wonder as I Wander," 1994, 42.

54. John Lovell, *Black Song: The Forge and the Flame; the Story of How the Afro-American Spiritual Was Hammered Out.*, First Printing (New York: Macmillan Pub Co, 1972), 294. Cited in Pinn, "I Wonder as I Wander," 1994, 43.

55. David Walker, *David Walker's Appeal, in Four Articles, Together with a Preamble, to the Coloured Citizens of the World, but in Particular, and Very Expressly, to Those of the United States of America*, ed. Charles M. Wiltse (New York: Hill and Wang, 1965; originally published in 1829), 18. Walker held that white missionaries must learn to do justice to their black neighbors at home before they would be fit to convert unbelievers abroad.

56. Rufus Burrow, Jr., *God and Human Responsibility: David Walker and Ethical Prophecy*, First edition (Macon, Ga: Mercer University Press, 2004), 138–139.

57. Wilson Jeremiah Moses, *Alexander Crummell: A Study of Civilization and Discontent* (New York: Oxford University Press, 1989), 220.

58. Crummel used Psalm 68:31 to support this idea. He interpreted the words "Ethiopia shall soon stretch forth her hands unto God" to imply the immanent conversion of Africa through the witness of African Americans. Alexander Crummell, "Hope for Africa," in *The Future of Africa: Being Addresses, Sermons, Etc., Etc., Delivered in the Republic of Liberia* (1862: Charles Scribner, 1862); Moses, Alexander Crummell, 78–79.

59. Pinn, *Why, Lord?*, 52.

60. Alexander Crummell, "The Destined Superiority of the Negro," in *The Greatness of Christ: And Other Sermons* (New York: Thomas Whittaker, 1882), 351. Cited in Pinn, *Why, Lord?*, 52.

61. Moses, *Alexander Crummell*, 139.

62. Pinn, *Why, Lord?*, 52.

63. Moses, *Alexander Crummell*, 199.

64. Maria Stewart, "Religion and the Pure Principles of Morality, the Sure Foundation on Which We Must Build," in *Maria W. Stewart, America's First Black Woman Political Writer: Essays and Speeches*, 4th Printing (Bloomington: Indiana University Press, 1987), 69. Pinn, *Why, Lord?*, 47, 55.

65. Martin Luther King, Jr., "Statement to the Press Regarding Nobel Trip," December 4, 1964, (The Archives of Martin Luther King, Jr., Center for Nonviolent Social Change, Inc., Atlanta, GA.), 1.

66. King, Jr., "Pilgrimage to Nonviolence," 224.

67. James H. Cone, *The Cross and the Lynching Tree* (Maryknoll: Orbis Books, 2011), 4.

68. Ibid., 5.

69. *In the Souls of Black Folk*, Du Bois devotes an entire chapter to Alexander Crummell. See W.E.B. Du Bois, "Of Alexander Crummell," in *The Souls of Black Folk* (CreateSpace Independent Publishing Platform, 2013), 106–11.

70. Baldwin, *Balm in Gilead*, 260.

71. W.E.B Du Bois, *The Conservation of Races* (Washington, D.C.: American Negro Academy, 1897), 12; See Wilson Jeremiah Moses, *Classical*

Black Nationalism: From the American Revolution to Marcus Garvey (New York: New York University Press, 1996), 236; Sweet, Black Images, 88, 120–121, 124; Lewis V. Baldwin, *There Is a Balm in Gilead*, 260. W.E.B. Du Bois, *The Negro* (New York: Oxford University Press, 1970), 146.

72. Du Bois, *The Conservation of Races*, 12.

73. Baldwin, *Balm in Gilead*, 262.

74. W.E.B. Du Bois, "The Souls of Black Folk," in *Three Negro Classics*, ed. John Hope Franklin (New York: Avon Books, 1965), 215.

75. Martin Luther King, Jr., *Stride Toward Freedom: The Montgomery Story* (HarperCollins, 1987), 224.

76. Baldwin, *Balm in Gilead*, 45.

77. See Martin Luther King, Jr., "Honoring Dr. Du Bois," *Freedomways*, 8, no. 2 (Spring 1968): 104–111.

2

BLACK CHURCH ROOTS

INTRODUCTION

Martin Luther King, Jr.'s approach to suffering was fundamentally shaped by his black church heritage and context. King was heir to three generations of pastors whose ministries were particularly oriented towards addressing black suffering. He also drew deeply from the wellspring of the black church music and prayer traditions which encompass nearly three hundred years of Christian reflection on the nature and purpose of black suffering in America. Moreover, the black church music and prayer traditions offered King a powerful medium through which to reinforce the hope of redemptive suffering in his own mind as well as to convey it in both parish and public ministry settings. The first part of this chapter aims to demonstrate that King's heritage provided the fundamental trajectory and shape of King's approach to suffering.

However, King's black Baptist pastoral context also helped determine his approach to black suffering. The social hardships of King's southern black congregants not only brought the question of theodicy to the forefront of his thinking and made it a repeated theme within his sermonic corpus, it influenced the way he framed the question. Keenly aware of his context, King tailored his language to resonate with prevailing black church paradigms such as the all-powerful God and the ultimate triumph of justice. The black church's basic optimism and traditional understandings of God's power and purposes in black suffering determined the kinds of theodical ideas King was willing to present before black church audiences.

KING'S BLACK CHURCH HERITAGE

Part 1: King's Pastoral Heritage

Martin Luther King, Jr., stood in a long line of black Baptist preachers whose legacies oriented him towards a ministry that particularly addressed black suffering.[1] King's Baptist roots extend as far back as 1846, when Willis Williams was converted and joined the Shiloh Baptist Church in the Penfield District of Greene County, Georgia.[2] Founded in 1795, Shiloh was among the oldest Baptist churches in the state, admitting both enslaved and free blacks as full members. When Williams joined Shiloh, the congregation numbered fifty white and twenty-eight black members.[3] However, despite their official status as full members, Shiloh's black membership was relegated to a status of complete subordination within the church. This loathsome circumstance became especially acute for Williams when his owner William N. Williams later joined the church. Despite race-based barriers to ministry licensure and ordination, Willis Williams would go on to become a gifted slave "exhorter" at Shiloh.[4] During a major revival in 1855, he helped to recruit many of the one hundred slaves who joined the congregation, a full one-tenth of the slave population of the Penfield District.[5] His success was in part due to his ability to identify with the daily hardships of his fellow slaves.[6] The increased numbers of blacks within the congregation made it more difficult for the whites to maintain their status of race-based superiority in church government and affairs. By the end of the Civil War, Shiloh had 144 black members compared to only 77 white members. With their newfound freedom and a sizable majority, the black membership eventually left the congregation—unwilling to accept the old order of subordination that the white membership demanded. Willis Williams joined other black former members of Shiloh in organizing a sizable black Baptist church in the Penfield district, a deliberate attempt to alleviate discrimination experienced within the church.[7] This response to black suffering marked the known beginnings of Martin King's black Baptist church roots.

Willis William's son, Adam Daniel (A.D.) Williams followed his father's footsteps by embracing a call to preach which specifically addressed the suffering of blacks. In the face of a declining economy and struggling to make a living as an itinerant preacher, A.D. Williams migrated to Atlanta in the winter of 1893. There, Williams enjoyed brief success as a local preacher before receiving a call to become the second pastor of the Ebenezer Baptist church in March 1894.[8] Williams quickly proved himself to be a capable leader, adding 65 members by the end of his first year as pastor. What he lacked in formal theological training he more than made up for in forceful and profound sermons that skillfully tackled the practical concerns of poor and working-class blacks.[9] A.D. Williams would claim that he had simply inherited his ministry gifts and perspective from his father Willis.[10] Combining Booker T. Washington's emphasis on black business development and W. E. B DuBois's view toward social action, Williams pioneered a kind of social justice-oriented gospel ministry especially aimed at addressing black suffering.[11] This black social gospel helped Williams address both the eternal destiny of the soul and the daily injustices felt by his congregants.

Under A.D. Williams' pastorate, Ebenezer weathered the infamous Atlanta massacre of 1906.[12] Incensed by sensationalized newspaper reports of black men attacking white women, mobs of angry whites stormed the city for four days savagely murdering dozens of black citizens and seriously wounding many more.[13] The riot relief committee's report to the Atlanta Chamber of Commerce succinctly described the grizzly scene. "About seventy persons were wounded and among these there was an immense amount of suffering. In some cases it was prolonged and excruciating pain. Many of the wounded are disfigured, and several are permanently disabled."[14] Local and national authorities especially depended on black ministers to keep the situation from escalating even further by attending to the grief, confusion, and anger of the black citizenry.[15] Uniquely attuned to the practical needs of the suffering, A.D. Williams' ministry brought much needed relief to parishioners and community members devastated by the carnage. Even in the wake of hardships like the 1906 massacre, Ebenezer continued to experience a steady growth in membership, eventually becoming one of the most prominent black churches in Atlanta. A.D. Williams continued to address the plight of the oppressed as a necessary function of his pastoral ministry. He helped to establish Atlanta's chapter of the National Association for the

Advancement of Colored People (NAACP) and, after it dehumanized blacks in its articles, Williams mobilized local congregations to boycott (and eventually bankrupt) *The Georgian*, one of Atlanta's most prominent newspapers.[16] Williams would go on to establish himself as one of the most influential black preachers in the South, modeling for a generation of black clergymen how to consistently apply the message of Christ to the problem of black suffering.[17]

While A.D. Williams was gaining influence in the city of Atlanta, James and Delia King (Martin King Jr.'s paternal grandparents) were struggling as sharecroppers in rural Stockbridge, Georgia.[18] Although James was not a particularly religious man, his wife Delia was a deeply committed Christian. She regularly brought the couple's nine children to worship services at the Floyd Chapel Baptist Church of Stockbridge. There, Delia's oldest son, Michael Luther King (later known as Martin Luther King, Sr.) fell in love with the soulful music and passionate preaching within the rural black Baptist church tradition.[19] These grace-filled rituals helped ameliorate the hardness of life in racist rural Georgia.[20] Under the pastorate of Rev. W.H. Rowe, Mike King grew to admire the willingness of black preachers to speak out fearlessly against the daily injustices experienced by blacks in the South.[21] Soon, he found himself secretly imitating "the gestures, cadences, and deeply emotive quality" of the traveling preachers in the area. And by 1917, he began to pursue a call to ministry himself.[22] By 1918, twenty-one-year-old Mike King had followed his older sister Woodie into Atlanta where he met Alberta Christine Williams, the daughter of A.D. and Jennie Williams. They began a seven year courtship that would lead to marriage.

A.D. Williams had a tremendous impact on King's ministry, particularly in orienting him towards addressing the problem of black suffering. Williams taught his son-in-law that as a faithful minister he must oppose the societal injustices experienced by his congregants.[23] King, Sr. recalled,

> For his part, the Reverend [A.D. Williams] kept a close eye on me, not just because I was now family, but also because of his deep interest in the ministries of younger men in Atlanta. It was through him that I came to understand the larger implications involved in any churchman's responsibility to the community he served. . . . In the act of faith, every minister became an advocate for justice. In the South, this

meant an active involvement in changing the social order all around us.[24]

Already well acquainted with the brutalities of the segregated South and the potential for black preachers to help alleviate them, King Sr. eagerly adopted A.D. Williams' social gospel approach to ministry. Williams particularly stressed the central role of suffering in achieving the goal of social progress. According to King, Sr., Williams considered the willingness to suffer to be among the most significant aspects of gospel ministry and had little tolerance for any preacher who attempted to evade it. He remembered,

> Reverend Williams made it clear to me from the time I moved into his home that he felt no sympathy for those who saw no mission in their lives, who could not understand, for instance, that progress never came without challenge, without danger and, at times great trial. These obstacles, however, could not stop the true man of God. A minister, in his calling, chose to lead the people of his church not only in the spiritual sense, but also in the practical world in which they found themselves struggling.[25]

Therefore, Williams handed King, Sr. a ministry perspective that included both a general orientation towards the social needs of the oppressed and particular recognition of the necessary role of personal suffering in meeting these social needs. As Williams' successor at Ebenezer, King Sr., immediately demonstrated a commitment to this view. In 1931, during the worst of the Great Depression, he revitalized the congregation through a series of successful membership and fundraising campaigns.[26] According to King, the key to the congregation's success was in the members' strength and willingness to endure suffering. "Our Sunday mornings had a joy about them," he wrote, "a passion in the songs, and a pleasure in the pastor's sermons that came from knowing what strength people could bring to hardship, what faith and fellowship."[27] Therefore, from the very beginning of his pastoral ministry King, Sr. emphasized faithful engagement with suffering as a key to Christian witness.

King, Sr. also applied this to the broader congregation. He firmly believed that Ebenezer's unique witness to the world lay in its ability to demonstrate faith in hardship. Convinced that this unique conviction would carry Ebenezer through the most trying times, King emphasized this belief early and often in his preaching ministry. He explained,

> And I preached that we wouldn't just make it through [hardships] but we would prosper, because this belief of ours was something special. "Ebenezer will give this world much that is special," I said, "because we walk any path proudly. We can be weary but continue on without a word of reproach. And we will, church," I preached. We surely will.[28]

For King, Sr., strength in suffering would be the enduring legacy of Ebenezer, its special contribution to the world. His statement seems to acknowledge that Ebenezer already had a reputation of handling adversity well, undoubtedly a testament to the thirty-seven-year ministry of A.D. Williams. Now King, Sr. exhorted Ebenezer to engage the hardships of southern racism during the Great Depression with a special dignity and love. His statements emphasize active engagement with suffering rather than the passive experience of it. Suffering was the inescapable reality for blacks living in the segregated south, especially during the period of the Great Depression. However, King, Sr. held that the Christian response would be to engage this suffering in a way that would teach the surrounding culture about God's purposes for it.

This became a core aspect of King, Sr.'s pastoral ministry and of Ebenezer's unique calling and identity as a congregation. King, Sr. continued,

> . . . I worked to give my congregation a continuing sense of our strength as God had provided it. We had been asked by Him to bear a great burden in our time. But we could rise above any misery and grief. Others might slip under the weight, Ebenezer determined not to.[29]

He held that God had called and empowered Ebenezer to weather the storms of racial adversity to help America "discover its future."[30] Therefore, King, Sr. continually encouraged Ebenezer to accept its congregational calling to rise above its misery for the sake of teaching the nation what God intended it to be. King, Jr. was only two years old when his father began preaching this message as the senior pastor of Ebenezer. As a virtual extension of his family, Ebenezer Baptist church also served as the primary context of King Jr.'s formative religious and intellectual development.[31] King's early experiences within Ebenezer laid the foundation for his sense of solidarity with southern blacks and his commitment to their plight.[32] It follows then, that he would have also been fundamentally shaped by Ebenezer's congregational calling to socially redemptive suffering. Additionally, King's grandmother Jennie Celeste Williams often told stories about the practical ministries of her late husband A.D. and father-in-law Willis Williams. Serving a largely didactic purpose, these stories would have ensured that King, Jr. was significantly informed by the values and legacies of his preaching ancestors.[33]

King's redemptive suffering theodicy represents the culmination of a century-long family tradition of pastoral ministries oriented towards the problem of black suffering. As we have shown, King's grandfather and father promoted the specific belief that suffering was a necessary means to achieve social progress. As the heir of three generations of preachers oriented towards black suffering, King would have been taught to understand pastoral ministry as (among other things) a calling to take up and practically address the issue of black suffering.[34] King would learn this lesson well. During Robert Keighton's preaching course at Crozer Seminary, King summarized his ministry in ways that closely reflected the ideals of his preaching forefathers. He noted,

> I feel that preaching should grow out of the experiences of the people. Therefore, I as a minister must know the problems of the people that I am pastoring. To[o] often do educated minister[s] leave the people lost in the fog of theological abstractions, rather than presenting that theology in light of people's experiences ... Above all I see the preaching ministry as a duel process. On the one hand I must change the soul of individuals so that their societies may be changed. On the other I must attempt to change the societies so that the individual soul will have a change. Therefore, I must be concerned about unemployment, slums, and economic insecurity. I am a profound advocator of the social gospel.[35]

In words that sound remarkably similar to A.D. Williams and King, Sr., Martin Luther King, Jr. described his ministry responsibilities as addressing the practical struggles of the congregation, identifying with the suffering, advocating for justice within the broader community, and attempting to change the social order. King expresses his strong conviction that preaching must "grow out of the experiences of the people." According to King, the faithful preacher must identify and relate to the struggles of the congregation. For him, this remained one of the most important components preaching ministry.[36] In his context, this approach to ministry would certainly have lent itself towards meaningful engagement with the problem of black suffering.

King did not receive this approach entirely from ministers within his family tree. After a period of intense religious skepticism, George Kelsey and Benjamin Mays renewed King's confidence in the potential for Christian ministry to intellectually and practically engage the problem of black suffering.[37] Unsatisfied by the "uncritical" approach to the Bible he had been taught in his youth,[38] King became skeptical of religion and initially pursued medicine and law as potential vocations at Morehouse College.[39] King's breakthrough came through the combined influences of George Kelsey and Benjamin Mays. Kelsey, Director of the Religious Studies Program at Morehouse, helped King work through his religious misgivings, formally introducing him to protestant liberalism and encouraging him that "behind the legends and myths of the Book [i.e., the Bible] were many profound truths which one could not escape."[40] Kelsey also encouraged King that modern ministers should engage with philosophy and delve deeply into the social concerns of the oppressed.

King found the example he sought in the preaching ministry of Benjamin Mays, President of Morehouse College. Applying the tenets of protestant liberalism to black suffering, Mays stressed the social responsibility of the Christian minister and the social implications of Christian doctrine. Profoundly impressed, King regularly sought Mays' counsel long after chapel services ended.[41] For King, Mays represented the ideal combination of intellectual and spiritual engagement in view of practical service to humanity.[42] As we have seen, King's father and grandfather already had considerable legacies of social engagement. However, Mays and Kelsey helped King reconsider the potential for Christian ministry to provide a platform for rigorous intellectual engagement aimed at addressing the problem of black suffering.[43] In so doing, they helped King better appreciate his own rich heritage of ministerial social engagement.[44]

We have also demonstrated that King's theodicy reflects the particular communal identity of the Ebenezer Baptist Church. Following A.D. Williams, Martin King, Sr. stilled the belief in redemptive suffering as an essential part of Ebenezer's congregational identity. Given the considerable place of Ebenezer as a formative influence in King Jr.'s life, it follows that this view of suffering would have been among the set of ideals that King, Jr. gradually absorbed from his earliest ecclesial environment. Additionally, King carried out the vast majority of his pastoral calling within the context of Ebenezer Baptist Church. In February 1948, he was ordained as the assistant pastor at Ebenezer right out of college. He would take up these pastoral duties mostly during his winter and summer breaks from Crozer Seminary and Boston University. After serving as the pastor of the Dexter Avenue Baptist Church for five years (1954–1959), King returned to Ebenezer where he served as co-pastor alongside his father from 1960 until his death in 1968. Although his work with the Southern Christian Leadership Conference (SCLC) increasingly took him away from local church life at Ebenezer, King primarily viewed his activism as an extension of his calling as a black Baptist pastor. He turned down a number of job offers from predominantly white universities and seminaries in order to maintain close ties with the black church community in general, and Ebenezer in particular.[45] Rather than the abstract musings of an ecclesiastically detached theologian, King's theodicy represents a century-long pastoral tradition and the deep reflection of a particular black church community about the meaning and purpose of black suffering. As a lifelong member of Ebenezer, a church which understood itself as divinely called to suffer in order to help America achieve social progress, King would have been primed to respond to the question of black suffering with a redemptive suffering theodicy.

Part 2: The Black Church Music Tradition Impacts King's Theodicy

King grew up imbibing the gospel songs, spirituals, and great hymns of the black church, a music tradition that reflects three centuries of sustained Christian reflection on the meaning of black suffering. With a musical pastor for a father and a gifted organist for a mother,[46] King was raised with a deep appreciation for black church music and its ability to convey hope amidst suffering. By the age of six, King was already singing "slow and sobbing hymns" at church conventions accompanied by his "Mother Dear" on piano. Known for his singing voice long before his sermonic oratory, congregants often wept and shouted for joy after hearing young King perform.[47] His father recalled that even as a young boy, King had a "passionate love of Baptist music."[48] He maintained this love for black church music during his college and seminary days, and was known to listen to "old-time spirituals" for hours at a time.[49] Therefore, early on, King understood the unique power of these "sorrow songs,"[50] as he called them, to express the hopeful groaning of a socially oppressed people of faith. In *Black Song,* James Lovell describes Negro spirituals as a communal blend of folklore and song that "tried, with inspired artistry, to pose the root questions of life, of before life, and of beyond life . . ."[51] Forged in the flames of chattel slavery, these songs wrestled deeply with the problem of evil.[52] King would appropriate this rhythmic theodical tradition to help give voice to the civil rights movement. He turned many spirituals into the freedom songs of the movement. He described these contextualized adaptations of the spirituals, as "playing a strong and vital role in our movement."[53] He explained,

> In a sense the freedom songs are the soul of the movement. They are more than just incantations of clever phrases designed to invigorate a campaign; they are as old as the history of the Negro in America. They are adaptations of the songs the slaves sang—the sorrow songs, the shouts of joy, the battle hymns and the anthems of our movement. I have heard people talk of their beat and their rhythm, but we in the movement are as inspired by their words . . . We sing the freedom songs today for the same reason the slaves sang them, because we too are in bondage and the songs add hope to our determination that 'We shall overcome, black and white together, We shall overcome someday.' . . . These songs bind us together, give us courage together, help us march together.[54]

King drew on black church music as a rich theological source which encapsulated the slave community's redemptive hope amidst suffering. For him, the genius of these songs lay in their unique ability to express both the extreme agonies and hope of black life in America.[55] In one version his sermon "A Knock at Midnight," delivered before Mt. Zion Baptist Church of Cincinnati, Ohio, King described the lessons learned from spirituals' strange blend of sorrow and joy.

> Our slave parents taught us so much in their beautiful sorrow songs, one of which you sang so beautifully this morning. They looked at the midnight surrounding their days. They knew that there were sorrow and agony and hurt all around. When they thought about midnight they would sing, "Nobody known the trouble I see, Nobody knows but Jesus." But pretty soon something reminded them that morning would

come, and they started singing, "I'm so glad, Trouble don't last always."[56]

Songs like "Nobody Knows De Trouble I've Seen," "Sometimes I Feel like a Motherless Child," and "I've Been 'Buked and I've Been Scorned," dance on the edge of despair before rejoicing in hopeful triumph.[57] Although they were staunchly hopeful, the spirituals avoided pat optimism. Laced with realistic doubts and fears, the spirituals acknowledged life's unresolved mysteries and tragedies. However, they almost always expressed clear-headed hope in the face of life's numerous tragedies. In his famous essay on the spirituals entitled "Sorrow Songs," W.E.B. Du Bois described the persistent hope held out in the spirituals.[58] He remarked, "Through all the sorrow of the Sorrow Songs there breathes a hope—a faith in the ultimate justice of things. The minor cadences of despair change often to triumph and calm confidence."[59] Following Du Bois,[60] King also identified the purpose of these songs as bringing hope to the socially oppressed, a faith in the ultimate triumph of justice.[61] When King spoke of the long arc of the moral universe bending toward justice and "when he sang, 'We Shall Overcome,' King was participating in the Christian optimism concerning the future of humankind and human society which the slaves gave expression to in their spiritual songs."[62]

Songs like "Didn't my Lord Deliver Daniel," "Balm in Gilead," and "We'll Understand it Better By and By" helped introduce King to the Black Church's hopeful attitude towards suffering. In "Didn't My Lord Deliver Daniel" the community raises the question of theodicy, asking,

> Didn't my Lord deliver Daniel
> Deliver Daniel, deliver Daniel
> Didn't my Lord deliver Daniel
> An' why not-a every man.
> He delivered Daniel from de lion's den
> Jonah from de belly of de whale
> An' de Hebrew chillun from de fiery furnace
> An' why not every man?[63]

The question within the refrain can be read both literally and rhetorically. Amidst their numerous frustrations and in light of God's mighty acts of deliverance, slaves wondered why they weren't yet free.[64] Here, the words "An' why not every man" reflect the classic problem of evil—given God's power to deliver, the slave community asked why they were not yet delivered? However, the refrain can also be read rhetorically, with a sense of hopeful expectation in the power and purpose of God to bring freedom. Since God was willing and able to deliver Daniel, Jonah, and the Hebrew chillun, why wouldn't he also be willing and able to deliver the rest of His people?

King probed the theodical depths of this song through Howard Thurman's *Deep River: Reflections on the Religious Insight of Certain of the Negro Spirituals*.[65] There, Thurman explained that spirituals like "Didn't My Lord Deliver Daniel" used Biblical narratives to address the deepest practical needs of the slaves, giving them real hope that God was still at work in the world as a deliverer. Thurman notes,

> The experiences of frustrations and divine deliverance, as set forth in the stories of the Hebrews in bondage spoke at once to the deep need in the life of the slave. . . . The outstanding significance of the Bible was that it provided the slaves inspiration and illumination as they sought to thread life's mystery with very few clues. What they found true in their experience lived for them in the sacred Book. God was at work in history . . . . God was the deliverer. The conception is that inasmuch as God is no respecter of persons, what He did for one race He would surely do for another . . . Daring to believe that God cared for them despite the cruel vicissitudes of life meant the giving of wings to life that nothing could destroy.[66]

A considerable portion of the spirituals were dramatized stories from the Old Testament intended to give the slaves hope that God would deliver them like he delivered the ancient Hebrews. Spirituals like "Didn't My Lord Deliver Daniel" would have even provided some unlettered lay preachers with enough knowledge of the Bible to preach sermons infused with the Black community's hopeful hermeneutic.[67] The power of God was at work among them as it had been among the ancients. King's theodical sermon "The Death of Evil upon the Seashore" stands well within this hermeneutic tradition highlighted in the spirituals.

The spiritual "Balm in Gilead" uses the rhetorical question posed by the book of Jeremiah to explain how hope can be forged from bleak experiences. The cry "Is There No Balm in Gilead?" was hammered out of Jeremiah's sense of discouragement and depression, a spiritual dilemma which stripped him of all superficialities and caused him to reflect on the very core of his faith. Howard Thurman explained that the slave caught the essence of this spiritual struggle and "straightened the question mark in Jeremiah's sentence into an exclamation point: 'There is a balm in Gilead!'"[68] King often quoted this spiritual when he "needed a lift."[69] The words reminded him of enduring hope in the midst of life's harshest trials.

> There is a balm in Gilead,
> To make the wounded whole.
> There is a balm in Gilead,
> To heal the sin-sick soul.[70]

Thurman describes "Balm in Gilead" as containing a note of "creative triumph"—a creative engagement with the suffering of life to produce hope.[71] He explains, "The basic insight here is one of optimism—an optimism that grows out of the pessimism of life and transcends it. It is an optimism that uses the pessimism of life as raw material out of which it creates its own strength."[72] Therefore, the key insight contained in this spiritual is very similar to King's theodical insight that unmerited suffering can be creatively engaged to help strengthen hope. In his sermon "A Knock at Midnight," King alluded almost directly to Thurman's interpretation of "Balm in Gilead." Confronted with the brutalities of slavery, King suggested that his slave forefathers did "an amazing thing, they took Jeremiah's question mark and straightened into an exclamation point."[73] In describing redemptive suffering theme contained in this spiritual, King explained, "Here we see a positive belief in the dawn which uses the midnight of life as a raw material out of which it creates its own strength. This was the growing edge of hope that kept the slaves going amid the most barren and tragic circumstances."[74] Having grown up hearing "Balm in Gilead" in Black Churches and having encountered Thurman's interpretation of it in "Deep River," King would have used "Balm in Gilead" to reinforce the idea that his trials could be creatively handled as the "raw material" out of which hope could be born.

Charles Tindley's hymn "We'll Understand it Better By and By," reflects a deep respect for the mystery of God's purposes in suffering. Tindley's hymn became so popular, it was eventually included both in *The Baptist Standard Hymnal* and *Gospel Pearls*, the standard music collections used by the churches in King's denomination, the National Baptist Convention. The song would have been standard fare at black Baptist churches like Ebenezer, and so King would have been intimately familiar with it.[75] The hymn brilliantly captures the hope reflected in the broader black church tradition that somehow, in ways not entirely understood right now, the longstanding trouble within the black experience will not have the final word.[76] The third stanza of the hymn says,

> Trials dark on every hand, and we cannot understand
> All the ways that God would lead us to that Blessed Promised Land;
> But he guides us with His eye and we'll follow till we die,
> For we'll understand it better by and by.

> By and by, when the morning comes.
> All the saints of God are gathered home,
> We'll tell the story of how we've overcome,
> For we'll understand it better by and by.[77]

In the spirit of this hymn, King's theodicy also included healthy respect for the mystery of God's purposes in trials. Although God worked through suffering, King readily acknowledged that it was not always clear exactly how He would do so. He confessed, "The existence of evil in the world still stands as a great enigma wrapped in mystery, yet it has not caused the Christian to live in total despair."[78] Convinced that one day believers would indeed overcome the suffering in this world, King held that God fulfills his mysterious benevolent purpose throughout history and within the lives of individuals in progressive "strides,"[79] which don't become entirely clear until their culmination. Therefore King's theodicy stands within the theodical tradition of this great hymn of the black church.

In this section we have demonstrated that the music of the black church significantly impacted Martin King's theodicy. King, Jr. developed a lasting appreciation for the spirituals and hymns of the black church through his family and church environment. Moreover, he self-consciously reflected on their theological significance through works like Du Bois's essay "Sorrow Songs" and Thurman's "Deep River" and "The Negro Spiritual Speaks of Life and Death." For King, songs like "Nobody Knows De Trouble I've Seen," "Sometimes I Feel like a Motherless Child," and "I've Been 'Buked and I've Been Scorned," highlighted the black church's unique ability to hold extreme highs and lows together, to see hopeful triumph even while acknowledging life's tragedies. Spirituals like "Didn't my Lord Deliver Daniel" used biblical narratives to reflect a common hope in the power of God still at work in history to fulfill good purposes through trials. King engaged Thurman's interpretation of Balm

BLACK CHURCH ROOTS

in Gilead to remind himself and others that dark times form the "raw material" which may be creatively engaged to strengthen hope. Finally, Charles Tindley's famous hymn "We'll Understand it Better By and By," reflects the black church's deep respect for the mystery of God's purposes in suffering, an attitude that King himself adopted and expressed through his own approach to theodicy.

Part 3: The Black Church Prayer Tradition Impacts King's Theodicy

King's outlook on suffering was also deeply impacted by the prayer tradition of the black church, a tradition born in the bellies of slave ships and refined within the cramped confines of slave quarters and in the sweltering heat of southern cotton fields.[80] King grew up in a household and church environment filled with prayer in the rhythmic style of his southern slave ancestors[81] and came to view prayer as "the lived theology"[82] of his people. Prayer offered the slaves a practical way to cope with the harsh realities of their daily lives, a place to "take one's burdens to the Lord and leave them there."[83] However, the Black prayer tradition also reflects the broader quest to make meaning out of the brutality of the black experience. Baldwin explains, "For people facing awful, traumatic experiences and unimaginable sorrow, prayer was a restless yearning for answers to the larger question of *meaning*, the *why* of the black experience [emphasis Baldwin's]."[84] Even in the face of seemingly senseless and unending hardships slaves prayed as a practical expression of their enduring hope that the Almighty was yet at work in and through their tragic circumstances.[85]

As a son of the black church, King inherited this nearly 300-year-old tradition and appropriated it to his own search for meaning. Baldwin notes, "King's own quest for meaning and healing drew on the resources of this heritage, and it explains why he felt that slave religion had much to teach about how to deal with the tragic events of everyday life."[86] During his darkest moments, King drew on the spiritual resources of the black church tradition, especially its prayer tradition.[87] A few months after the Montgomery Bus Boycott began, King received a barrage of threatening phone calls and letters. One such phone call bothered him so much that he felt himself "ready to give up." Alone in his kitchen, he prayed to the God made known to him in the black church tradition. This detailed recollection of his now famous "kitchen vision," reveals the way the black prayer tradition informed King's approach to theodicy. For these reasons, it is worth quoting at length.

> . . . I never will forget one night, very late—it was around midnight. And you can have some strange experiences at midnight. The phone started ringing and I picked it up. On the other end was an ugly voice. That voice said to me, in substance, "nigger, we are tired of you and your mess now, and if you aren't out of town in three days, we're going to blow your brains out and blow up your house." I'd heard these things before, but for some reason that night, it got to me. I turned over and tried to go to sleep, but I couldn't go to sleep. I was frustrated, bewildered. Then I got up and went back to the kitchen and started warming some coffee, thinking that coffee would give me a little relief. Then I started thinking about many things—*I pulled back on the theology and philosophy that I had just studied in the universities, trying to give philosophical and theological reasons for the existence and reality of sin and evil, but the answer didn't quite come there* [emphasis mine] . . . And I got to the point where I couldn't take it any longer—I was weak. And something said to me, 'You can't call on Daddy now, he's up in Atlanta, a hundred and seventy-five miles away. You can't even call on Mamma now. *You've got to call on that something and that person that your Daddy used to tell you about— that power that can make a way out of no way.* . . . *And I bowed down over that cup of coffee, I never will forget it. Oh yes, I prayed a prayer, and I prayed out loud that night* [emphasis mine] . . .[88]

King wrestled deeply with the problem of evil that night. Edgar Sheffield Brightman's theistic finitude must have been among the philosophical concepts King attempted to "pull back on" that night. However, vexed by his own weaknesses, King would have derived little comfort from the idea of a limited deity. Unconsoled by the protestant liberal approaches to theodicy he learned at Crozer Seminary and Boston University, King ultimately appealed to the black church's traditional concept of all-powerful, all-knowing, ever present God, the one his Daddy used to tell him about. Humbled by his dependence upon the matchless power of God, King resorted to prayer. As he recounted the Kitchen vision, King deliberately reminded his black church audience of his posture and manner of prayer. "And I bowed down over that cup of coffee . . . Oh yes," he said, "I prayed a prayer, and I prayed out loud that night." With this, King deliberately drew on the tradition of taking his burdens to the Lord in the most humble way possible. Apparently, in his most intense moments of crisis, King resorted to his prayer roots in the black church.

Within the black prayer tradition, God is most often understood as being able to "do as He pleases," to "open doors no man can close and close doors no man can open," and being able to "build up where no man can tear down, and tear down where no man can build up."[89] These common expressions convey the sense that God possesses a power beyond the limits of His finite creation. Despite his tutelage under Edgar Brightman, King often directed prayer to the God of absolute power and infinite intelligence.[90] However, King's carefully chosen wording conveys more than the traditional idea that God has unlimited power. It also conveys a specific sense in which God uses His power. God uses His power to "make a way out of no way." In other words, God fulfills his good purposes (i.e., "makes a way") using the raw material of adversity (i.e., "out of no way"). Alone in the kitchen, King was not seeking to escape his circumstances; rather he sought to understand God's good purposes in and through them. Informed by the black prayer tradition, King called on the God who could transform his bleak circumstances into something redemptive.

As a pastor, King found prayer to be a vital instrument in offering the members of Dexter Avenue and Ebenezer a renewed sense of meaning, healing, and courage to face their trials. For King, prayer was a positive catalyst for redemptive transformation in the hearts and minds of God's people and the means by which many of redemptive promises are fulfilled. In the common black church vernacular, "prayer changes things."[91] Prayer also served a didactic purpose for King, providing a fitting venue to convey his redemptive suffering theodicy.[92] For instance, in 1959 King offered this prayer near the end of a "Palm Sunday Sermon on Mohandas K Gandhi."

> And God grant that we shall choose the high way, even if it will mean assassination, even if it will mean crucifixion, for by going this way we will discover that death would be only the beginning of our influence.[93]

Here, the cross of Christ is viewed as the paradigmatic example of redemptive suffering. The cross was central to King's theodicy, because it serves as the ultimate empowering revelation of God's intention and power to creatively transform unmerited suffering into redemption.[94] For King, the answer to the problem of evil is a direct result "of what Christ did with evil on the cross."[95] Within the black church context, a thoroughly cruci-centric tradition,[96] there couldn't be a more powerful symbol with which to make meaning out of unmerited suffering. King's enslaved forbearers also prayed to Jesus as a "fellow sufferer at the hands of the unjust oppressor."[97] Therefore, King's theodical prayer took up an old theme within the black prayer tradition and served as a powerful means to appropriate it to his contemporary circumstance.

Much like the "sorrow songs" of the black church, King also found the prayer tradition of the black church to be a powerful weapon in the struggle for civil rights—a practical way that physical force could be met by the power of "soul force." In *The Prayer Tradition of Black People*, Harold Carter observed, "Martin Luther King, Jr., knew that facing life on one's knees had been historically the only potent weapon black people had to face life's many problems . . . Dr. King used this long prayer tradition to teach black people that the one who faces life with a prayer is not weak." [98] With a view towards the theological potency of the black prayer tradition, King made prayer a central focus of the movement, a quintessential expression of non-violent resistance.[99] During marches in Birmingham and Selma, Alabama, King knelt to pray directly in front of police officers who forcefully grabbed him and hauled him to jail for "illegally" protesting.[100] Hence, prayer served as a practical embodiment of King's theodical conviction that redemptive power is available through creatively engaging suffering. Following King, Civil Rights activists often prayed fervently after being arrested for participating in the movement—a strategy to creatively engage their suffering with a view towards social redemption.[101] King also used prayer as a means to communicate the message of redemptive suffering within his speeches. In a speech delivered on July 26, 1965, from a truck bed parked at Chicago's City Hall, King offered this prayer.

> . . . We pray especially for every white citizen of this great city. Instill in them an awareness of the deep scars, the terrible hurt, and the tragic disappointment that segregation has inflicted upon the Negro . . . For those who are still caught in the dark valley of prejudice, we pray that Thou will guide them to sunlit paths of open-hearted good will.
>
> We pray also for every Negro citizen of Chicago. Save us from the patience that would accept less than first class citizenship, but imbue

us with a faith which the forces of ill cannot dampen, a hope that the long night of struggle ahead cannot extinguish, and a creative redeeming love that will enable us to continue our struggle non-violently.[102]

King's "Prayer for the City of Chicago," features some of the core components of his theodicy. By "creative redeeming love," King means the power by which God works through suffering, creatively transforming it in order to fulfill his redemptive purposes. In this context, King meant creatively engaging suffering through non-violent direct action protests. By way of creative suffering, King hoped God would guide the white citizens of Chicago to "sunlit paths of open-hearted good will." In private, ecclesial, as well as public settings, prayer served as a powerful means to reinforce and communicate the substance of King's redemptive suffering theodicy.

With this, we have seen that the black church prayer tradition made a significant impact on King's theodicy. Marked by the question of the meaning of black suffering, the black church prayer tradition reinforced the idea, in King's mind, that God powerfully fulfills his purposes through creatively transforming adversity. In his darkest moments, King prayed to the God most often petitioned in black prayer, the God who could "make a way out of no way." Furthermore, King drew on the crucicentrism of the black prayer tradition to powerfully convey his theodicy in ecclesial settings. Finally, King used prayer as a practical embodiment of the theological conviction that suffering could be engaged creatively to yield redemptive benefits.[103] With this, we turn from King's black church heritage to his black church context.

KING'S BLACK CHURCH MINISTRY CONTEXT IMPACTS HIS THEODICY

The black Baptist context in which King served as a pastor deeply impacted his theodicy, not only raising the issue but helping to determine his sermonic emphases on divine omnipotence and the inevitable triumph of justice. Less than nine months after being installed as the twentieth pastor of the Dexter Avenue Baptist Church, King addressed the question of theodicy head-on in a sermon entitled "The Death of Evil upon the Seashore" in which he likened the death of evil to the death of the Egyptian army at the Red Sea.[104] Reflecting the optimism characteristic of the black church, King exhorted the congregation to trust that God will ultimately defeat evil.[105] "... in the long struggle between good and evil," he said, "good eventually emerges as the victor. Evil is ultimately doomed by the powerful insurgent forces of good."[106] The eventual triumph of good over evil remains among the most deeply cherished beliefs in the black church tradition. King reaffirmed this belief by suggesting that the death of evil was already being gradually realized throughout the modern history of the American Negro. He viewed the U.S. Supreme Court's 1954 Brown v. Board of Education decision as proof that the evil of segregation was destined to die.[107] He continued, "As we look back we see segregation caught in the rushing waters of historical necessity. Evil in the form of injustice and exploitation cannot survive."[108] King explained that God intends to achieve a world in which human beings live in just and harmonious relations and recognize the true dignity of one another. According to King, God fulfills this purpose by seeking to "lift men from the bondage of some evil Egypt, carrying them through the wilderness of discipline, and finally to the promised land of personal and social integration."[109] So King remained staunchly optimistic about God's power to bring about the eventual downfall of segregation.

Two months into the Montgomery Bus boycott, King found himself facing numerous death threats and other racially motivated hardships. Forced to think even more deeply about the problem of black suffering, King delivered, "Our God is Able," his most explicit homiletical reflection on the problem of evil up to that point.[110] There, King offered Dexter Avenue a textbook description of the classic problem of evil. He explained,

> There are times when each of us is forced to question the ableness of our God. When we notice the stark and colossal realities of evil ... we find ourselves asking why does all this exist if God is able to prevent it ... We can say that in spite of all these glaring dimensions of evil, and the occasional doubts that come to all of us there is a perennial conviction that "our God is able."[111]

Much like in "The Death of Evil upon the Seashore," King affirms that evil will ultimately be conquered by the power of God.[112] He credits this belief with having sustained him through doubts about the outcome of the struggle for social justice. Amidst the intensifying heat of racism, King encouraged Dexter Avenue to remain hopeful in God's power to destroy the evil of segregation:

> Let us notice again that God is able to subdue all the powers of evil . . . Evil must ultimately give way to the powerful insurgent forces of Good. This is ultimately the hope that keeps us going. Much of my ministry has been given to fighting against social evil. There are times when I get despondent, and wonder if it is worth it. But then something says to me deep down within God is able, you need not worry. So this morning I say to you we must continue to struggle against evil, but don't worry, God is able. Don't worry about segregation. It will die because God is against it. Whenever God is against a thing, it cannot survive.[113]

In all of these sermonic examples, King projects a virtually unqualified confidence in the power of God to triumph over the evils of racism. Although King admitted times of "occasional doubt," he maintained an unwavering hope, an absolute certainty in the demise of segregation beneath the matchless power of God. This kind of language is fairly typical of the black church, reflecting King's homespun roots. However his theodical language within the black church marks a notable shift from some of his musings in graduate school just the year prior, and so highlights just how the King's black church context influenced these specific points of emphasis.

King's pastorate at Dexter Avenue came just on the heels of his graduate studies with the personalist philosopher Edgar Sheffield Brightman. Brightman's particular version of personalism included a distinctive idea known as "theistic finitism," an attempt to resolve certain difficulties raised by the problem of evil. According to Brightman, God has an infinite will for the good, however there is a mysterious "Given" part of God's nature which hinders God's ability to bring to fulfillment the full expression of God's will. According to Brightman, the "Given" is not created or produced by God's will and cannot be understood as an act of self-limitation.[114] Although he was suspicious of theistic finitism during his days at Crozer Seminary, King gradually became more sympathetic to the concept while studying under Brightman himself at Boston University. When asked to evaluate the finite God idea in Brightman's philosophy of religion course, King still expressed some reservations. He wrote,

> ... Dr. Brightman does not completely escape dualism. It is true that he escapes cosmic dualism, but only to leave a dualism in the nature of God. Does not such dualism leave faith in a supreme God endangered and triumph over the nonrational Given uncertain? What evidence that God is winning a gradual mastery over the limitations in his nature?[115]

King raises a concern about believing in God as the Supreme Being capable of ensuring the triumph of justice and goodness, in this case through gradually mastering the limitations in God's own nature. However, by the time he wrote the final exam for Brightman's course, King's reservations had all but vanished. He said,

> At present I am quite sympathetic with this idea [theistic finitism]. After a somewhat extensive study of the idea, I am all but convinced that it is the only adequate explanation for the existence of evil ... It is the most empirical explanation we can set forth in relation to the God idea.[116]

It is difficult to say exactly what provoked this sudden change in King's tone toward theistic finitism. During the class, Brightman may have offered compelling support for his theory that King hadn't previously considered. Perhaps, as a graduate student at Boston, King did not feel at liberty to disagree with his advisors point of view as forcefully as he did at Crozer.[117] Whatever the reasons, King's comments most likely reflect his sincere opinion at the time. In the final analysis, King did eventually adopt some version of finitism, however he adapted his language to stress the elements of his view that would resonate with his black church audience.[118] Among white liberals like Brightman, King was comfortable acknowledging his appreciation for philosophical answers provided by theistic finitism. However, in the heat of the struggle for freedom and before black church audiences, King unequivocally stressed the matchless power of God.

King appears to have carefully concealed any sympathies with finitism from his black church audience at Dexter Avenue.[119] King's earliest versions of "The Death of Evil" and "Our God is Able" don't offer the slightest hint that God is in any way hindered in conquering the evils of racism and segregation, especially by anything intrinsic to the divine nature.[120] Although King was more willing to employ language that sounded like theistic finitism before predominantly white audiences, his

BLACK CHURCH ROOTS

black church context completely prevented him from endorsing it from the pulpit.[121] Generally, African Americans have held fast to the traditional view of the "all-powerful God,"[122] who is able to "do anything but fail."[123] Historically, this belief has offered a strong sense of security amidst the many uncertainties of black life in America.[124] Steeped in traditional black church notions of divine omnipotence, King knew his congregation would have likely rejected any idea that God could be hindered from conquering the evils of racism in Montgomery. Although he re-conceptualized traditional views of divine omnipotence during his formal theological studies, King avoided presenting these ideas before black church audiences.[125] Rufus Burrow explains, "King knew that the predominantly Black audience could not handle this [concept of theistic finitism] as well [as White predominantly audiences]. For their historical experience was such that the more traditional doctrine of the omnipotent omni-benevolent God gave them more reason to be optimistic in a racist society."[126]

So King's strategy reflects the considerable influence the black church exercised on him. King rejected divine omnipotence in the traditional absolute sense, essentially holding that God has infinite concern for the good as well as power sufficient to actualize it in a concrete way.[127] Rather than equivocate or risk describing God in way that would be completely unfamiliar (and potentially off-putting) to his congregation, King emphasized the aspects of his theodicy with which black church folks could relate. Essentially, King held that God has matchless power, rather than all power. However, as the Supreme Being, God's power is sufficient to ensure the triumph of justice. Therefore, King focused his sermons on God's ability to bring good out of evil rather than God's inability to do the impossible or the absurd, and on God's power to triumph over evil rather than any internal hindrances to the fulfillment of God's good purposes. King described God as perfectly willing and able to deliver oppressed people even while inviting humans to cooperate in the effort. Despite re-conceptualizing the traditional sense of omnipotence, King's sermonic emphases on the problem of evil faithfully reflect the traditional black church source of optimism, the God who is able to "make a way out of no way."[128] The practical needs and expectations of traditional black church audiences pressed him to continue to wrestle with theodicy and to speak of God's power in a way that would resonate. This context served to counterbalance the finitistic language he used in graduate school and among predominantly white protestant liberal audiences.

CONCLUSION

This chapter has demonstrated that Martin Luther King, Jr.'s black church heritage and context significantly impacted his redemptive suffering theodicy. King was the product of a considerable line of black Baptist ministers whose legacies primed him to respond to the question of black suffering with a redemptive suffering theodicy. We also discovered that King drew on the black church music and prayer traditions as sources and tools to reinforce the message of redemptive suffering in private, church, and public settings. King's black church pastoral context also influenced his theodicy. Faced with the daily struggles of black congregants in the segregated South, King used his redemptive suffering theodicy to offer hope and make meaning out of their painful experiences. In "The Death of Evil upon the Seashore" and "Our God is Able" King demonstrated a staunch confidence in the power of God to overcome racism. However, prevailing black church beliefs about the absolute power of God prevented King from fully and consistently appropriating Brightman's theistic finitude within his theodicy. King's church roots and context provide the first and most important resource for understanding his approach to suffering. However, in the academy, King found theological resources beyond the fundamentalism of his immediate preaching forefathers—resources to satisfy his burgeoning intellectual curiosity, ground his social conscience, and hone his theodicy. In the next two chapters we consider King's use of protestant liberalism to develop his approach to black suffering.

NOTES

1. Farris, *Through It All*, 3–4.
2. Clayborne Carson, "Introduction," in *The Papers of Martin Luther King, Jr.: Volume I: Called to Serve, January 1929–June 1951*, First Edition, vol. 1, The Papers of Martin Luther King, Jr. (Berkeley: University of California Press, 1992), 1. This section is particularly indebted to Calyborne Carson's thorough

chronology of the King family history in his introduction to Vol. 1 of the Papers of Martin Luther King, Jr.

3. Ibid.

4. G.S. Ellington, "A Short Sketch of the Life and Work of Rev. A.D. Williams of Ebenezer Baptist Church," in *Programme of the Thirtieth Anniversary of the Pastorate of Rev. A.D. Williams of Ebenezer Baptist Church* (Atlanta, 1924); Cited in Carson, "Introduction to the Papers of MLK," 2. Slave exhorters were often unlicensed preachers who took up the call specifically to evangelize the slave population.

5. Carson, "Introduction to the Papers of MLK," 2.

6. King, Sr., *Daddy King*, 84. William's son Adam would later gain renown as a powerful preacher who uniquely applied the teachings of Scripture to the social plight southern Blacks. He attributed his considerable gifts and ministry outlook to his father Willis.

7. Carter G. Woodson, *The History of the Negro Church* (Washington, D.C.: The Associated Publishers, 1921), 192, 196–198; Bartow Davis Ragsdale, *Story of Georgia Baptists* (Atlanta: Foote and Davies, 1938), 3:65, 3:312; Arthur F. Raper, *Preface to Peasantry: A Tale of Two Black Belt Counties* (Chapel Hill: University of North Carolina Press, 1936), 356; Clarence M. Wagner, *Profiles of Black Georgia Baptist* (Atlanta: Bennett Brothers, 1980), 65. Cited in Carson, "Introduction to the Papers of MLK," 4.

8. Carson, "Introduction to the Papers of MLK," 6.

9. Ellington, "Thirtieth Pastoral Anniversary of A.D. Williams"; Cited in Carson, "Introduction to the Papers of MLK," 7–8.

10. King, Sr., *Daddy King*, 84.

11. Carson, "Introduction to the Papers of MLK," 10.

12. King, Sr., *Daddy King*, 85.

13. Mark Bauerlein, *Negrophobia: A Race Riot in Atlanta, 1906* (San Francisco: Encounter Books, 2002), 110–77.

14. Atlanta Chamber of Commerce, *Annual Report* (Atlanta, 1907). Cited in Bauerlein, *Negrophobia*, 239.

15. Bauerlein, *Negrophobia*, 116–17.

16. King, Sr., *Daddy King*, 85–86.

17. Highly influential in black Baptist denominational life, A.D. Williams went on to serve as the President of Atlanta's Baptist Minister's Union, Moderator and Treasurer of the Atlanta Baptist Association, Home Mission Board Secretary, Foreign Mission Board Representative and Executive Board member of the National Baptist Convention, which remains the largest black Church convention the nation. Baldwin, *Balm in Gilead*, 160–61.

18. King, Sr., *Daddy King*, 23.

19. Ibid., 26–27.

20. Ibid., 26; Carson, "Introduction to the Papers of MLK," 21.
21. Carson, "Introduction to the Papers of MLK," 23.
22. King, Sr., *Daddy King*, 27.
23. Ibid., 82; Carson, "Introduction to the Papers of MLK," 26.
24. King, Sr., *Daddy King*, 82.
25. Ibid.
26. Ibid., 93–94; Carson, "Introduction to the Papers of MLK," 30.
27. King, Sr., *Daddy King*, 93.
28. Ibid., 94.
29. Ibid.
30. Ibid.
31. King, Jr., "Autobiography of Religious Development," 361; Baldwin, *Balm in Gilead,* 160, 162–63. Oates, *Let the Trumpet Sound*, 4.
32. Baldwin, *Balm in Gilead*, 160.
33. The matriarchs of the King family, his great aunt Ida Worthem, grandmother Jennie Williams, and mother Alberta King, embodied the best of the black storytelling tradition in the South. Rather than mere entertainment, the family history and tales they recounted were meant to pass along the traditions and values of the King family, the black church, and wider black community. Ibid., 108.
34. Lewis V Baldwin, *The Voice of Conscience: The Church in the Mind of Martin Luther King, Jr.* (Oxford: Oxford University Press, 2010), 28.
35. Martin Luther King, Jr., "Preaching Ministry," (September–November 1948) in *The Papers of Martin Luther King, Jr.: Volume VI: Advocate of the Social Gospel, September 1948–March 1963*, ed. Susan Englander and Troy Jackson, 1st ed. (Berkeley: University of California Press, 2007), 72.
36. In another preaching paper submitted at Crozer, King criticized the great Karl Barth on exactly this point. He noted, ". . . the preaching of theology must be presented in light of the experiences of the people. This Barth fails to do." Martin Luther King, Jr., "Karl Barth," in *The Papers of Martin Luther King, Jr.: Volume VI: Advocate of the Social Gospel, September 1948–March 1963*, ed. Susan Englander and Troy Jackson, 1st ed. (Berkeley: University of California Press, 2007), 103.
37. Kelsey was the Director of the Religious Studies Department (1945–1958) at Morehouse and Mays was the President of Morehouse (1940–1967). As ordained clergymen, they both felt called to apply their considerable intellectual gifts to addressing to the social plight of American Negroes. See George D. Kelsey, *Racism and the Christian Understanding of Man*, 1st Edition (New York: Scribner, 1965); Mays, *The Negro's God as Reflected in His Literature*.
38. Oates, *Let the Trumpet Sound*, 19.

39. Martin Luther King, Jr., "My Call to the Ministry," in *The Papers of Martin Luther King, Jr.: Vol. VI: Advocate of the Social Gospel: September 1948–March 1963*, ed. Clayborne Carson and Susan Carson (Berkeley: University of California Press, 2007), 368.

40. King, Jr., "Autobiography of Religious Development," 362.

41. King considered Mays as one of his fathers in ministry and requested that, if he should precede Mays in death, that Mays would eulogize him. In Mays, King saw what he thought "a real minister to be," spiritually sound, theologically informed, intellectually astute, and socially engaged. Oates, *Let the Trumpet Sound*, 20.

42. Baldwin, *The Voice of Conscience*, 37–39.

43. Oates, *Let the Trumpet Sound*, 23.

44. Despite Mays' considerable influence, King often credited his father with inspiring him to pursue the ministry. Most likely, Mays' example helped King reconsider Christian ministry as a viable platform for sustained and informed engagement with social inequities. King, Jr., "Autobiography of Religious Development," 363.

45. James H. Cone, "Martin Luther King, Jr, Black Theology—Black Church," *Theology Today* 40, no. 4 (January 1, 1984): 412.

46. King's mother, Alberta, founded the Ebenezer Baptist church choir and served as its organist for forty years. She also served as the organist for the Women's Auxiliary of the National Baptist Convention from 1950–1962. Carson, Armstrong, and Englander, *The Martin Luther King, Jr., Encyclopedia*, 173.

47. Martin Luther King, Jr.'s mother, Alberta King, was often known as "Mother Dear." Oates, *Let the Trumpet Sound*, 9–10.

48. King, Sr., *Daddy King*, 127. Cited in Baldwin, *Balm in Gilead*, 32.

49. At Morehouse, King became a member of both the Glee club and the Atlanta University-Morehouse-Spelman Chorus. Baldwin, *Balm in Gilead*, 32. Sara V. Richardson, who knew King during his seminary days, recalled, "He loved old-time spirituals, and would sit for hours listening to Calvary's choirs singing them." Sara V. Richardson, Private Interview with Sara V. Richardson, interview by Lewis V. Baldwin, May 29, 1987. Cited in Baldwin, *Balm in Gilead*, 38. See also Reddick, *Crusader Without Violence*, 73.

50. King may well have gotten this phrase from W.E.B. Du Bois, who famously referred to the spirituals as "sorrow songs" in his poetic masterpiece *The Souls of Black Folk*. Du Bois, "The Souls of Black Folk," chap. XIV.

51. John Jr Lovell, Black Song: *The Forge and the Flame the Story of How the Afro-American Spiritual* (New York: MacMillan, n.d.), 17.

52. Ibid., 293–301.

53. Robert Shelton, "Songs A Weapon in Rights Battle," *New York Times*, August 20, 1962.

54. Martin Luther King, Jr., *Why We Can't Wait* (New York: Harper and Row, 1964), 61. Cited in Baldwin, "MLK, Black Church, and Black Messianic Vision," 101.

55. Baldwin, "MLK, Black Church, and Black Messianic Vision," 101.

56. Martin Luther King, Jr., *A Knock at Midnight* (Mt. Zion Baptist Church, Cincinnati: Nashboro, n.d.). Cited in Baldwin, "MLK, Black Church, and Black Messianic Vision," 102.

57. King would have gotten "I've been Buked and I've Been Scorned," through the music ministry at Ebenezer. Benjamin C Ridgeway, *Atlanta's Ebenezer Baptist Church* (Charleston, SC: Arcadia Publishing, 2009), 71. If not directly through Ebenezer or Calvary Baptist Church (Chester, PA) he would have certainly learned "Sometimes I Feel like a Motherless Child," and "Nobody Knows De Trouble I've Seen," from the works of Howard Thurman. Howard Thurman, "The Negro Spiritual Speaks of Life and Death," in *Deep River and the Negro Spiritual Speaks of Life and Death* (Richmond, Indiana: Friends United Press, 1975), 25–26.

58. Du Bois also went on to describe the future society that the spirituals looked toward. "Sometimes it is faith in life, sometimes a faith in death, sometimes assurance of boundless justice in some fair world beyond. But whichever it is the meaning is always clear: that sometime, somewhere, men will judge men by their souls and not by their skins." Du Bois, "The Souls of Black Folk," chap. XIV. In words that sound remarkably similar to Du Bois' description of the spirituals, King also set forth his dream for a just society. "I have a dream that my four little children will one day live in a nation where they will not be judged by the color of their skin but by the content of their character." Martin Luther King, Jr., "I Have a Dream (1963)," in *A Testament of Hope: The Essential Writings and Speeches of Martin Luther King, Jr.* (San Francisco: Harper San Francisco, 1991), 219.

59. Du Bois, "The Souls of Black Folk," chap. XIV.

60. King read Du Bois' essay "Sorrow Songs" many times throughout his life. Baldwin, *Balm in Gilead*, 45.

61. Civil rights demonstrators often sang freedom songs when faced with the brutal tactics of the opposition. Additionally, King and other leaders of the movement used spirituals, hymns, and gospel songs to relieve pressure during crises and particularly intense staff meetings and retreats. Coretta Scott King, *My Life with Martin Luther King, Jr.*, Revised (New York: Puffin, 1994), 9.

62. Kenneth L. Smith and Ira G. Zepp, *Search for the Beloved Community: The Thinking of Martin Luther King Jr.* (Valley Forge: Judson Press, 1998), 112. Baldwin, "MLK, Black Church, and Black Messianic Vision," 100–101. Even King's most famous and often quoted speech, "I Have A Dream" culminated

BLACK CHURCH ROOTS

with hope held out in the Negro spiritual "Free at Last." King, Jr., "I Have a Dream (1963)," 220.

63. See Howard Thurman, "Deep River," in *Deep River and the Negro Spiritual Speaks of Life and Death* (Richmond, Indiana: Friends United Press, 1975), 14.

64. Pinn, "I Wonder as I Wander," 1994, 42.

65. King crossed paths with the great Howard Thurman while finishing his graduate studies at Boston University. King had a profound appreciation for Thurman's theological insights. After delivering a lecture at Boston University, Thurman signed King's personal copy of *Deep River* along with the inscription "The test of life is often found in the amount of pain we can absorb without spoiling our joy." Martin Luther King, *The Papers of Martin Luther King, Jr.: Volume VI: Advocate of the Social Gospel: September 1948–March 1963*, ed. Clayborne Carson and Susan Carson (Berkeley: Univ. of California Press, 2007), 229.

66. Thurman, "Deep River," 15.

67. Harold Courlander, *Negro Folk Music* U.S.A. (New York: Dover, 1992), 37.

68. Thurman, "Deep River," 56.

69. King, *My Life with Martin Luther King, Jr.*, 9.

70. Wilma Townsend et al., eds., *Gospel Pearls* (Nashville, TN: Sunday School Publishing Board, 1921), No. 158.

71. Thurman, "Deep River," 56.

72. Ibid.

73. King, Jr., *A Knock at Midnight*. Cited in Baldwin, "MLK, Black Church, and Black Messianic Vision," 102.

74. Martin Luther King, Jr., "A Knock at Midnight (1958)," in *The Papers of Martin Luther King, Jr.: Volume VI: Advocate of the Social Gospel, September 1948–March 1963*, ed. Clayborne Carson and Susan Carson (Berkeley: University of California Press, 2007), 502.

75. A. M. Townsend, ed., *The Baptist Standard Hymnal with Responsive Readings: A New Book for All Services* (Nashville, TN: Sunday School Publishing Board, 1924), No. 502.; Townsend et al., *Gospel Pearls*, No. 107.

76. Cone, "Martin Luther King, Jr, Black Theology—Black Church," 420.

77. Townsend et al., *Gospel Pearls*, No. 107.

78. King, Jr., "Religion's Answer to the Problem of Evil," 432.

79. Martin Luther King, Jr., "Looking Beyond Your Circumstances," in *The Papers of Martin Luther King, Jr.: Volume VI: Advocate of the Social Gospel, September 1948–March 1963*, ed. Susan Englander and Troy Jackson, 1st ed. (Berkeley: University of California Press, 2007), 230.

80. Harold A. Carter, *The Prayer Tradition of Black People*, Reprint (Valley Forge, PA: Judson Press, 2002), 28–31.

81. Lewis V Baldwin, *Never to Leave Us Alone: The Prayer Life of Martin Luther King, Jr.* (Minneapolis, MN: Fortress Press, 2010), 10, 20.

82. Ibid., 12.

83. This common folk expression highlights the practical way prayer inculcated a sense of hope in the face of adversity and relieved Black Christians from the numerous burdens of their lives.

84. Baldwin, *Never to Leave Us Alone*, 13.

85. Ibid.

86. Ibid.

87. Tasked with delivering the keynote speech at the very first mass meeting of the Montgomery Bus Boycott at the last minute, King nearly completely succumbed to anxiety and self-doubt. Desperate for courage, and with only fifteen minutes to prepare the most important speech of his life, King turned to God in prayer. King, Jr., "Pilgrimage to Nonviolence," 59.

88. David J. Garrow, *Bearing the Cross: Martin Luther King, Jr., and the Southern Christian Leadership Conference* (New York: William Morrow & Co, 1986), 57–58. King, Jr., "Pilgrimage to Nonviolence," 134–35. Baldwin, *Balm in Gilead*, 187–88. King recounted this story in his theodical sermon, "Our God is Able." Martin Luther King, Jr., *"Thou, Dear God": Prayers That Open Hearts and Spirits*, ed. Lewis V. Baldwin (Boston: Beacon Press, 2012), 76.

89. Mays, *The Negro's God as Reflected in His Literature*, 83; Carter, *The Prayer Tradition of Black People*, 38.

90. In a prayer composed for a radio broadcast for Ebenezer, King appealed to the black church prayer perspective on God. He began his prayer, "O, thou Eternal God, out of whose *absolute power and infinite intelligence* the whole universe has come into being [emphasis mine]." King, *Advocate of the Social Gospel*, 137; King, Jr., *Thou, Dear God*, 7.

91. Baldwin, *Never to Leave Us Alone*, 59.

92. Ibid., 58.

93. Martin Luther King, Jr., "Palm Sunday Sermon on Mohandas K. Gandi," in *The Papers of Martin Luther King, Jr.: Volume V: Threshold of a New Decade: January 1959–December 1960*, ed. Tenisha Armstrong and Clayborne Carson (Berkeley, California: University of California Press, 2005), 156. Cited in King, Jr., *Thou, Dear God*, 47.

94. Cone, *The Cross and the Lynching Tree*, 73–76.

95. King, Jr., "Religion's Answer to the Problem of Evil," 432–33.

96. Cone, *The Cross and the Lynching Tree*, 73–74.

97. Carter, *The Prayer Tradition of Black People*, 47.

98. Ibid., 66–67.

99. Ibid., 106–7. King routinely called for prayer vigils to end segregation and led young protestors to pray in front of courthouses. The most famous of these prayer vigils may be the so-called, "Prayer Pilgrimage for Freedom," held May 17, 1957. There, 25,000 demonstrators gathered to pray for the full implementation of the three-year-old "Brown v. Board of Education" decision. Carson, Armstrong, and Englander, *The Martin Luther King, Jr., Encyclopedia*, 274.

100. King: *A Filmed Record . . . from Montgomery to Memphis* (New York: Kino Lorber, 2013).

101. Carter, *The Prayer Tradition of Black People*, 66–67.

102. Martin Luther King, Jr., "A Prayer for Chicago," *Chicago Defender*, April 16, 1966, 10. Cited in King, Jr., *Thou, Dear God*, 172.

103. Humor is another significant theodical resource that King inherited from the black church tradition. African Americans have long been noted for their ability to laugh and find humor amidst the harshest social circumstances. King inherited this ability, often using humor to unwind from the constant pressures of the struggle. King could regale his wife with humorous stories for hours on end, and his closest personal associates have often noted his considerable ability to relieve the tensest moments with a joke or a comical impression. However, humor was not merely a survival tactic. Like singing and prayer, it was a practical embodiment of King's theodicy. Laughter conveyed a sense of hope and optimism in the face of hard times. Through humor and laughter, King actively engaged the painful circumstances in which he found himself, effectively turning these situations on their head. A *Time* magazine report featured this instance of King's use of humor, "The jetliner left Atlanta and raced through the night toward Los Angeles. From his window seat, the black man gazed down at the shadowed outlines of the Appalachians, then leaned back against a white pillow. In the dimmed cabin light, his dark, impassive face seemed enlivened only by his big, shiny, compelling eyes. Suddenly, the plane shuddered in a pocket of severe turbulence. The Rev. Martin Luther King Jr. turned a wisp of a smile to his companion and said: "I guess that's Birmingham down below." "America's Gandhi: Rev. Martin Luther King Jr.," *Time*, January 3, 1964, http://content.time.com/time/magazine/article/0,9171,940759,00.html; Donald T. Phillips, *Martin Luther King, Jr., on Leadership: Inspiration and Wisdom for Challenging Times*, Reissue edition (New York: Business Plus, 2000). During personal correspondences, Rufus Burrow Jr, and Lewis Baldwin suggested that I briefly explore King's theodical use of humor. Although space will not allow me to do so in this study, this needs to be explored further.

104. First delivered at Dexter Avenue July 24, 1955, King preached "The Death of Evil upon the Seashore" several times throughout his career. After some revisions, he included it in a published volume of representative sermons entitled

Strength to Love. Martin Luther King, Jr., *Strength to Love*, Reprint (Glascow: Collins/Fount Paperbacks, 1963), 76–85.

105. Dr. Benjamin Mays, one of King's closest mentors, found that the ultimate triumph of good over evil and the vindication of the righteous rank among the most deeply held beliefs within the black church tradition. Mays, *The Negro's God as Reflected in His Literature*, 24–25, 88–89. Rev. Francis Grimke also expressed this widely held sentiment suggesting, "Whether we realize it or not, God is on the throne; and sooner or later, he will make even the wrath of man to praise Him." Carter G. Woodson, *Negro Orators and Their Orations* (Washington, D.C.: The Associated Publishers, 1925), 705. Cited in Mays, *The Negro's God as Reflected in His Literature*, 194–96. King would reemphasize this point two months later in sermon called "Looking beyond Your Circumstances." King, Jr., "Looking Beyond Your Circumstances," 228.

106. Martin Luther King, Jr., "The Death of Evil upon the Seashore," in *The Papers of Martin Luther King, Jr.: Volume III: Birth of a New Age, December 1955–December 1956*, ed. Clayborne Carson, Stewart Burns, and Peter Holloran (Berkeley: University of California Press, 1997). King made a similar point in King, Jr., "Looking Beyond Your Circumstances," 228.

107. King, Jr., "The Death of Evil," 261.

108. Ibid., 261–62.

109. Ibid., 262. King's cryptic comment about God carrying people through "the wilderness of discipline" reveals his commitment to the idea of pedagogical suffering. In an attempt to make meaning out of the frequent hardships faced by his parishioners, King suggested that they would have to endure a certain measure of disciplinary pain (meant to teach them as well as their oppressors) before fully enjoying the promised land of integration. This disciplinary view of pain describes it as a means to build character. Martin Luther King, Jr., "How to Believe in a Good God in the Midst of Glaring Evil," in *The Papers of Martin Luther King, Jr.: Volume VI: Advocate of the Social Gospel, September 1948–March 1963*, ed. Susan Englander and Troy Jackson, 1st ed. (University of California Press, 2007), 248.

110. The fact that the sermons were delivered at the beginning of the year January 1, 1956, owes to the significance of this issue on the minds and hearts of King and his congregation. Martin Luther King, Jr., "Our God Is Able," in *The Papers of Martin Luther King, Jr.: Volume VI: Advocate of the Social Gospel, September 1948–March 1963*, ed. Susan Englander and Troy Jackson, 1st ed. (Berkeley: University of California Press, 2007), 243–46. King, Jr., "How to Believe in A Good God," 247–49.

111. King, Jr., "A Way Out," 243, 245.

112. Ibid., 245.

113. Ibid., 245–46.

114. Brightman suggests that the "Given" probably also limits God's ability to know the precise details of the future. Edgar S. Brightman, *A Philosophy of Religion*, Reprint (Westport: Greenwood Press, 1940), 336–337; Harris Franklin Rall, *Christianity: An Inquiry into Its Nature and Truth* (New York: Charles Scribner's Sons, 1940), 320; King, Jr., "Religion's Answer to the Problem of Evil," 425–426.

115. Martin Luther King, Jr., "A Comparison and Evaluation of the Philosophical Views Set Forth in J.M.E. McTaggart's *Some Dogmas of Religion*, and William E Hocking's *The Meaning of God in Human Experience* with Those Set Forth in Edgar Brightman's Course on 'Philosophy of Religion,'" in *The Papers of Martin Luther King, Jr.: Volume 2: Rediscovering Precious Values July 1951–November 1955*, ed. Clayborne Carson et al. (Berkeley: University of California Press, 1992), 85.

116. Martin Luther King, Jr., "Final Examination Answers, Philosophy of Religion," in *The Papers of Martin Luther King, Jr.: Rediscovering Precious Values July 1951–November 1955*, ed. Clayborne Carson and Peter H. Holloran (Berkeley: University of California Press, 1994), 109.

117. King, Jr., "A Comparison and Evaluation of McTaggart, Brightman, and Hocking," 85. Brightman offered some fairly adamant comments to King in response to the questions he raised. Therefore, as a student, King may not have felt that he really had the academic freedom to stress the points at which disagreed with Brightman.

118. Rufus Burrow, Jr., *God and Human Dignity: The Personalism, Theology, and Ethics of Martin Luther King, Jr.* (Notre Dame: University of Notre Dame Press, 2006), 95.

119. Watley, *Roots of Resistance*, 41–43.

120. In a revised version of "The Death of Evil," published in 1963, King suggested that if God defeated evil in a sudden "overbearing way," he would undermine his ultimate purpose to use free creatures. However, even this revised version, aimed at a broader audience, avoids Brightman's version of theistic finitism by appealing to God's self-limitation. King immediately followed the section by suggesting that God's power fulfills the righteousness that "weak and finite" humans never could. Martin Luther King, Jr., "The Death of Evil Upon the Seashore," in *The Papers of Martin Luther King, Jr.: Volume VI: Advocate of the Social Gospel, September 1948–March 1963*, ed. Clayborne Carson, Susan Englander, and Troy Jackson (University of California Press, 2007), 512.

121. Burrow, Jr., *God and Human Dignity*, 95.

122. Mays, *The Negro's God as Reflected in His Literature*, 83.

123. Burrow, Jr., *God and Human Dignity*, 95, 101.

124. Mays, *The Negro's God as Reflected in His Literature*, 85, 92.

125. Burrow, Jr., *God and Human Dignity*, 101.

126. Ibid., 96.

127. Ibid., 99.

128. King often used this common folk expression of the black Church tradition. The phrase reflects the widely held belief within the black church that God is able to bring good outcomes out of evil circumstances and to rescue his people out of seemingly impossible situations. Wolfgang Mieder, *"Making a Way Out of No Way": Martin Luther King's Sermonic Proverbial Rhetoric* (New York: Peter Lang, 2010), 1.

3

EARLY ENGAGEMENT WITH PROTESTANT LIBERALISM

INTRODUCTION

Martin Luther King, Jr's family lineage, cultural heritage, and church environment already fit him with a basic hopefulness concerning God's good purposes through black suffering. However, his engagement with Protestant liberalism at Crozer Seminary gave King a theological and metaphysical framework upon which to hang what until then had been more or less "homespun" theodical ideas.[1] King arrived at Crozer ready to embrace liberalism primarily due to Morehouse influences like George Kelsey and Benjamin Mays who combined modern critical methods with a deeply practical concern for black suffering. Applying the best of liberal thought to the black condition, Kelsey and Mays renewed King's confidence in the church and Christian ministry to address social and spiritual needs. However, early experiences with racism, strong black church sensibilities, and the influence of George Kelsey fashioned King to be skeptical of some aspects of Protestant liberalism such as its unqualified optimism concerning human nature and progress. So King remained conscientious about which aspects of liberalism best harmonized with the basic redemptive suffering outlook he inherited from his family, church, and cultural environments. At Crozer, King encountered higher critical sources such as John Skinner and R.H. Charles, the atonement theories of A.C. Knudson and Anders Nygren, and the liberal theodicies of Harris

Franklin Rall and Edgar Brightman, using them to develop his basic redemptive suffering theodicy in significant ways.

This chapter will argue that King's theodicy represents a true synthesis of the liberal ideas he encountered at Crozer with the homespun ideas he acquired from his family, church, and cultural influences. After considering the state of contemporary scholarship on the subject, I will make the case by demonstrating the formative influence of Morehouse Professor George Kelsey on King's critical approach to Protestant Liberalism. Next, I will analyze King's formal reflections on the problem of evil during his years at Crozer to show that they reflect a true synthesis of traditional African American religious beliefs and Protestant Liberalism. Therefore, King's redemptive suffering theodicy does not represent a mere recapitulation of traditional black church theodicies or a complete shift to Protestant Liberalism. Rather, King's theodicy represents a careful blending of both traditional African American and liberal sources.

Although King's engagement with Protestant liberalism at Crozer has been well documented, scholars have often neglected how King's Morehouse years prepared him to criticize certain aspects of liberalism even as he embraced others. For instance, Smith and Zepp's classic work on King's intellectual sources *Search for the Beloved Community* essentially begins at Crozer, almost entirely overlooking the impact of Morehouse on King's critical engagement with liberalism.[2] John Ansboro's *Martin Luther King, Jr.: The Making of a Mind*, another extensive treatment of King's engagement with Protestant liberalism, falls prey to the same mistake. Although Ansboro treats King's later appropriation of George Kelsey's theology of race,[3] he omits the significant influence Kelsey exercised on the young King at Morehouse, an influence which prepared him early to critique certain aspects of Protestant liberalism by means of Christian realism. Consequently, these sources depict King as indiscriminately embracing Protestant liberalism until he finally discovered Niebuhr's realism during his senior year at Crozer.[4] However, King had already been handed a form of liberalism from George Kelsey at Morehouse marked by traditional black Baptist cultural and communal concerns and qualified by a healthy dose of Christian realism. King's earliest introduction to liberalism at Morehouse prepared him to embrace and critically assess the liberal tradition he would later encounter at Crozer seminary.[5]

AT MOREHOUSE: KING'S CRITICAL INTRODUCTION TO PROTESTANT LIBERALISM

At Morehouse, Professor George Kelsey introduced King to Protestant liberalism to help ground his already substantial social consciousness and help him think critically about his faith claims.[6] Embarrassed and intellectually unfulfilled by the emotionalism of his southern black Baptist roots, the young King had become intensely skeptical towards Christianity—especially the traditional form typified by his father. However, in George Kelsey, King found a stimulating blend of familiar old-fashioned country Baptist oratory with a tough-minded approach to theological issues.[7] Moreover, he found a thinker particularly adept at using liberalism to draw out the implications of the Christian gospel for racial and social reform[8] even as he (following Reinhold Niebuhr) remained realistic about the potential for human progress in these areas.[9] According to Daddy King, Kelsey "saw the pulpit as a place both for the drama, in the old-fashioned, country Baptist sense, and for the articulation of philosophies that address the problems of society."[10] Kelsey's two-semester course on the Bible promoted a higher critical approach which cast the stories of the Bible as legends that convey inescapable truths.[11] King, Jr. was captivated by liberalism's use of modern techniques as well as its seemingly relentless search for truth. Through George Kelsey and Morehouse president Benjamin Mays, King had finally found an expression of Christianity which left him intellectually and emotionally fulfilled, and which addressed his pressing social concerns. Later, he would credit Kelsey with helping to remove the "shackles of fundamentalism" from him[12]—by which he largely meant the "uncritical" approach to the Bible exemplified by his father, Sunday School teachers, and other "unlettered" church leaders at Ebenezer.[13]

At first glance, King's comment could appear misleading. However, George Kelsey never taught King to reject the traditional faith of his black Church heritage. Rather, he encouraged King to synthesize and develop his homespun theology and faith with the scientific tools of modern thinking. Under Kelsey's mentorship, King learned to apply the critical thinking he had learned throughout his Morehouse experience to the realm of religion and faith. As Clayborne Carson explains, "Kelsey encouraged King to synthesize the religious notions of his upbringing with the secular education he received."[14]

Kelsey advanced a form of Protestant liberalism which he could integrate with traditional African American socio-cultural and religious experiences and concerns. This blending meant Kelsey rejected the parts of liberalism which did not harmonize with these experiences and concerns. For instance, Kelsey sharply criticized the unqualified evolutionary optimism of most early twentieth-century liberals. Liberalism's prevailing view of humanity simply didn't resonate with his experiences with racism personally or socially. Reared in the country town of Griffin, Georgia, during the height of the Jim Crow era, Kelsey was all-too-familiar with pervasive social sin and the tendency of societies to morally idealize more than they can realistically achieve.[15] In "Protestantism and Democratic Intergroup Living," a lecture delivered in 1946 (the very same year King took Kelsey's class at Morehouse), Kelsey offered this critique of Protestant liberalism. He noted,

> Protestantism is also weak on the side of too easy an adjustment to modern culture . . . . Liberal Protestantism stresses the immanence of God, overemphasizes the humanity of Jesus, overestimates the capacity of man for virtue, and identifies the best in Anglo-Saxon, bourgeois culture with the ideals of the Gospels. Liberal Protestantism therefore lacks resources necessary for the effecting of transformations in society that meet the demands of Protestant idealism at its best. On the contrary, it inspires sociological complacency through an espousal of evolutionary optimism.[16]

True to his traditional black Baptist roots,[17] Kelsey charges liberalism with "too easy an adjustment to modern culture," essentially holding that it has veered too far away from traditional ideas of divine transcendence, human sin, and concern for the poor and socially oppressed—three longstanding core convictions within the black religious tradition.[18] From the black perspective, Kelsey could also clearly see liberalism's prevailing ethnocentrism—its idealization of white middle-class culture, at the expense of the gospel call for the relief of socially oppressed and the poor. Like many African Americans, Kelsey's experiences with racism also fit him with a basic realism which checked any unqualified optimism about the human capacity for virtue. Kelsey found this rose-colored outlook on the human condition to be out-of-step with black experiences and unhelpful to social reform. In fact, he insisted that evolutionary optimism actually undermines social reform through inspiring "sociological complacency." Without the proper acknowledgment of the pervasiveness, persistence, and depth of sin, society is lulled into a false optimism and will never take steps radical enough to promote true social equality.[19] Through theologically grounded social insights like this, Kelsey offered King a unique blend of higher critical and African American social concerns.

Following Kelsey and Benjamin Mays, King enthusiastically embraced the critical methods of liberalism with a view towards applying them to black social and religious life. During his junior year at Morehouse, King wrote an article for the school newspaper the *Maroon Tiger* entitled, "The Purpose of Education" in which he contended that the function of education is "to teach one to think intensively and to think critically."[20] However, King cautioned against education apart from moral formation. "The most dangerous criminal," he warned, "may be the man with gifted reason, but with no morals."[21] King went on to argue that the goal of critical thought is the development of character and intellect towards the betterment of society. In a paper entitled "Ritual," written during his senior year at Morehouse, King again demonstrated his deep commitment to higher critical methods, this time using them to analyze his own black Baptist tradition. He explained, "The present study represents an attempt to apply the scientific [method to an] analysis of ritual. Being a pre-theological student it would ordinarily be expected of me to defend certain aspects of sacred ritual, therefore becoming unscientific; but I will attempt to be as unbiased and scientific as possible."[22] Based on his critical research, King went on to admit the uncertain origins of the rite of Christian baptism and to suggest that the sacraments exercise an emotional hold over the faithful even after the intellectual basis of their faith have been shaken. These comments demonstrate King's attempts to embrace liberalism's supposed objectivity and modern "scientific" methods even when they challenge his traditional Baptist beliefs.

However, like George Kelsey, King was also willing to critique liberalism where it proved out-of-step with black experiences and social concerns. In 1948, during his very first semester at Crozer, King penned two essays entitled "The Weakness of Liberal Theology." There, King chided liberals for failing to consistently and effectively apply their theological ideals to practical social matters. Inspired by black social gospelers like Kelsey and Mays, King suggested that many liberals were so preoccupied with the science of higher criticism that they neglected to question the practical relevance.[23] Therefore, King's initial critique involved liberals' failure to do what Kelsey and Mays did so well—apply theology to the everyday concerns of the masses. In February 1950, in a seminary paper entitled "How Modern Christians Should Think of Man," King also took aim at liberalism's overly optimistic view of human sin. Like Kelsey, King's experiences with "the vicious problem of racism" served as a reality check on his views about sin and human progress, a kind of homespun Christian realism that kept him from uncritically asserting the unlimited and unqualified potential for human virtue. He noted, "Some of the experiences that I encountered there made it very difficult for me to believe in the essential goodness of man."[24] And like Kelsey, King appealed to Niebuhr's formulations in support of his rejection of evolutionary optimism. He noted, "The tendency of some liberal theologians to see sin as a mere 'lag of nature' which can be progressively eliminated as man climbs the evolutionary ladder seems to me quite perilous . . . Dr. Reinhold Niebuhr has pointed out with great illumination how men sin through intellectual pride and arrogance."[25]

Throughout his career, King would maintain the same basic critical approach to liberalism he learned early from George Kelsey. He affirmed liberal ideas in so far as they helped him develop and give further expression to his social and religious conscious and easily melded with prevailing black experiences. In "Pilgrimage to Nonviolence," King reflected on his early engagement with Protestant liberalism. There, King affirmed the helpfulness of Protestant liberal works such as Rauschenbusch's *Christianity and the Social Crisis* for helping him develop his homespun ideas and for addressing the social needs of the oppressed. Reflecting on his time at Crozer Seminary, King recalled, "I came early to Rauschenbusch's *Christianity and the Social Crisis*, which left an indelible imprint on my thinking by giving me a theological basis for the social concern which had already grown up in me as a result of my early experiences."[26] So King engaged Protestant liberal thinkers like Rauschenbusch with a view towards further developing the religious ideas and social consciousness handed him in his youth. King's homespun realism caused him to be wary of liberalism's optimistic view of human nature and progress.[27] However, despite such misgivings, King largely embraced liberalism as an intellectually fulfilling and socially relevant expression of the Christian faith.

In Protestant liberalism, King found a powerful tool that could be synthesized with his homespun beliefs to help him address the practical realities of black suffering. Far from shedding the fundamental theological foundation he adopted in his youth, King insisted that even in moments of doubt, he could never turn from the moral principles he grew up under.[28] King thought of himself as having kept this fundamental belief structure largely intact, even while having developed it using modern methods.[29] Therefore, as we turn to consider the impact of liberalism on King's theodicy at Crozer, we should not expect any fundamental shifts. Rather, this engagement will reflect a further development of the basic redemptive suffering themes King had already received throughout from his upbringing and college education in Atlanta.

AT CROZER: KING'S CRITICAL APPROPRIATION OF LIBERALISM TO THEODICY

Endowed with a renewed confidence in the capacity of Christian ministry and Protestant liberalism to address black suffering, Martin King Jr. entered Crozer Seminary in September 1948 ready to "serve society."[30] King's Crozer years mark a period of intense philosophical and theological reflection on the problem of evil. Although he almost never made direct reference to his family and cultural roots during in his academic writings on theodicy as Crozer, his basic approach to theodicy and the unique insights he offered reveal a mind fundamentally shaped by the black church and the black experience in America. Moreover, during his Crozer years, King was never far from the black church tradition, often preaching in black churches such as Calvary Baptist Church. As a frequent houseguest and guest preacher for Rev. J. Pius Barbour, a longtime family friend, King remained engaged with the religious outlook and social struggles of his people.[31] Hence, the questions that attended black suffering such as what good can come from it, why would God allow it, and how can it be effectively engaged were often at the forefront of his academic writings.

King broached the issue of theodicy during his very first semester at Crozer, in a paper entitled "The Significant Contributions of Jeremiah to Religious Thought" written for James Bennett Pritchard's class on the Old Testament.[32] There, King suggested that Jeremiah's greatest religious contribution, the concept of personal religion, arose out of his struggles with theodicy. King described the prophet Jeremiah as "an actor in a unique tragedy" and a man struggling through "moments of disillusionment" and "inner conflict."[33] According to King, Jeremiah was in "perpetual pain because of the stubbornness of his people . . . and their tragedy caused his tears to flow day and night."[34] However, King asserted that Jeremiah's emphasis on personal religion was forged through his painful struggles.[35] Through the pain of rejection and isolation Jeremiah held fast to God, and thus surpassed all of his prophetic predecessors with the unique insight that religion is a direct personal relationship between the Lord and the individual soul. So, for King, redemptive suffering helps account for the very existence of personal religion itself.

Although John Skinner, King's primary higher critical source, did not include such explicit statements about the role of suffering in individual religion, King centralized the issue of redemptive suffering in a way that reflects his black Baptist heritage. King followed Skinner's interpretation of Jeremiah's influences almost exactly, except that he stressed the transformative impact of suffering much more than Skinner. Homespun influences such as the Negro spiritual "Balm in Gilead" had already fundamentally shaped King with a redemptive suffering interpretation of Jeremiah's ministry.[36] These sources reflect the longstanding belief within the black community that God can use the tragedies of life as raw material out of which to forge some redemptive quality to the soul. Skinner's critical assertions about the tumultuous events behind the text of Jeremiah fit well with King's belief that suffering can be creatively engaged to produce spiritual transformation and deep religious insight. King synthesized this homespun belief with Skinner's critical liberal interpretation of Jeremiah to produce an important further development to his redemptive suffering theodicy, the idea that God's redemptive suffering helped give rise to the very idea of personal religion itself, a testament to the great power and purpose of redemptive suffering. King would apply this insight to the betterment of society. For King, the enduring message of Jeremiah is that the religious insights forged through suffering experiences pushed Jeremiah beyond the social status quo of his day. So King drew out an important social implication of his theological assertions. Indeed, using religion to resist the social status quo would mark King's lifelong efforts to alleviate black suffering. With this, we see that right from the beginning of his education at Crozer, King synthesized and developed his homespun redemptive suffering ideas with liberal tools in order to apply them to the current social situation.

In another early paper entitled "The Ethics of Late Judaism as Evidenced in the Testaments of the Twelve Patriarchs," King used higher critical tools to broach the topic of redemptive suffering through the ethics of forgiv   Following the higher critical scholar R. H. Charles, King suggested that the pseudepigraphical work *The Testament of the Twelve Patriarchs* marks a significant development over the Old Testament's ethics of forgiveness and that Jesus Himself may have drawn from it in formulating His own teaching on the subject. King described forgiveness as a non-violent response to suffering which graciously reconciles and restores an offender to communion with the offended party. Suffering is therefore engaged in such a way as to produce a "deeper and sweeter" relationship than before the offense occurred.[37] According to King, responding to unearned suffering with bitterness only "poison[s]" the offender and brings guilt to the victim.[38] Therefore, victims of sin must respond to their offenders with "love and kindness" in order to bring about repentance.[39] Even if the guilty party does not immediately admit fault, they can be made to feel a sense of shame and be led to repentance through the continually loving response of a victim. King held that this teaching from the *The Testament of the Twelve Patriarchs* has had a profound impact on the history of development of the Christian tradition and that "no one can fully destroy its relevance today."[40]

King's higher critical examination of the *Twelve Patriarchs* only helped him develop a homespun value that had already been instilled in him in his formative years. Informed by his family, communal, and religious influences, King already possessed a firm commitment to the centrality of forgiveness as a Christian value and that hatred must be responded to with love.[41] Years earlier, King's paternal grandmother, Delia Lindsay King ensured that her son Martin (Michael) "Daddy" King Sr. embraced the ethics of forgiveness. Tempted to hate white people for the pain they caused her throughout her life, Daddy King was rebuked by his mother on her deathbed, who admonished him that "Hatred . . . makes nothin' but more hatred, Michael. Don't you do it."[42] He recalled the lasting influence of his mother on his commitment to non-violence. "All those years back in the country, my mother, who had never learned to read or write or hear about philosophies and governments, told me things that moved across all the history of this nation as great wisdom. She told me not to hate."[43] Daddy and Alberta King, in turn, passed this lesson along to their son, Martin Jr., who would later use higher criticism to develop the idea further.

King's engagement with R.H. Charles' work on *The Testaments of the Twelve Patriarchs* helped him nuance the homespun ideas about forgiveness. Through his critical engagement with Charles, King articulated the idea that suffering is not redemptive *per se*. Early in his seminary paper, King acknowledged that "forgiveness does not take away the fact of sin."[44] Forgiveness does not undo the sinfulness of wrongs committed. In other words, offenses and the suffering they cause are not good in and of themselves. Rather, they provide opportunities for creative and redemptive engagement, for grace and forgiveness to be extended. This is a point often overlooked in King's theodicy—namely, that suffering in and of itself is not redemptive, rather it is the creative response to suffering which brings about the redemptive outcome. In his paper, King freely admits that if suffering is engaged with bitterness, it will only further corrupt the offender and bring "a double sin" upon the victim.[45] By "double sin," King most likely meant the guilt of having responded in bitterness and thereby caused the offender to become even more corrupt. Rather than bitterness, one must choose to respond with love and forgiveness in order to realize repentance, the redemptive benefit of suffering.

In a sermon entitled "The Meaning of Forgiveness," probably delivered sometime during his days at Crozer, King applied the lessons from his paper directly to the social plight of African Americans. The last point of the sermon asks the question, "What then is forgiveness [?] . . . forgiveness is a process of life *and* [emphasis King's] the Christian weapon of social redemption . . . Here then is the Christian weapon against social evil. We are to go out with the spirit of forgiveness, heal the hurts, right the wrongs, and change society with forgiveness . . . This is the solution of the race problem."[46] According to King, forgiveness was the only redemptive response to oppression that could alleviate the social plight of blacks in America. He would continue to develop this aspect of his theodicy into a central concept he would later call "creative suffering." The concept appears in King's famous "I Have a Dream" speech where he used it to inspire the beleaguered participants in the non-violent movement. He said,

> I am not mindful that some of you have come here out of excessive trials and tribulation. Some of you have come fresh from areas where your quest for freedom left you battered by the storms of persecution and staggered by the winds of police brutality. You have been the veterans of creative suffering. Continue to work with the faith that unearned suffering is redemptive.[47]

King's words essentially repeated the same point made in his early seminary paper on the ethics of *The Testament of the Twelve Patriarchs*, that unearned suffering can be non-violently engaged so as to help produce a redemptive outcome. Much like forgiveness, the non-violent direct action tactics of the civil rights movement were a creative response to the suffering of systemic and personal racism. Without romanticizing the brutality his hearers experienced, King offered hope that their pain had a redemptive purpose. The forgiveness or non-violent response of the protestors did not deny the fact of sin or undo the sin of racism; rather it took the occasion of sin as an opportunity to respond in love and kindness, and therefore to help bring about a redemptive outcome, personal and societal repentance. Therefore, King's synthesis of homespun beliefs concerning forgiveness and higher critical study on *The Testament of the Twelve Patriarchs* marks a significant point in the development in his redemptive suffering theodicy aimed at addressing black suffering.

In "A View of the Cross Possessing Biblical and Spiritual Justification," King described the atonement in terms of redemptive suffering. Christ is the paradigmatic martyr whose righteous engagement with unearned suffering brings about moral transformation in the hearts of sinners. Following personalist theologian A.C. Knudson's article "A View of Atonement for the Modern World," King highlighted the Abelardian or "Moral Influence Theory" as the single theory of the atonement fit to meet the needs of the modern world. He dismissed the historic Christos victor view with its emphasis on cosmic powers as promoting a kind of mythological dualism "incompatible with a thoroughgoing Christian theism."[48] Next, he suggested that Anselmian or Latin-type theories (satisfaction and penal substitution) were inadequate because they hinge on the transference of guilt and merit—abstract realities which King insisted cannot be "detached" from one person and transferred to another. "Penalty," he wrote, "has been treated in such an abstract manner that it may be transferred to an innocent person. Mechanical relations have taken the pace of personal relations. But the atonement will not be understood in such abstract and speculative terms . . ."[49]

Concerned with practical concrete realities, King favored the moral influence theory, which seemed to him to address most directly the concrete realities of human sin and serve as the best expression of God as a loving Father seeking to redeem His alienated children. For King, the fundamental obstacle to reconciling sinners to God does not exist in malevolent cosmic powers or in the wrath of God, but in sinners themselves. He explained, "According to this theory, the atoning work of Christ was a revelation of the heart of God not intended to remove obstacles to forgiveness on God's side, of which there was no need, but designed to bring sinful men to repentance and win their love to Himself."[50] Therefore, for King, and most theological liberals of his day, the atonement is fundamentally about overcoming humanity's enmity against God, reconciling it to its loving Father. Fundamentally, the sufferings of Christ have a pedagogical purpose, a moral display which compels a moral transformation. The key to the cross of Christ is in being the perfect revelation of divine love and righteousness, a revelation so compelling that enemies are drawn into communion with the divine. Additionally, King viewed this revelation of divine love as the redemptive suffering paradigm which excites sinners to sacrificial love towards one another. Not only is the cross of Christ the model of redemptive suffering, but the power behind it as well. King's comments in this paper are so illustrative of his early redemptive suffering theodicy they are worth quoting at length:

> The cross represents the eternal love of God seeking to attract men into fellowship with the divine. The chief source of the inspiring and redeeming power of the cross is the revelation of the divine love and righteousness . . . It is this aspect of the death of Christ that alone gives it profound moral significance. Any theory that does not recognize this fact is quite inadequate. The true meaning of the atonement must be interpreted in light of the incarnation, whose purpose and cause was, in the words of Abelard, 'that he light illuminate the world by his wisdom and excite it to the love of himself . . . our redemption, therefore is that supreme love of Christ shown to us by His passion, which not only frees us from slavery to sin but acquires for us true liberty of sons of God . . . so that kindled by so great a benefit of divine grace, charity should not be afraid to endure anything for his sake.' The spiritual

> justification of this view is found in the emphasis that it places on the sacrificial love of God. As stated above, the death of Christ is a symbol or revelation of the eternal sacrificial love of God. This is the agape that Nygren speaks of in his Agape and Eros . . . The divine love, in short, is sacrificial in its nature. This truth is symbolized, as stated above, by the death of Christ, who, because of his unique relation to God and his moral perfection, made his truth more efficacious than any other martyr. Here is the doctrine of the atonement presented in moral, spiritual, and personal form. This seems to me to be the only theory of atonement adequate to meet the needs of modern culture. Some of life is an earned reward, a commercial transaction, quid pro quo, so much for so much, but that is not the major element. The major element arrives when we feel some beauty, goodness, love, truth poured out on us by the sacrifices of others beyond our merit and deserving.[51]

In this passage, King stressed the power of the cross as a revelation of God's love and of human righteousness which excites human transformation. This makes Christ the paradigmatic example of redemptive suffering that reconciles sinful humans with God, giving them the ultimate example of righteousness and power to live for God. In one of the most important developments we have seen in his theodicy, King placed the cross directly at the center of his redemptive suffering theodicy. It was the cross of Christ which ultimately grounded King's hope that unearned suffering is redemptive.[52] The cross makes meaning out of unearned suffering, proving it to have a redemptive purpose and power if engaged in righteousness and as an act of sacrifice. As King explained, the "major element" of life rests in the impact made upon us by the undeserved sacrifices of others. Additionally, the cross directs our engagement with unearned suffering through providing the most instructive example of redemptive suffering. It teaches us concretely how to sacrifice for the sake of an enemy, how to engage hate with love, and how to engage suffering in a way that brings about a moral change. It also provides the most compelling example of redemptive suffering, thereby reconciling sinners to God and transforming them morally.[53]

King articulated the particular form of this redemptive love using Anders Nygren's description of *agape* from his classic two-volume work *Agape and Eros: A Study of the Christian Idea of Love*. In it, Nygren argued that *agape*, rather than *eros* or *philia*, is the specific kind of love demonstrated at the cross. Whereas *eros* is an essentially acquisitive, self-interested, ego-centric form of love, *agape* is a sacrificial, self-giving, theocentric, unconditional, and spontaneous form of love.[54] Agape sacrifices for the sake of God and the other rather than for self.[55] Christ's sufferings brought redemption because they were the revelation of divine *agape*, the highest form of self-giving love.

With this, King gained confidence in *agape* as the particular form of creative engagement that could make suffering experiences redemptive. If suffering experiences can be transformed, it must be accomplished through the redemptive power of *agape*. Throughout his studies at Boston University[56] and during the campaign for non-violence, King would develop this early theme, repeatedly highlighting *agape* as a key aspect of his redemptive suffering formulation as the powerful creative force that makes suffering redemptive.[57] In his writings on Christian altruism, George Washington Davis (King's academic advisor at Crozer) essentially agreed with Nygren's emphasis on self-sacrifice. However, Nygren's focus on the spontaneous nature of *agape* would not allow any room to acknowledge human dignity as a cause for sacrificial self-giving. By contrast, Davis insisted Christian altruism could be motivated by the fundamental value of the human personality it serves.[58] With a strong commitment to human dignity instilled during his formative years, King would propound a version of *agape* that employed Davis' insights as a kind of corrective to Nygren's original version. He would adopt the positive elements of Nygren's agape while leaving behind his negative assessment of human worth.[59]

Although King's adoption of the moral influence theory and concepts like *agape* reflect his deep engagement with the liberal tradition, the atonement aspect of King's theodicy still reflects the development of homespun ideas.[60] The black church tradition has a long history of understanding the cross as theodicy, a way to make sense of their staunch faith in light of the evils they encountered in white power structures.[61] Therefore, King was remaining true to his black church roots by centralizing the cross within his theodicy. Back at Ebenezer, King had grown up in a thoroughly cruci-centric tradition.[62] Worshippers in the black Baptist tradition reflected on the cross as one of the most important themes of their Christian experience, the central saving event which offered redemption and shed light on their experiences of suffering. James Cone explains,

> At Ebenezer, young Martin heard a lot of singing and preaching about the cross. Black Christians sang, "Surely He Died on Calvary," as if they were actually there. They felt something redemptive about Jesus' cross—transforming a cruel tree into a "Wondrous Cross.". . . Though wonderful and beautiful, Jesus' cross was also painful and tragic. Songs and sermons about the "blood" were stark reminders of the agony of Christ's crucifixion—the symbol of the physical and mental suffering he endured as "dey whupped him up de hill" and "crowned him wid a thorny crown." Blacks told the story of Jesus' passion, as if they were at Golgotha suffering with Him. 'Were you there when they crucified my Lord?' 'Dey nailed him to de cross'; 'dey pierced him in de side'; 'and de blood came twinklin' down' . . . They proclaimed what they felt in song and sermon and let the truth of their proclamation bear witness to God's redemptive presence in their resistance to oppression . . . As a child, Martin King heard his father and other ministers preach about Jesus' death and his power to save not only from personal sins but also from 'the hatred, the violence, the vitriolic and vituperative words of the mobs, . . . aided and abetted by the law and law enforcement officers.' Ministers often preached sermons about Jesus' crucifixion, as if they were telling the story of black people's tragedy and triumph in America . . . . Black ministers preached about Jesus' death more than any other theme because they saw in Jesus' suffering and persecution a parallel to their own encounter with slavery, segregation, and the lynching tree.[63]

Reared in this environment, King would have been fit to view the cross as the paradigmatic revelation of redemptive suffering which brings transformation. As Cone explained, black ministers saw in Jesus' suffering a parallel to their experiences of suffering. The cross offered them hope that suffering could be redemptive. King's native church environment depicted the cross in graphic fashion with a view towards spiritually transforming all who would imaginatively behold the scene. Traditional black Baptist preachers like King, Sr. and Sandy Ray were particularly adept at describing the agonies of Golgotha.[64] In sermonic crescendos, they would tell how they "hung him high" and "stretched him wide." This powerful imagery could move an audience to tears and shouts of joy through imaginatively placing them in the scene. Songs like "Were you there when they crucified my Lord," were also meant to transform the worshipper through a lyrical and melodic portrayal of the sufferings of Christ. As worshippers imagined witnessing Christ being nailed to the tree, pierced in the side, and laid in the tomb, they were moved to awe by the wondrous love of God. They sang, "Sometimes it causes me to tremble, tremble, tremble, Were you there when they crucified my Lord?"[65] Placing the congregation at the scene, as it were, helped them to be gripped and transformed by this divine revelation of love—a direct application of the moral influence theory.

This was also a strong emphasis during the Lord's Supper. Christ's sufferings were remembered through graphic details and, in a sense, beheld through partaking of the elements. Thus, through preaching, singing, and the Lord's Supper, black Baptist congregations not only centralized the cross but viewed its revelation of God's sacrificial love as a means of transformation. Additionally, black congregations understood the cross as profoundly mysterious, something to behold and marvel at, but not to analyze scientifically in the higher critical sense. With this background, it is no surprise that King adopted the moral influence atonement theory and applied it as a central grounding theme in his redemptive suffering theodicy.[66] A basic form of the moral influence theory had long been inculcated in him through his black church roots. Therefore, at this stage, King refined his basic outlook on atonement, appropriating the moral influence theory to the question of theodicy. King would develop this theme further in a paper entitled "Religion's Answer to the Problem of Evil" where the cross appears as the definitive answer to the problem of evil.

Written for George Washington Davis' Advanced Philosophy of Religion course during King's final semester at Crozer, "Religion's Answer to the Problem of Evil" examines ancient and modern approaches to theodicy. For King, belief in a personal, perfectly good and powerful God must be squared with the "cruel" facts of nature, human immorality, and the prevalence of suffering in our world. Almost immediately, King broaches the subject using black suffering as the experiential framework and theistic personalism as the philosophical framework for the question. King's introductory comments follow Rall's *Christianity: An Inquiry into its Nature and Truth* almost word-for-word, making the same basic points about natural and moral evil.[67] However, when we compare Rall's introductory comments to King's, we find that King shifted Rall's language at certain key points in order to emphasize his own practical socio-cultural and personalist concerns. He explained:

> The problem of evil has always been the most baffling problem facing the theist. Indeed, it is the belief in a personal God which constitutes the problem in all its known acuteness . . . If we look through the pages of history what do we find? Jesus on the cross and Caesar in a palace; truth on the scaffold and wrong on the throne; the just suffering while the unjust prosper. How explain all this in the face of a good and powerful God? If the universe is rational, why is evil rampant within it? If God is powerful and perfectly good why does he permit such devastating conditions to befall the lives of men? Why do the innocent suffer? How account for the endless chain of moral and physical evils? These are the questions which no serious minded religionist can overlook. Evil is a reality. No one can make light of disease, slavery, war, or famine.[68]

King deliberately inserted abolitionist James Russell Lowell's words "Truth forever on the scaffold, wrong forever on the throne" into his argument in order to contextualize theodicy within the framework of black suffering. Although Rall never mentioned slavery in his book, King broached the matter in order to help address the concrete social plight of blacks in America. Penned in 1845, Lowell's poem "The Present Crisis" addresses the problem of evil with a view toward ending American slavery. Although Lowell personally held mixed opinions about African Americans, his poem predicts the eventual doom of slavery and the inevitable triumph of freedom.[69] Lowell's bleak description of the current state of affairs "Truth forever on the scaffold, Wrong forever on the throne" is answered by the hopeful words "Yet that scaffold sways the future, and, behind the dim unknown, standeth God within the shadow, keeping watch above his own."[70] Lowell's imagery of the scaffold swaying the future has redemptive suffering overtones that would have strongly resonated with blacks caught in the grip of systemic oppression. Lowell's poem had such a profound social impact that the official magazine of the National Association for the Advancement of Colored People (NAACP) was named "The Crisis" in honor of it. Editor of "The Crisis," W.E.B DuBois, used the very same words from Lowell's poem to introduce his essay "Of the Dawn of Freedom" in his classic compilation *The Souls of Back Folk.*[71] With a longstanding family connection with the NAACP and having been immersed in the works of Du Bois at Morehouse, King, Jr. was almost certainly familiar with Lowell's poem. Fond of Lowell's line about truth being on the scaffold and yet that scaffold swaying the future, King would later use it often in sermons and speeches as a shorthand way to raise question of theodicy before answering it with a redemptive suffering approach.[72]

King's use of an abolitionist poem to raise the question of theodicy demonstrates that black suffering served as the particular context of his redemptive suffering approach. Moreover, King explicitly mentions slavery alongside disease, famine, and war as one of the tragedies that gives rise to theodicy. Although Harris Rall never mentioned slavery in his list of theodicy-raising phenomena,[73] King interjected the issue, demonstrating his intent to take up and apply his theodicy within the particular framework of the black experience. His introduction shows that King engaged the philosophical question of theodicy from a black perspective, ever mindful of the practical implications for the social plight of African Americans.

Theistic personalism appears prominently within King's introduction as another fundamental component of his theodical perspective. King interjected the issue into Rall's argument, insisting that "it is the belief in a personal God which constitutes the problem [of evil] in all its known acuteness. At the heart of all high religion there is the conviction that there is behind the universe an ultimate power which is perfectly good."[74] Theistic personalism holds that "persons are the highest intrinsic values" and that "God is personal."[75] King embraced this philosophy early in his academic career in order to give formal metaphysical categories to help ground his social and religious consciousness. Whereas Rall made no explicit mentioned of personalism within his opening, King deliberately interposed the point about belief in a personal God to ground theodicy within a personalist perspective.[76] For him, the problem of evil is the problem of how to account for the presence of evil and suffering in a world governed by a *personal* God ultimate in power and perfect in goodness. Therefore, belief in a personal God grounds theodicy, giving it its very force. King's personalist convictions are evident even in the way he conceptualized theodicy—as an exclusively theistic and an especially personalist enterprise.

Following personalist luminary Edgar Sheffield Brightman, King called evil a "principal of fragmentariness, of incoherence, of mockery," and "the Satan that laughs at logic," he was quoting Brightman.[77] Here, King was simply reflecting Brightman's view that the existence of evil is perplexing and illogical, and yet theists have not been content to avoid the issue. He adopted Brightman's responses to most of the modern approaches to theodicy. For instance, King agreed with Brightman's opinion that human freedom may explain some moral evils, but human freedom itself is not sufficient to explain "the force of temptation or the debasing consequence of moral evil."[78] He also followed Brightman in rejecting the idea that non-moral evils are retributive or disciplinary since they seem to be meted out so disproportionately and superfluously to the innocent.[79] With Brightman, King also rejected the idealist notion that evil is only incomplete good, since, according to King, it raises the possibility that good might be incomplete evil.[80] King explained "even if the whole could be proved to be good, the question would still remain as to whether destructive means justify constructive ends. As Dr. Rall laconically states, 'the Christian faith which follows Jesus in his belief in the sacredness of a moral personality cannot let even God (God, indeed, least of all) use human beings as mere means to some supposedly higher ends.'"[81] Finally, King follows Brightman in dismissing the view that evil is a necessary contrast to good. According to King, this would imply that God deliberately created evil to highlight the good via juxtaposition. Not only would this impugn the character of the perfectly good God, it would devalue human persons by making their destruction a means to another end.[82] Therefore, King rejected this view on the grounds that it contravenes the central tenet of personalism, i.e., that persons have the highest intrinsic value. Virtually all of King's responses to modern theodicies closely follow Brightman's personalist analysis. Therefore King approached the entire question of theodicy from a thoroughly personalist lens, even using it to critique other modern theories.

King's family and black church roots oriented him towards conceptualizing theodicy in an essentially personalist way. As Rufus Burrow explains, King's personalism was a "homespun personalism."[83] By "homespun personalism," Burrow means that King's family, church, and community roots fit him with the fundamental tenets of personalism long before he ever encountered them in seminary or graduate school. These formative influences taught King to view God as the supreme personal being and that God's image bearers have been divinely endowed with an inalienable dignity. These values are deeply rooted within African and African American traditional thought as well as the black church tradition.[84] In his helpful article, "Personalism and Traditional Afrikan Thought," Rufus Burrow points out that traditional African proverbs, rituals, folktales, songs, and myths are essentially personalistic and may have even spawned personalism.[85]

When Daddy King consoled young M.L. at the death of his maternal grandmother, Jennie Parks Williams, his homespun theodical insight was essentially personalistic in nature. He told King, Jr. "God has His own plan and His own way, and we cannot change or interfere with the time he chooses to call any of us back to Him."[86] Daddy King assured his grieving son that the personal loving God has a specific redemptive plan and that He wouldn't take Jennie in response to something as trivial as sneaking to a parade or neglecting his homework. The understanding was that Jennie, as a person, is sacred and precious, such that her death must be a part of some mysterious divine purpose, a grand cosmic plan. Her death wasn't an act of divine retribution or the result of a pitiless impersonal cosmic force. King, Sr. described Jennie has having been called back to God—a thoroughly personalistic understanding of the meaning behind her death. His belief in the sacredness of human persons and the goodness of the personal God compelled Daddy King to suggest that the black community had been "asked by Him [God] to bear a great burden during our time . . . . So many of us had come from places where Negroes were not regarded as part of the human race. We knew better. We could be set back, knocked down, and kicked around. But we'd live. And in our living, America would discover its future."[87] King, Sr.'s comments cast God as a personal being asking His precious people to suffer for the sake teaching other sacred persons about the true value of human worth. Therefore, personalism helped make up the very fabric of King, Jr.'s early theodical consciousness. Academic personalism simply gave him a philosophical framework to express and develop the theodical beliefs handed to him through his family, church, and communal environment.[88]

King also critiqued Brightman's personalism where it did not fit with black experiences and social needs. Therefore, whereas King closely followed Brightman's assessment in almost every other theodical point, he rejected Brightman's theistic finitism.[89] Theistic finitism explains the existence of evil by proposing some limitation on the power of God.[90] Although Brightman was one of the leading modern proponents of this idea, King, informed by his black church sensibilities, remained ambivalent towards it. Using Rall and Brightman, King traced the roots of the idea back to Plato's Timaeus where the divine is limited by the "principles of order and control," and the "uncreated discordant and disorderly aspects of being." For Plato, according to King, God wills the good and works to bring it about as far as is possible within the limits imposed by certain uncreated conditions inherent in the nature of being itself.[91] For modern theistic finitists like Edgar Brightman, God's will to realize the good is hindered by something within God's own self.[92] Brightman simply couldn't resolve senseless and non-disciplinary evils with the idea of absolute divine omnipotence and omni-benevolence. He had watched a loved one die a slow painful death, and couldn't reconcile this with an absolutely powerful God.[93] Furthermore, although moral evils may be explained by human freedom (a self-imposed limitation consequent upon creating free beings)[94] natural evils must be explained by something more. For Brightman, non-disciplinary evils and natural evil may be explained by a mysterious "Given" within God's own nature.[95] This is an "unwilled, nonvoluntary consciousness"[96] within the divine consciousness that hinders the perfect expression of God's infinite will for the good. Brightman insists that God is yet infinite in space and time, unlimited in overall knowledge, and even infinite in willing good and loving purposes. For this reason, Brightman's concept is often termed the finite-infinite God. Although he is not limited by anything external to Himself, this "Given" aspect of God's own nature prevents him from perfectly actualizing the infinite good He wills. The "Given" must be within God's own nature, rather than external to it in order to avoid the problem of metaphysical dualism. At this point in his career, King rejected idea of a finite God on the formal grounds that it humanized God too much, suggests an internal dualism within God that doesn't resolve the problem of evil, and doesn't absolve God of having made creatures that He knew would eventually suffer from "surd" or senseless non-disciplinary evils.[97] King then concludes his criticism, "With such a view faith in the supreme God is endangered and the triumph of good left uncertain."[98]

Although he essentially borrowed these formal criticisms from scholars like Rall and personalist A.C. Knudson,[99] King's church and family roots may actually be behind his initial reticence towards theistic finitism. As we have noted, in "Religion's Answer to the Problem of Evil," King tracked closely with Brightman's analysis of theodicy. However, at this point, he abruptly diverged from Brightman. Whatever his reasons, we know King's black church sensibilities wouldn't have allowed him to easily swallow the idea of a limited God.[100] With few exceptions, the black church has understood God as absolutely powerful, able to do whatever He pleases.[101] The frustrating and unimaginably painful realities of black life in America have never shaken the black communal confidence in the absolute power of God. Hope for freedom has often been deeply rooted in the idea that God is able to save his people from seemingly impossible situations and defeat the powerful forces which oppress God's people. Biblical stories of miraculous deliverances strengthened these ideas. Black Christians identified with the Israelites standing at the Red Sea trusting in God's absolute power to deliver them from bondage. This kind of faith is not so concerned with resolving detailed philosophical tensions as clinging to the supreme object of deliverance. Although (by this time) King was no biblical literalist, his understanding of the character and nature of God was greatly influenced by the black church and his early childhood experiences. As Daddy King comforted young M.L. over the death of Jennie Williams, he didn't offer the slightest hint of a limited God. On the contrary, he insisted "we cannot change or interfere with the time he chooses to call any of us back to Him."[102] Rather than any internal hindrances, King's comfort was located in the absolutely powerful hand of God to enact His ultimate plan. With this basic theological outlook already in place, King couldn't easily accept Brightman's hypothesis.

King's doctrine of God is another significant theodical development featured in "Religion's Answer to the Problem of Evil" which demonstrates a synthesis of liberalism and homespun beliefs. Having analyzed various modern approaches to the problem of evil, King develops his doctrine of God to propose his own soul-making approach to theodicy. King borrowed Harris Rall's concept of divine goodness to nuance his understanding of God's character in allowing suffering. Rall describes divine goodness as creative, redemptive, and goodwill. Divine goodness is creative in the sense that it is active, self-giving, and spares no pain in itself or its object in sharing its own life with humanity. It is redemptive in the sense that it opposes all evil, and it is goodwill in that it has its "high and fixed" purpose and aims at the supreme good of humanity.[103] Rall held that goodness will inflict whatever pain it must to realize its high and transformative purpose in the life of the object of love. This is basically a "soul making" theodicy, that is a theodicy which views the spiritual growth (the soul making) of humans as justification for the existence evil. Absolute goodness and power are fully compatible with this view since it sees suffering as instrumental in the attainment of God's

EARLY ENGAGEMENT WITH PROTESTANT LIBERALISM

good purposes. King adopted this understanding of divine goodness, coupling it with a view of power that emphasized the attainment of ultimate purposes.[104] King understood God's power as "God's ability to fulfill his purpose," not simply to achieve certain results but to accomplish them in the specific way that conduces to redemptive transformation.[105] He explained that virtues like ingenuity, discipline, and resourcefulness could not be cultivated except by way of hardship and struggle. God's power can only be properly understood in light of the divine purpose. Thus, God's restraint in the face of suffering is justified and demonstrates power rather than weakness since it helps fulfill his redemptive purpose in the lives of his creatures. King notes that the cross is the ultimate example of this. He explained,

> No one knows what it cost God to refrain from intervention when wicked men put his beloved Son to death. But restraint was not weakness. The Cross became the power of God unto salvation.[106]

And he concluded the paper saying,

> The Christian answer to the problem of evil is ultimately contained in what he does with evil, itself the result of what Christ did with evil on the cross.[107]

God's decision to allow suffering can only be understood in light of God's ultimate purposes. King described God as refraining from intervening while Christ endured unimaginable suffering for the sake of redeeming humanity. Although King freely embraced the mystery, the cross brings hope that God has an ultimate redemptive plan and that, according to that plan, He will bring good out of suffering.

Thus, King's proposed solution to theodicy highlights the goodness of God working toward some ultimate mysterious plan, an idea King had already received back in Atlanta. Blacks have almost always held to the absolute goodness of God, viewing their collective and individual hardships as a part of His mysterious cosmic plan. This deep conviction has sustained African Americans during their darkest moments and long shaped the black community's collective response to its suffering and oppression. Benjamin Mays explains, "How much this idea has saved the Negro from violent, revolutionary tendencies can never be known. But it can hardly be doubted that the idea has helped the race to cling on and endure afflictions rather than die in despair."[108] Daddy King drew on this belief when attempting to make sense out of Jennie Williams' death for King, Jr. He counseled his son, "God has His own plan and His own way, and we cannot change or interfere with the time he chooses to call any of us back to Him."[109] In this single sentence, King taught his grief-stricken son that Jennie's death was a part of an ultimate and mysterious divine plan that cannot be thwarted. Though painful, Jennie's death was a necessary part of that plan. Additionally, in correcting M.L.'s misguided belief that Jennie's death was divine retribution, King Sr. was essentially appealing to a common understanding of divine goodness. Although God does punish sin, God's fundamental character is love. He would not exact such a harsh punishment on M.L. for such a small matter as sneaking off to a parade. M.L. was encouraged to trust in the goodness of God at work in and through these painful events to fulfill some grand purpose.

CONCLUSION

The most significant developments in King's theodicy occurred as he used liberal concepts to enhance the foundational ideas that he brought to Crozer. George Kelsey introduced King to liberalism as an intellectually satisfying and socially relevant framework to enhance the homespun faith he embraced at Ebenezer. However, Kelsey modeled and King accepted a critical approach to liberalism which rejected elements that did not fit with black experience and religious sensibilities. Therefore, King arrived at Crozer in 1948 ready to refine and enhance his basic redemptive suffering theodicy within his formal academic writings. Early in his studies, King engaged higher scholar John Skinner to strengthen his homespun theodical interpretation of Jeremiah, suggesting that the prophet's suffering produced his most significant religious insight, the idea of personal religion. Through encountering R.H. Charles' work on the ethics of forgiveness in *The Testaments of the Twelve Patriarchs,* King developed a more nuanced understanding of the way suffering may be engaged to produce a redemptive outcome—a deep conviction handed down to him from his paternal grandmother by way of his father. King also used the works of A.C. Knudson and Anders Nygren to centralize the moral influence atonement theory within his theodicy, building on the basic crucicentric approach to theodicy highlighted in his native black church tradition. Finally, whereas King had early been introduced to a homespun personalist approach to theodicy through his father's explanation of his maternal grandmother's death, at Crozer he employed Harris Franklin Rall and Edgar Brightman to advance a personalist approach to the entire question of theodicy, even as he—influenced by his black church roots—rejected Brightman's theistic finitism. King's Crozer years do not represent a rejection of his native black church tradition or a mere recapitulation of the tradition masked in the categories of liberalism. Rather, King's theodicy at Crozer reflects consistent, careful, and critical engagement with liberalism to build on the theodical foundation he inherited in Atlanta.

NOTES

1. Rufus Burrow helpfully describes "homespun ideas" as theological concepts King imbibed through his family, church, and college environment before formally engaging them in Seminary. Rufus Burrow, Jr., *God and Human Dignity: The Personalism, Theology, and Ethics of Martin Luther King, Jr.* (Notre Dame: University of Notre Dame Press, 2006), 6; Rufus Burrow, *Martin Luther King, Jr. for Armchair Theologians* (Louisville: Westminster John Knox Press, 2009), 44.

2. Appealing to L.D. Reddick's chapter on King's Morehouse days in *Crusader Without Violence*, Smith and Zepp note, "the story of King's intellectual pilgrimage at Morehouse college has been told as fully as possible at this time." Kenneth L. Smith and Ira G. Zepp, *Search for the Beloved Community: The Thinking of Martin Luther King Jr.* (Valley Forge: Judson Press, 1998), 3. Although it briefly touches on King's admiration for George Kelsey, Reddick's chapter never considers King's early engagement with Protestant liberalism. Lawrence Dunbar Reddick, *Crusader Without Violence: A Biography of Martin Luther King, Jr*, 1st ed. (New York: Harper and Brothers Publishers, 1959), 74.

3. John J. Ansbro, *Martin Luther King, Jr.: The Making of a Mind*, 1st ed. (Maryknoll: Orbis Books, 1984), 106–109.

4. Inspired by the cultural studies genre of King scholarship, pioneered by Lewis Baldwin and James Cone, Ira Zepp would later lament this "limited" perspective on King's intellectual journey. Kenneth L. Smith and Ira G. Zepp, "Preface to the Third Printing," in *Search for the Beloved Community: The Thinking of Martin Luther King, Jr.* (Valley Forge, Pa.: Judson Press, 1998), xvii–xix.

5. Martin Luther King, Jr., "An Autobiography of Religious Development," in *The Papers of Martin Luther King, Jr.: Volume I: Called to Serve, January 1929–June 1951, vol. 1*, First Edition, The Papers of Martin Luther King, Jr. (Berkeley: University of California Press, 1992), 363; Lewis V Baldwin, *The Voice of Conscience: The Church in the Mind of Martin Luther King, Jr.* (Oxford: Oxford University Press, 2010), 46–47.

6. Several Morehouse professors significantly impacted King's intellectual and spiritual development alongside George Kelsey. Other notables include Benjamin Mays, Gladstone Chandler, Samuel Williams, Walter Chivers, C.B. Dansby, N.P. Tillman, and Lucius Tobin who also helped shape King's outlook in a host of areas. However, Kelsey was primarily responsible for influencing King to embrace the higher critical methods of Protestant liberalism. Reddick, *Crusader Without Violence*, 73–74; Lewis V. Baldwin, *There Is a Balm in Gilead: The Cultural Roots of Martin Luther King, Jr* (Minneapolis: Fortress Press, 1991), 26–29; William D. Watley, *Roots of Resistance: The Nonviolent Ethic of Martin Luther King, Jr* (Valley Forge: Judson Press, 1985), 18.

7. Martin Luther King, Sr., *Daddy King: An Autobiography*, 1st ed. (New York: William Morrow & Co, 1980), 141; Clayborne Carson, "Introduction," in *The Papers of Martin Luther King, Jr.: Volume I: Called to Serve, January 1929–June 1951*, vol. 1, First Edition, The Papers of Martin Luther King, Jr. (Berkeley: University of California Press, 1992), 42.

8. See especially, George D. Kelsey, *Racism and the Christian Understanding of Man*, 1st Edition (New York: Scribner, 1965).

9. On February 7, 1946, Kelsey delivered a lecture entitled Protestantism and Democratic Intergroup Living at the Community Race Relations Institute. There, just before quoting Niebuhr at length, Kelsey highlighted the inherent inability of humans to realize their highest ideals. Likely, following Niebuhr's famous formulations in Moral Man and Immoral society, Kelsey also stressed the inherent selfishness of social groups and their inability to achieve genuinely loving relationships. George D. Kelsey, "Protestantism and Democratic Intergroup Living," *Phylon* 8, no. 1 (1947): 79–80.

10. King, Sr., *Daddy King*, 141.

11. King, Jr., "Autobiography of Religious Development," 362.

12. Ibid., 363.

13. Ibid., 361.

14. Clayborne Carson, Tenisha H. Armstrong, and Susan Englander, *The Martin Luther King, Jr., Encyclopedia*, ed. Susan A. Carson and Erin K. Cook (London: Greenwood Press, 2008), 168.

15. Kelsey, "Protestantism and Democratic Intergroup Living," 80.

16. Ibid., 79–80.

17. Kelsey's black Baptist roots ran especially deep. An ordained Baptist minister, Kelsey was also educated in black Baptist institutions Cabin Creek High School and Morehouse College before pursuing graduate studies at Andover Newton and Yale.

18. Benjamin E. Mays, *The Negro's God as Reflected in His Literature* (New York: Russel & Russel, 1938), 91, 117, 154, 195.

19. King was so impressed with these sorts of theologically based social insights that he began to seriously consider Christian ministry as a vocation. With a renewed confidence in Christian ministry as a platform for serious intellectual inquiry and to promote social reform, King formally pursued a call to ministry at Ebenezer Baptist church, in October 1947 and requested an application to Crozer seminary the very same month.

20. Martin Luther King, Jr., "The Purpose of Education," in *The Papers of Martin Luther King, Jr.: Volume I: Called to Serve, January 1929–June 1951*, ed. Clayborne Carson and Ralph E. Luker (Berkeley, California: University of California Press, 1992), 124.

21. Ibid.

22. Martin Luther King, Jr., "Ritual," in *The Papers of Martin Luther King, Jr.: Volume I: Called to Serve, January 1929–June 1951*, ed. Clayborne Carson and Ralph E. Luker, vol. 1 (Berkeley, California: University of California Press, 1992), 128.

23. Martin Luther King, Jr., "The Weakness of Liberal Theology I," in *The Papers of Martin Luther King, Jr.: Vol. VI: Advocate of the Social Gospel: September 1948–March 1963*, ed. Clayborne Carson et al. (Berkeley: University of California Press, 1992), 80.

24. Martin Luther King, Jr., "How Modern Christians Should Think of Man," in *The Papers of Martin Luther King, Jr.: Volume I: Called to Serve, January 1929–June 1951*, vol. 1, First Edition, The Papers of Martin Luther King, Jr. (Berkeley: University of California Press, 1992), 274.

25. Ibid., 278.

26. Martin Luther King, Jr., "Pilgrimage to Nonviolence," in *Stride Toward Freedom: The Montgomery Story* (San Francisco: HarperCollins, 1987), 91.

27. Ibid.

28. King, Jr., "Autobiography of Religious Development," 363.

29. Although King shed his father's literalistic approach to scripture, this did not prevent him from being ordained in February 1948 and serving alongside his father as assistant pastor of Ebenezer Baptist Church. King, Sr., J.H. Edwards and other members of the ordination committee took exception to the younger King's refusal to accept the Bible as literally true. This issue came to a head when King, Jr. denied the virgin birth before the committee. Despite his unorthodox views, King was still the son of a prominent pastor and heir to a renown

preaching legacy in Atlanta. Therefore, church politics and the influence of committee members Benjamin Mays and Lucius Tobin (Morehouse College Chaplain) took priority over such doctrinal disagreements. Baldwin, *The Voice of Conscience*, 46, 274.

30. Martin Luther King, Jr., "Application for Admission to Crozer Theological Seminary," in *The Papers of Martin Luther King, Jr.: Volume I: Called to Serve, January 1929–June 1951*, ed. Clayborne Carson and Ralph E. Luker (Berkeley, California: University of California Press, 1992), 144.

31. Stephen B. Oates, *Let the Trumpet Sound: A Life of Martin Luther King, Jr.*, Reprint (New York: Harper Perennial, 1994), 29.

32. Martin Luther King, Jr., "The Significant Contributions of Jeremiah to Religious Thought," in *The Papers of Martin Luther King, Jr.: Volume I: Called to Serve, January 1929–June 1951* (Berkeley, California: University of California Press, 1992), 181. At the beginning of the paper, King reaffirmed his commitment to higher criticism by questioning the factual "infallibility" of the book of Jeremiah while also strongly affirming its indispensable moral lessons.

33. Ibid.

34. Ibid., 182.

35. Ibid., 189.

36. Howard Thurman, *"The Negro Spiritual Speaks of Life and Death," in Deep River and the Negro Spiritual Speaks of Life and Death* (Richmond, Indiana: Friends United Press, 1975), 56.

37. Martin Luther King, Jr., "The Ethics of Late Judaism as Evidenced in the Testaments of the Twelve Patriarchs," in *The Papers of Martin Luther King, Jr.: Volume I: Called to Serve, January 1929–June 1951* (Berkeley, California: University of California Press, 1992), 206.

38. Ibid.

39. Ibid.

40. Ibid., 207.

41. The Christian value of forgiveness (particular towards whites) is deep within the black church tradition. Famed abolitionist and woman's rights activist Sojourner Truth expressed this in a sermon called "When I found Jesus," where she recalled her conversion to Christianity. "Praise, praise, praise to the Lord! An' I begun to feel such a love in my soul as I never felt before—love to all creatures. An' then, all of a sudden it stopped, an' I said, Dar's de white folksdat have abused you, an' beat you, an' abused your people—think o' them! But then there came another rush of love through my soul, an' I cried out loud—'Lord, I can love *even de white folks*! [emphasis Gilbert's]'" Olive Gilbert, *Narrative of Sojourner Truth* (New York: Arno Press, 1968), 158–159. Cited in JoAnne Marie Terrell, *Power in the Blood?* (Maryknoll, N.Y.: Orbis, 1998), 31.

42. King, Sr., *Daddy King*, 74.

43. Ibid., 195–196.

44. King, Jr., "Twelve Patriarchs," 206.

45. Ibid.

46. Martin Luther King, "The Meaning of Forgiveness," in *The Papers of Martin Luther King, Jr.: Volume VI: Advocate of the Social Gospel, September 1948–March 1963*, ed. Susan Englander et al., vol. VI (Berkeley: University of California Press, 1992), 580–581.

47. Martin Luther King, Jr., "I Have a Dream (1963)," in *A Testament of Hope: The Essential Writings and Speeches of Martin Luther King, Jr.* (San Francisco: Harper SanFrancisco, 1991), 219.

48. Martin Luther King, Jr., "A View of the Cross Possessing Biblical and Spiritual Justification," in *The Papers of Martin Luther King, Jr.: Volume I: Called to Serve, January 1929–June 1951* (Berkeley, California: University of California Press, 1992), 264–265.

49. Ibid., 266.

50. Ibid., 264.

51. Ibid., 266–267.

52. Later, King would also highlight the resurrection as proof that unearned suffering is redemptive. See Martin Luther King, Jr., "Questions That Easter Answers," in *The Papers of Martin Luther King, Jr.: Vol. VI: Advocate of the Social Gospel: September 1948–March 1963*, ed. Clayborne Carson et al. (Berkeley, California: University of California Press, 1992), 286–292.

53. King would continue to develop this moral influence understanding of the atonement in sermons like "Palm Sunday Sermon on Mohandas K. Gandi," and "Love in Action," where he highlighted the cross as the paradigmatic symbol of the redemptive suffering. Martin Luther King, Jr., "Palm Sunday Sermon on Mohandas K. Gandi," in *The Papers of Martin Luther King, Jr.: Volume V: Threshold of a New Decade: January 1959–December 1960*, ed. Tenisha Armstrong and Clayborne Carson (Berkeley, California: University of California Press, 2005), 145–157; Martin Luther King, "Love in Action," in *The Papers of Martin Luther King, Jr.: Volume VI: Advocate of the Social Gospel, September 1948–March 1963*, ed. Clayborne Carson et al. (Berkeley, California: University of California Press, 1992), 486–494.

54. Ansbro, *Martin Luther King, Jr.*, 11–15.

55. See Anders Nygren, *Agape and Eros: A Study of the Christian Idea of Love*, 2 vols. (London: Society for Promoting Christian Knowledge, 1932).

56. Although, King agreed with Nygren in many respects, he disagreed with Nygren's dismal view of human value. King would eventually adopt George Washington Davis and Harold DeWolf's conception Ansbro, *Martin Luther King, Jr.*, 17.

57. In 1957, before a packed audience at the University of California at Berkeley, King explained, "Agape is understanding, creative, redemptive good will for all men. Biblical theologians would say it is the love of God working in the minds of men, It is an overflowing love which seeks nothing in return. And when you come to love on this level you begin to love men not because they are likable, not because they do things that attract us, but because God loves them and here we love the person who does the evil deed while hating the deed that the person does. It is the type of love that stands at the center of the movement that we are trying to carry on in the Southland—agape." Martin Luther King, "The Power of Nonviolence," in *A Testament of Hope: The Essential Writings and Speeches of Martin Luther King, Jr.*, ed. James Melvin Washington (San Francisco: Harper San Francisco, 1991), 13. See also Martin Luther King, Jr., "Contemporary Continental Theology," in *The Papers of Martin Luther King, Jr.: Rediscovering Precious Values, July 1951–1955*, ed. Clayborne Carson et al., vol. 2 (Berkeley, California: University of California Press, 1992), 127; Martin Luther King, "A Comparison of the Conceptions of God in the Thinking of Paul Tillich and Henry Nelson Wieman," in *The Papers of Martin Luther King, Jr.: Rediscovering Precious Values, July 1951–1955*, ed. Clayborne Carson et al., vol. 2 (Berkeley, California: University of California Press, 1992), 441.

58. George Washington Davis, "God and History," *The Crozer Quarterly* 20, no. 1 (January 1943): 32; George Washington Davis, "Some Theological Continuities in the Crisis Theology," *Crozer Quarterly* 27, no. 3 (July 1946): 219. Cited in Ansbro, *Martin Luther King, Jr.*, 16–17.

59. Ansbro, *Martin Luther King, Jr.*, 17.

60. Taking aim at the more traditional theories, King described penal satisfaction and penal substitutionary models as "bizarre," "inadequate," and even "immoral." In so doing, King essentially distanced himself from the atonement theories most prevalent within his native black Baptist tradition. King, Jr., "A View of the Cross Possessing Biblical and Spiritual Justification," 264–266.

61. Terrell, *Power in the Blood?*, 4.

62. James H. Cone, *The Cross and the Lynching Tree* (Maryknoll: Orbis Books, 2011), 73–74.

63. Ibid., 74–75.

64. Sandy Ray was Martin King, Sr.'s best friend during his days at Morehouse and became one of King, Jr's chief preaching role models. King, Sr., *Daddy King*, 77–79; Carson, Armstrong, and Englander, *The Martin Luther King, Jr., Encyclopedia*, 284.

65. Wilma Towsend et al., eds., *Gospel Pearls* (Nashville, TN: Sunday School Publishing Board, 1921), 150.

66. Following A.C. Knudson, King also rejected the popular *Christos Victor* view of the atonement as being inadequate. With its emphasis on the Christ's

defeat of the cosmic powers, King found the theory more "mythological" than "theological." He also thought the theory introduced a dualism "incompatible with a thoroughgoing theism." King, Jr., "A View of the Cross Possessing Biblical and Spiritual Justification," 263–265; Albert C Knudson, "A Vew of Atonement for the Modern World," *Crozer Quarterly* 23, no. 23 (January 1946): 53.

67. Even King's use of John Stuart Mills is lifted directly from Rall's introduction. Harris Franklin Rall, *Christianity: An Inquiry into Its Nature and Truth* (New York: Charles Scribner's Sons, 1940), 313.

68. Martin Luther King, Jr., "Religion's Answer to the Problem of Evil," in *The Papers of Martin Luther King, Jr.: Volume I: Called to Serve, January 1929–June 1951*, vol. 1, First, The Papers of Martin Luther King, Jr. (Berkeley: University of California Press, 1992), 416–417.

69. James Russell Lowell, "The Present Crisis," in *English Poetry III: From Tennyson to Whitman*, vol. 42, The Harvard Classics (New York: P.F. Collier & Son, 1909), 51.

70. Ibid., l. 39–40.

71. W. E. B Du Bois, "Of the Dawn of Freedom," in *The Souls of Black Folk* (New York: Dover, 1994), 9.

72. King used Lowell's imagery in some of his most famous speeches and sermons such as "Facing the Challenge of a New Age," (1956), "Love, Law, and Civil Disobedience," (1961), and "Remaining Awake through a Great Revolution," (1968). See Martin Luther King, Jr., *A Testament of Hope: The Essential Writings and Speeches of Martin Luther King, Jr.*, ed. James Melvin Washington (San Francisco: Harper SanFrancisco, 1991), 52, 141, 207, 243–244, 277, 507; King, Jr., "Religion's Answer to the Problem of Evil," 417.

73. Rall never mentions slavery in his list of moral evils. He wrote, "The world seems positively immoral. The Innocent suffer for the deeds of the evil. A handful of men, selfish, ambitious, foolish, blind, bring on a world war; and all around the world the common folk who want only to live and love and labor in peace pay for these misdeeds with starvation, disease, and death, and the curse lasts on through generations still unborn." Rall, *Christianity: An Inquiry into Its Nature and Truth*, 313–314.

74. King, Jr., "Religion's Answer to the Problem of Evil," 416.

75. Rufus Burrow, Jr., "Afrikan American Contributions to Personalism," *Encounter* 60, no. 2 (March 1, 1999): 146.

76. Rall, *Christianity: An Inquiry into Its Nature and Truth*, 313.

77. Edgar S. Brightman, *A Philosophy of Religion*, Reprint (Westport: Greenwood Press, 1940), 259.

78. King, Jr., "Religion's Answer to the Problem of Evil," 418; Brightman, *A Philosophy of Religion*, 260–261. Although King agreed with Brightman about the overuse of human freedom to explain evil, he omitted Brightman's criticism

of the Bible's description of temptation (James 1:14). The fact that King quoted the surrounding sentences may indicate that he deliberately chose to avoid criticizing the Bible at this point. If so, this probably reflects his fundamentalist Baptist roots. Although King moved away from Biblical literalism, he remained sensitive to the prevailing literalistic hermeneutical approach of his black church context—a dynamic that will crop up again as he approached the concept of theistic finitism.

79. King, Jr., "Religion's Answer to the Problem of Evil," 418–419; Brightman, *A Philosophy of Religion*, 419–420. King held the disciplinary/retributive view in his formative years. Convinced that his maternal Grandmother Jennie Williams' death was divine punishment for disobeying his father, the young King was driven to the brink of despair. Here, we see that King used Brightman's argument to debunk the retributive/disciplinary explanation for non-moral evil. King, Sr., *Daddy King*, 109; Oates, *Let the Trumpet Sound*, 12–13.

80. King, Jr., "Religion's Answer to the Problem of Evil," 420; Brightman, *A Philosophy of Religion*, 264–265.

81. King, Jr., "Religion's Answer to the Problem of Evil," 420; Rall, *Christianity: An Inquiry into Its Nature and Truth*, 316. King almost certainly meant to ask whether constructive ends justify destructive means.

82. King, Jr., "Religion's Answer to the Problem of Evil," 420–421.

83. Burrow, Jr., *God and Human Dignity*, 6.

84. Ibid., 70.

85. Rufus Burrow, Jr., "Personalism and Afrikan Traditional Thought," *Encounter* 61, no. 3 (June 1, 2000): 323–324.

86. King, Sr., *Daddy King*, 109.

87. Ibid., 94.

88. Martin Luther King, Jr., *Stride Toward Freedom: The Montgomery Story* (Harpercollins, 1987); Burrow, Jr., *God and Human Dignity*, 6–7.

89. This was not a critique of personalism generally, since some personalists like Harold DeWolf did not promote theistic finitism.

90. King, Jr., "Religion's Answer to the Problem of Evil," 422; Rall, *Christianity: An Inquiry into Its Nature and Truth*, 317; Edgar Sheffield Brightman, *The Finding of God* (New York: The Abingdon Press, 1931), 184.

91. King, Jr., "Religion's Answer to the Problem of Evil," 422–423; Brightman, *A Philosophy of Religion*, 288–289; Rall, *Christianity: An Inquiry into Its Nature and Truth*, 317.

92. King, Jr., "Religion's Answer to the Problem of Evil," 424–425; William Pepperell Montague, *Belief Unbound: A Promethian Religion For The Modern World* (New Haven: Yale University Press, 1931), 74,83,84,91; Rall, *Christianity: An Inquiry into Its Nature and Truth*, 319–320.

93. Rufus Burrow, Jr., "The Personalistic Theism of Edgar S Brightman," *Encounter* 53, no. 2 (March 1, 1992): 171–172.

94. Brightman, *A Philosophy of Religion*, 303.

95. King, Jr., "Religion's Answer to the Problem of Evil," 425–426; Brightman, *A Philosophy of Religion*, 337.

96. Brightman, *A Philosophy of Religion*, 337–338.

97. King, Jr., "Religion's Answer to the Problem of Evil," 426. According to Brightman, "surd evils" are evils that have no instrumentality and cannot conduce to any disciplinary good. Burrow, Jr., "The Personalistic Theism of Edgar S Brightman," 170; Brightman, *A Philosophy of Religion*, 246.

98. King, Jr., "Religion's Answer to the Problem of Evil," 426.

99. Burrow, Jr., *God and Human Dignity*, 97.

100. According to Brightman, God is the most powerful being in the universe. Although not absolutely powerful, he possesses matchless or unsurpassable power. Therefore, he is able to accomplish his divine purposes, but only in cooperation with His creatures. Among other problems, Brightman held that postulating that God has all power actually impugns the character of God by making him directly responsible for the existence of evil. During his graduate studies under Brightman, King would become more agreeable to theistic finitism. However, at this stage of his career, he was not prepared to accept it. Brightman, *A Philosophy of Religion*, 303; Burrow, Jr., "The Personalistic Theism of Edgar S Brightman," 172.

101. Mays, *The Negro's God as Reflected in His Literature*, 74.

102. King, Sr., *Daddy King*, 109.

103. Rall, *Christianity: An Inquiry into Its Nature and Truth*, 323; King, Jr., "Religion's Answer to the Problem of Evil," 427.

104. Later, King would repeatedly use Rall's formula of creative, redemptive, goodwill to describe *agape*, the divine love. For instance in "Loving Your Enemies," delivered at Dexter Avenue Baptist Church in 1957 King explained, "Love is creative, understanding goodwill for all men. . . . agape is something of the understanding, creative, redemptive goodwill for all men . . . Love is understanding, redemptive goodwill for all men, so that you love everybody, because God loves them. You refuse to do anything that will defeat an individual, because you have agape in your soul." Martin Luther King, Jr., "Loving Your Enemies," in *A Knock at Midnight: Inspiration from the Great Sermons of Reverend Martin Luther King, Jr.*, ed. Clayborne Carson and Peter Holloran (New York: Warner Books, 1998).

105. King, Jr., "Religion's Answer to the Problem of Evil," 428.

106. Ibid., 428–429.

107. Ibid., 432–433.

108. Mays, *The Negro's God as Reflected in His Literature*, 153.

109. King, Sr., *Daddy King*, 109.

4

LATER ENGAGEMENT WITH PROTESTANT LIBERALISM

INTRODUCTION

When Martin Luther King, Jr. arrived at Boston University for graduate studies in 1951, his theodicy represented an eclectic blend of homespun ideas enhanced by the evangelical liberalism he encountered at Crozer Seminary. For King, Boston University provided an opportunity for intense reflection in the birthplace and bastion of Boston personalism. Under the watchful eye of the ailing Edgar Sheffield Brightman, King took the opportunity to develop his theodicy even further, wrestling through issues like theistic finitism, which he initially broached at Crozer.

Coretta Scott King recalled that redemptive suffering was one of the many fascinating ideas swirling around King's brilliant mind during his tenure at Boston. Deeply moved by his critical reflections on redemptive suffering, King would often describe to her the theodical hope behind ideas like non-violent militancy and redemptive love. As early as their courtship in Boston, Coretta King remembered Martin King applying these ideas to the black struggle for freedom. "Even if you get beaten by not defending yourself," she remembered, "he said, somehow your suffering helps to redeem the other person and to purge your hatred of that person."[1] According to Martin King, redemptive suffering was a powerful force which could "break the chain of hatred" and provide the platform for true brotherhood to begin—the establishment of the beloved community. King often tested theological and philosophical concepts like redemptive suffering outside of the classroom in conversations at the dialectical society (a gathering of local black graduate students that met in King's Boston area apartment) and in sermons delivered in black churches like Ebenezer.[2] After Brightman's sudden death in 1953, King continued to think through the problem of evil under the guidance of Brightman's younger protégé, the Methodist minister L. Harold DeWolf. And, by the time he finished his studies at Boston University, King's redemptive suffering theodicy was basically fully formed and ready for practical application in the fledgling civil rights movement.

King's matriculation at Boston University represents his most rigorous and sustained period of formal academic reflection on the problem of evil. Much like at Crozer, at Boston, King sharpened his theodicy by carefully appropriating Protestant liberal concepts from a wide array of sources that resonated with his critical mind as well as his black cultural and religious sensibilities. This chapter argues that despite his varied sources, theodical developments, and struggles with concepts like theistic finitism, King's Boston years left the basic structure of his redemptive suffering theodicy intact. To make the case, I will examine King's academic reflections on theodicy during his matriculation at Boston University. As he honed his theodicy, King engaged diverse forms of personalism such as the absolutism of Borden Bowne and Harold DeWolf (which he ultimately adopted), the finitism of Edgar Brightman, and even the atheistic personalism of J.M.E. McTaggart. He also gleaned theodical insights from idealists like William Hocking and especially G.W.F. Hegel, and finally through comparing Henry Wieman and Paul Tillich's approaches to theodicy in his doctoral dissertation. Although King's final theodical approach closely resembled Bowne and DeWolf's, it was not merely a product of the liberalism he encountered at Crozer or Boston. Rather, King carefully culled and synthesized liberal concepts which supported the fundamental theodical outlook he inherited from his black church and family roots. At Boston, King took a particular focus on the doctrine of God, developing the fundamental theodical approach he received during his formative years through that lens. According to King, the omni-benevolent and omnipotent personal God uses human engagement with unearned suffering to bring about redemptive transformation according God's mysterious and all-encompassing purpose.[3]

AT BOSTON UNIVERSITY: LATER THEODICAL DEVELOPMENTS

During his first term at Boston University's school of theology, King dealt with theodicy through comparing the philosophies of J.M.E. McTaggart (a proponent of atheistic personalism), Edgar Brightman (a theistic finitist), and William Ernest Hocking (a theistic absolutist). King explained that the question of theodicy led these thinkers to develop differing doctrines of God. He noted that for McTaggart and Brightman "the existence of evil in the world is incompatible with the belief in an omnipotent being who is also good."[4] The traditional theodical dilemma can be explained like this. Either God wishes to prevent evil but is unable to do so; or has the power to prevent evil but is unwilling to do so.[5] McTaggart and Brightman chose to question God's power, whereas Hocking chose to question the very concept of evil itself.

Part 1: King's Theodicy and the Atheistic Personalism of J.M.E. McTaggart

According to King, the question of theodicy led McTaggart to atheistic personalism, one of the most atypical forms of personalism. As its name implies, atheistic personalism denies the existence of a personal creator God. However, McTaggart was still considered a personalist in the sense that he maintained that only eternal persons truly exist.[6] According to McTaggart, the only real substances are "selves, parts of selves, and groups of selves."[7] For him, person is the ultimate reality. Though he denied the existence of a personal God, McTaggart admitted the reality of the "Absolute" which for him is "a unity of persons, not a personal unity."[8] McTaggart's "Absolute" is related to its individual selves much like a college is related to its individual students—the absolute is essentially the organized system of individuals taken together as a single unit.[9] As a thoroughgoing theistic personalist, King insisted that McTaggart's harmonious system of selves needs a personal God to explain itself and bind it together as a unity. Furthermore, King suggested that McTaggart's atheism is inconsistent with his idealism, since his system of selves would need a supreme mind in which to exist.[10]

King clarified his position on divine omnipotence (and its theodical implications) as he engaged McTaggart's criticisms of the doctrine.

McTaggart understood the doctrine of divine omnipotence to mean that God can do anything whatsoever, even the philosophically impossible or absurd. In *Some Dogmas of Religion,* McTaggart took aim at this version of divine omnipotence, showing how it leads to certain absurd conclusions. McTaggart essentially lampooned the doctrine by positing absurd scenarios such as whether God could create a being that he couldn't destroy or create a man who was simultaneously not a man.[11] King noted, "Indeed, the reader gets the impression sometimes that McTaggart is simply indulging in logical trifling, that the discredited doctrine is unworthy of serious consideration and may be caricatured to any extent. McTaggart's insistence on taking omnipotence as implying the power to make contradictions true makes his whole discussion at this point rather profitless."[12] In response, King offered his own understanding of the doctrine of divine omnipotence. He explained, "When God is said to possess omnipotence, the meaning is that there is nothing which can prevent Him from realizing any purpose His wisdom and goodness, e.g., decided Him to attempt."[13] For King, God can realize anything God purposes to do according to the divine nature. He dismissed the idea that God can act contrary to the divine nature or do the non-doable.

However, King's main problem with McTaggart's argument to absurdity is that it hinges on an overly abstract understanding of the doctrine—an approach out-of-step with the typical practical emphases within the black church tradition. King explained, "Certainly few, if any, modern theologians believing in the omnipotence of God would take omnipotence in such an absolutely abstract sense."[14] Informed by the black church tradition, King was primarily concerned with the practical implications of divine omnipotence rather than the philosophical inconsistencies with the doctrine. With its tangible need for liberation, the black church has traditionally held that God can do anything God wants to do. God can rescue God's people no matter how unlikely it appears and no power can thwart God's good and wise purposes. However, it is difficult to say whether this also implies that blacks have traditionally believed God can do the absurd, ridiculous, or contradict his own nature. Such speculations seem foreign to the black church way of doing theology. We can say that King's deep concern for the practical implications of divine omnipotence resonate strongly with the black church way of approaching the issue of omnipotence. Although King wrestled deeply with the philosophical issues related to theodicy, he did so with a view towards its practical implications for present circumstances.

Part 2: King's Theodicy and the Theistic Finitism of Edgar Brightman

Whereas the question of theodicy led McTaggart to atheistic personalism, it led Edgar Brightman to a "modified theism."[15] Brightman began his theological career as a theistic absolutist, much like his renowned personalist mentor Borden Parker Bowne as well as Harvard's Josiah Royce. However, influenced by William James's pragmatism, Hegel's dialectic, Darwin's evolutionary theory, Joseph Leighton's temporal limitations on God, and especially a series of personal tragedies, Brightman eventually rejected theistic absolutism in favor of theistic finitism.[16] Burrow suggests that Brightman may have considered the facts of evil much more carefully than Bowne. "Bowne gave considerable attention to divine goodness," he said, "but failed to give adequate attention to the facts of evil and God."[17] On the other hand, "Brightman meets the traditional dilemma regarding God's power and goodness in the fact of massive suffering head-on."[18]

The prevalence of evils, particularly non-moral or natural evils, led Brightman to suggest that although God is willing to prevent suffering, God is hindered from eliminating evil as God's infinite goodness and wisdom would dictate. Brightman held that God is limited by an uncreated, internal, non-rational factor in the divine nature he called the "Given." The "Given" renders God unable to realize God's perfect will in the immediate, thereby resolving the question of evil. According to Brightman, the hindrance is not located in the goodness or wisdom of God, but in the ability of God to bring God's purposes to pass. King had already rejected theistic finitism at Crozer, following Harris Franklin Rall and A.C. Knudson's critiques.[19] However, under the tutelage of Brightman himself, King became more amenable to the idea. He noted that Brightman's concept had the advantage of preserving the omni-benevolent character of God in the face of evil and suffering. Additionally, King thought Brightman's view gave metaphysical grounding to the Christian ideal of sacrificial love. Brightman's limited God sacrifices and struggles with this aspect of the divine nature to realize the best for God's creatures. In a sense, it is out of God's own suffering to overcome the "Given" that God's will is ultimately realized in the world.

Despite these philosophical advantages, King still ultimately rejected Brightman's theory, convinced that theistic finitism could not give sufficient assurance and the practical hope that oppressed people need. According to King, Brightman's concept implied that evil in the world is ultimately beyond God's purpose and control. He noted, "Dr. Brightman's conception of the finite God begins with the contention that evil in the world is apparently outside the purpose of God and to some extent beyond his control."[20] When grading King's paper, Brightman underlined the words "beyond His control" and wrote, "beyond His Creation."[21] This highlights the tension between King and Brightman's respective approaches to theistic finitism. Brightman thought his theory absolved God of any moral responsibility for the existence of evil in the world. For him, the major issue was abstract philosophical coherence. Positing a limitation on God's power simply meant that God cannot be held liable for the facts of evil and suffering in the world—evil lies beyond God's creation. However, for King the major issue was practical deliverance. Putting a limitation on God's power casts doubt on God's ability to alleviate the suffering in the world—evil lies beyond God's control. King's concern for practical deliverance and freedom for the oppressed essentially trumped his concern for the philosophical advantages of Brightman's theory. At this stage in his career, King was willing to live with the mystery of moral tension as long as he could be assured that good would triumph over evil.

Although Brightman insisted that God's partial control of the "Given" gives sufficient assurance that the good will ultimately triumph, King was not altogether convinced. King explained that "in some instances, the 'Given,' with its purposeless processes constitutes so great an obstacle to the divine will that God's endeavors are temporarily defeated."[22] God finds innovative ways to advance and realize his purposes even using the "Given" instrumentally as much as possible. However, according to the theory, God is in the process of realizing God's own perfection. This was too much for King to accept. He suspected that Brightman's "Given" set up a dualism within the very nature of God and created a dichotomy between God's nature and His Will, two aspects of the divine life which are intimately connected. According to King, this idea also undermined faith in the supreme God and (even more troubling) left the triumph of good over evil a matter of uncertainty. Despite the philosophical payoffs, King could not accept the concept of a God in constant tension with Himself. He wondered, "What evidence is there that God is winning a gradual mastery over the limitations in his nature?"[23] Again, King demonstrates his concern for the concrete facts of life. Although King would come to see history as moving in a positive direction, at this point he felt that the facts of evil in the world don't seem to indicate that the limited God is gaining any gradual mastery over evil.[24]

Part 3: King's Theodicy and the Absolute Idealism of William Hocking

King found reason to be optimistic about the progress of history as he considered the absolute idealism of William E. Hocking. Hocking helped King firmly ground his theodical hope in God as creator and in the fundamental character of the universe itself. Hocking held that Christian hope demands some kind of judgment about the fundamental character of reality. According to Hocking, monism implies that there is a fundamental character to the universe—a moral unity to the world. Since reality itself is unified in overcoming evil, we can be confident that goodness will ultimately triumph. Hocking explained, "No man can be content to accept evil as finality: each must have his theory of evil as a means of bringing that evil under the conception of the whole—and so of disposing of it."[25] Hocking's way of doing this was to surmise that evil was somehow less real than good. This was not a denial or downplaying of the brutal facts of experience. Hocking took tragedy seriously,[26] and yet he took goodness even more seriously—insisting that it is even more deeply embedded within the very fabric of world. The optimist has caught sight of this fundamental truth about the character of reality, a truth that is beyond immediate observation.[27] Having acknowledged the uncertainty of immediate observation, Hocking based his optimism on a hope that present evils will, in the end, turn out to be goods in a broader context. Reality is fundamentally good. Accordingly, evils, even ghastly ones, are really goods when viewed from an ultimate perspective. As the absolute mind beholds present evils from an ultimate timeless perspective, He creates continuity between present evils and future purpose thereby transmuting them into goods.[28]

Moreover, Hocking affirmed divine omnipotence in a way that minimized the need for dramatic cosmic interventions and emphasized the need for cosmic companionship. Although Hocking's view didn't exclude miraculous interventions, he offered a kind of theodical hope that highlighted God's presence with and word to the sufferer—a hopeful word often communicated through the "still small voice." Hocking held that human peace of mind comes as God communicates God's divine perspective on our suffering in a way we can receive, a still small voice which communicates with an irresistible "might of meaning."[29] The idea of experiencing God in this way would have deeply resonated with King. His conversion was not a sudden and abrupt divine intervention, but consisted in the subtle and gradual intaking of the Christian ideals he grew up under.[30] Likewise, rather than a dramatic call, King described his calling to ministry as "an inescapable urge to serve society."[31] Already familiar with experiencing God as still small voice, King would have gravitated to Hocking's description of omnipotence. According to Hocking, God's omnipotence brings comfort by communicating an ultimate perspective on suffering external to the experience itself.[32] For Hocking, theodicy is grounded in the moral character of the universe itself and in God's ultimate purposes—a perspective that can only come from outside the arena of human effort and experience.[33] Additionally, the black church tradition has from its inception derived comfort through divine companionship. The idea that God is present to His creatures has given blacks confidence, resolve, hope, and a sense of optimism amidst countless tragedies. Because God is ever present to all things, all things would work towards the ultimate triumph of good.[34] King was already fashioned through his church and cultural roots to embrace theodical hope through cosmic companionship.

Hocking's approach to theodicy also resonated with King's already strong sense of optimism and the ways he personally experienced God in the world. Having been raised in a deeply religious and "uplifting" environment, King entered graduate studies with a basic optimism about the universe itself.[35] This was one of King's most basic theological convictions. Despite the facts of evil, King held (along with so many others in the black church tradition) that injustice violated the very fabric of reality itself, that God infused a moral character within creation which cannot suffer evil permanently. However long it may take and however unlikely it may appear, all things are working towards the ultimate elimination of evil. King often appealed to the moral character of the universe to give theodical hope to beleaguered congregants—perhaps most famously in his sermon "Rediscovering Precious Values." In words which deeply resonate with Hocking's approach, King explained,

> All I'm trying to say to you is our universe hinges on moral foundations. God has made it so. God has made the universe based on a moral law. So long as a man disobeys it he is revolting against God . . . This universe hinges on moral foundations. There is something in this universe that justifies Carlyle in saying, "No lie can live forever." There is something in this universe that justifies William Cullen Bryant in saying, "Truth Crushed to the Earth will rise again." There is something in this universe that justifies James Russel Lowell in saying "Truth forever on the scaffold, Wrong forever on the throne, Yet that scaffold sways the future, Behind the dim unknown stands God, Within the shadow keeping watch above his own."[36]

Just as Hocking insisted, theodical hope is connected with something in the very warp and woof of the universe itself. The key is in seeing and communicating the truth which lies beneath the surface of life's tragic experiences—the truth that apparent evils are less real, and are actually transmuted into goods when seen from an ultimate perspective.[37] Even more than the brute power of God to miraculously intervene in suffering, King's hope was grounded in the universe being "hinged" on moral foundations. Like Hocking, King knew the facts of pain that gave rise to the question of theodicy often hid the reality of this moral foundation. Truth seems "forever on the scaffold" and wrong seems "forever on the throne." Hence, King also stressed the reality of cosmic companionship. King reminded the wearied saints that their God is standing just "behind the dim unknown," just "within the shadow keeping watch above his own."[38]

With this, we see that King's early engagement with liberalism during his Boston years sharpened his basic theodical outlook in ways that continued to resonate with his black church roots. Through engaging the atheistic personalism of McTaggart, King refocused his definition of omnipotence, insisting that God can do whatever accords with God's goodness and wisdom, whatever God wills to do, rather than the philosophically absurd or undoable—a definition that is not out-of-step with the traditional absolutism within the black church tradition. King's continued rejection of Brightman at this stage in his career also reflects his black church roots. For King, placing limitations on the power of God comprised the practical hope of the oppressed saints in the black church that God is in control of all things and potentially imperiled the triumph of good over evil. Finally, King's analysis of Hocking's ideal absolutism helped him focus his theodical emphasis on the fundamental nature of the universe itself and cosmic companionship. King begins to describe theodical hope in terms of God as omni-benevolent creator who offers constant companionship and speaks through a still small voice, more so than God as dramatic miraculous intervener who only intervenes during specific moments of crisis.

By the end of King's course with Brightman, his attitude towards theistic finitism shifted considerably. Although he initially rejected Brightman's concept, King appears to have embraced the idea by his final examination in Brightman's course on the Philosophy of Religion. Brightman asked his students to define the "finite God" idea and offer a critical analysis on philosophical and religious grounds. After defining the concept, making some comparisons to Plato's thought, King described his newfound affinity for Brightman's theory. He didn't offer any criticisms of the theory. Rather, he affirmed Brightman's idea explaining,

> At present, I am quite sympathetic with this idea. After a somewhat extensive study of the idea I am all but convinced that it is the only adequate explanation for the existence of evil. Moreover, it is significant and adequate from a religious point of view because it establishes the Christian idea of sacrificial love on metaphysical grounds. It is the most empirical explanation that we can set forth in relation to the God idea. It makes a thorough distinction between good and evil, given an explanation for the existence of both. This theistic absolutism fails to do.[39]

This quote is perhaps King's strongest statement in favor of finitism, making it appear that he wholeheartedly embraced the theory. However, it would be a mistake to assume that King was a finitist in the final analysis. As Rufus Burrow has well documented, King vacillated on the issue of theistic finitism throughout his career. At this point, Brightman's personal influence on King was at its peak. In the classroom, Brightman would have cast his theory in the best possible light, and as a good student, King would have given it the most charitable reading possible. However, that doesn't mean that King was ultimately convinced. As we

LATER ENGAGEMENT WITH PROTESTANT LIBERALISM

have seen, King had significant misgivings about finitism tracing back at least as far as his days at Crozer. He suggested then, as well as at Boston, that Brightman's "Given" concept set up a duality within the very nature of God and his limitations on divine power undermined faith in the supreme God and imperiled the ultimate triumph of good. In other words, he felt that Brightman's concept humanized God too much. There is no evidence that King's concerns ever went away. Even in this, his most positive statement about finitism, King never mentions how finitism resolves the issue of dualism or gives assurance that the cause of goodness would eventually prevail. In his final examination answers, rather than rehearse his criticisms yet again, King focused on the positive aspects of Brightman's theory. The "Given" accounts for natural evils, which can't be explained on the basis of divine self-limitation due to human freedom. It also protects the character of God by absolving him of any responsibility for the existence of evil. It makes a clear distinction between good and evil, not casting evil as some form of partial or unfulfilled goodness. It also, according to King, makes the best rational sense out of the empirical facts of experience. It appears as though the omni-benevolent God must be somehow limited in immediately alleviating the massive amounts of evil and suffering in the world.

Perhaps most importantly for King's theodicy, theistic finitism provided a metaphysical basis for sacrificial love. Brightman's idea described God as creatively engaging the limitations of the "Given," struggling through them in order to realize his ultimate redemptive purposes and perfecting Himself in the process. This is almost exactly parallel to how King thought suffering may be engaged in human life to bring redemptive transformation. King described that for Brightman, "God is a struggling God. . . . His will didn't create this 'Given' but it has to work with it."[40] Burrow explains that the divine struggle with the "Given" brings suffering into God's own experience in a way that is analogous to our own painful experiences. He notes,

> Brightman theorized that just as the cosmic drag in the evolutionary process and in human nature retards and hinders the expression of value producing opposition and struggle in all experience, the nonrational Given within God's own nature causes an eternal problem for God . . . Even God was not free to escape suffering entirely. Therefore, God is perceived as a redemptive participant in human suffering.[41]

Therefore, the creaturely struggle to realize redemptive purposes through pain is grounded in the divine struggle. However, for Brightman, God suffers as we suffer, but participates in our suffering. He suffers as human beings suffer the pain of conditions allowed to exists because of the limitations of the "Given." Brightman's theory offered a tantalizing philosophical justification for King's redemptive suffering perspective. It provided a metaphysical basis for redemptive suffering and highlighted divine immanence in a way that affirms that God literally feels the pain of human beings. Brightman articulated this in an article entitled, "The Essence of Christianity." There, he noted that "It is safe to say that no one at any stage of Christian development has ever read the story of Good Friday and of Easter without seeing in it the drama of faith in the spiritual value of sacrifice. Out of voluntary submission to undeserved suffering come resurrection and redemption. Here is the universal faith essential to all Christians everywhere."[42] Therefore for Brightman, redemptive suffering was not only harmonious with his notion of theistic finitism, but it was right at the heart of Christian faith itself. Like King, Brightman also viewed the cross of Christ as the paradigmatic example of unmerited suffering bringing about redemption.

However, despite such similarities, King still could not accept Brightman's finitism since it justified sacrifice at the expense of God's supremacy in all things. King was a theologian of action who deeply considered the practical implications of any philosophy. Locating the duality within the nature of God (as finitists hold) rather than external to God (as absolutists hold) would potentially undermine the hope of oppressed people who believed that the supreme God could defend and deliver them from any evil force.[43] Brightman's finitism would have hardly been accepted within King's black church context. Although King might have told the saints that God struggles with them and somehow participates in their suffering, he couldn't imagine telling black congregants that the reason such atrocities exist is because God cannot overcome the obstacles within God's own nature. In the minds of many blacks accustomed to traditional understandings of omnipotence, this would make God appear somewhat weak and not wholly set against the forces of evil since its existence is due to something within the divine nature.

Part 4: King's Theodicy and Hegel's Dialectic

King would find another philosophical basis for redemptive suffering in Hegel's famous dialectic, the principle that truth lies within the tension of opposites. At Morehouse, sociology professor Walter Chivers already taught King to apply Hegel's formula to the black experience.[44] At Boston, King's class with Brightman and Peter Bertocci offered the opportunity to delve more extensively into Hegel's thought.[45] Bertocci suggested that the principle of dialectal unity traces back at least as far as the Greek philosopher Heraclitus.[46] Heraclitus held that the tension of opposites is essential to reality and development. He explained, "It should be understood that war is the common condition, that strife is justice, and that all things come to pass through compulsion of strife."[47] He also noted, "Opposition brings concord. Out of discord comes the fairest harmony."[48] Therefore, Heraclitus was a kind of precursor to Hegel's methodology and teleology of development through struggle. King studied Hegel's *Phenomenology of Mind*, *Philosophy of History,* and *Philosophy of Right* tracing the dialectal movements of the "Absolute" in history and in human thought.[49] According to Hegel, the Absolute's dialectical movements result in the realization of greater freedom and truth. The Absolute passes on from one position or thesis in history and thought, on to an opposing antithesis. The tension between the two opposing positions (thesis and antithesis) exposes the limitations of both respective polarities, with a more complete truth resting within the synthesis of the two partial truths.[50] The claim of each partial truth to being comprehensive is annulled, while their partial truths are preserved in the synthesis. Hegel chose the term *Aufhebung* (or sublation) to describe the interaction between thesis and antithesis. Each resultant synthesis becomes its own thesis, destined to be interrelated with a corresponding antithesis and shown to be partial in the total pursuit for freedom and truth.[51] Through *Aufhebung* there is a greater, more elevated manifestation of the Absolute in human history and community.

Although King rejected Hegel's absolute idealism as "rationally unsound," he embraced his dialectal method and teleological interpretation of history. This methodology and teleology gave King a helpful philosophical grounding for redemptive suffering.[52] In *Stride Toward Freedom*, King recalled that Hegel's dialectal process "helped me see that growth comes through struggle."[53] King would hold fast to the dialectal method throughout his involvement with the freedom struggle, applying it to make sense of out opposing views and to offer hope to the participants in the freedom struggle. The idea that growth comes through struggle provided meaning to the prevalent opposition to the freedom movement as well as the chaos of the times. Drawing on lessons learned in Bertocci's class, King explained, "Long ago the Greek philosopher Heraclitus argued that justice emerges from the strife of opposites, and Hegel, in modern philosophy preached a doctrine of growth through struggle. It is both historically and biologically true that there can be no birth and growth without birth and growing pains."[54] Spiritual development and transformation comes precisely through the tension of engagement with the opposition. The Hegelian dialectic helped King recognize the usefulness of non-violent direct action, a synthesis which combined the partial truths of passive acquiescence on the one hand, and militant resistance on the other. Accordingly, transformation would not come purely through suffering, but through the tension created as one resisted suffering non-violently. In this understanding, the tension created from resistance to evil yields a development, a redemptive transformation within persons that would not otherwise be present. In communities, powerful socio-political and economic structures (i.e., a thesis) must be confronted by a unified uprising of oppressed people (i.e., antithesis). As a result of this tension, a new reality may emerge, a synthesis that combines the best in both positions.[55] Pain and suffering are often an unavoidable part of the conflict and tension at the heart of this historical process. Therefore, suffering often accompanies positive developments in history, the necessary context out of which redemptive realities arise. Thus, the dialectal method provided a substantial philosophical grounding for King's redemptive suffering theodicy. True to his black church heritage and context, King preferred to attribute the existence of evil to hindrances outside of the divine nature such as the necessary tension at the heart of the historical process.

Part 5: King's Theodicy and the Theistic Absolutism of Borden Bowne and Harold DeWolf

After Edgar Brightman's death, King studied the works of Borden Bowne and worked with Harold DeWolf to articulate a personalist approach to theodicy much more harmonious with the traditional ideas he received back in Atlanta.[56] Unlike Brightman and other theistic finalists, Bowne and DeWolf insisted that God is infinite in goodness and in power. Although God has imposed self-limitations due to human freedom such limitations don't count against God's omnipotence.[57] For King, freedom was one of the most important elements in the value of personality. God's power achieves its purpose to sustaining human freedom (and with it value), even at the cost of suffering so that divine omnipotence is demonstrated precisely through allowing certain forms of suffering.[58] However, human freedom can't account for natural evils. But rather than attempt to resolve all of the tensions, King opted to affirm God's omnipotence, insisting that the answer to the problem of evil is ultimately mysterious. God allows sufferings, not because He is powerless to stop it, but for his own inscrutable good purposes.[59] And so, as Rufus Burrow notes, "King explicitly rejected Brightman's mature conception of God, i.e., the finite-infinite God, choosing instead the traditional absolutist view of Afrikan-American theism and that of personalists Borden P. Bowne (1847–1910) and L. Harold DeWolf (1905–1986)."[60]

Through critiquing the theodicies of Henry Nelson Wieman and Paul Tillich in his doctoral dissertation, King sharpened his approach a bit more. King explained that, according to Wieman, the problem of evil depends on the erroneous assumption that God is the creator of all existence. Having doubted that God is the fundamental ground of all existence, Wieman posited a finite God whose power is limited by forces external to his nature, forces that He did not create.[61] Although King agreed with Wieman's emphasis on the goodness of God, he balked at Wieman's limitation on God's power.[62] King insisted that Wieman's denial of the Creator-God "raises more problems than it solves."[63] It fails to explain the source of consciousness or value. Though Wieman insisted that his conception of God is supra-personal, King suggested that such a limited conception is subpersonal. Having so limited the power of God, King concluded that Wieman's theodicy was "inadequate."[64] Tillich, on the other hand, called God's goodness into question. First he suggested that natural evils in the world are simply the result of our creaturely finitude. King responded that this suggestion is "no solution to the problem" since it would imply that as the creator of our creaturely finitude, God is also the creator of evil.[65] Secondly, Tillich located a non-rational limitation within God's own nature called the "abyss," that he contended is responsible for the evils in the world. Following DeWolf, King leveled the same major criticism against Tillich's abyss as he leveled against Brightman's "Given," namely that it set up a metaphysical dualism within the nature of God itself.[66]

In his *Theology of the Living Church*, written about the same time as King matriculated at Boston, DeWolf also critiqued both Brightman and Tillich at this very point—mentioning internal metaphysical dualism as the greatest weakness of theistic finitism.[67] This supposed internal dualism would set up "a self-contradictory relationship at the very source of being," where we can appeal to none greater for an explanation.[68] By contrast, DeWolf proposed that absolutism depends more heavily on mystery, yet involves less inherent contradictions than finitism.[69] For absolutists like DeWolf, there is no being or aspect of being beyond the control of God's rational will. All being is either directly or indirectly attributable to "the perfection of God's good purpose."[70] God only allows suffering according to his mysterious all-encompassing purposes. Suffering then is a part of God's holy will. Suggesting that God wills a suffering circumstance is quite different than merely admitting, as the finitist does, that God has partial control over it.[71] It conveys the sense that God's mysterious purposes are being infallibly worked out through suffering situations. It also conveys the sense that sufferers are not enduring something that God is powerless to prevent, but the faith of the faithful is deepened precisely as they accept their suffering as a part of God's will.[72] DeWolf insisted that the theodical questions in Scripture find their force with the belief in an absolutely powerful God.[73] Redemptive meaning emerges precisely out of the tension that God has the power to prevent suffering and yet allows it. Anguish then is interpreted as serving God's mysterious redemptive purpose. For King, this was the biblical faith that sustained the humble believers among whom he would serve.

King would affirm the mystery of suffering as he considered the problem of suffering from Scripture. In his qualifying examination on the theology of the Bible (taken just before starting work on his dissertation), King traced Old Testament approaches to the problem of evil. True to his higher critical leanings, King characterized the biblical authors as offering competing accounts of the existence of natural evils. He noted that the deutoronomic writers built an entire philosophy of history on the principle that natural evils were punishment due to sin. King suggested that the prophets Habakkuk and Jeremiah were the first to seriously question this outlook. Habakkuk's question arose as he considered the rampant injustice within the nation and Jeremiah's query as he considered his own personal mistreatment. Both figures were perplexed as they saw the righteous suffering and the wicked prospering, the very opposite of what the Deutoronomic view was supposed to have predicted. King explained that though they raised the question, the problem was not solved for them intellectually. In the end, it was a matter of faith—essentially the same view King offered years earlier at Crozer in "The Significant Contributions of Jeremiah to Religious Thought" and "Religion's Answer to the Problem of Evil."[74]

In this essay response, King developed his approach with additional biblical reasons to be hopeful about the mystery of theodicy. He explained that there is "something of a solution to the problem [of evil] found in the prologue of the book of Job." He continued, "Here it is affirmed that in the council of God the suffering of Job had a purpose although Job didn't know it. May it not be true that the natural evil in the world has a purpose that our limited minds cannot comprehend at the moment?"[75] The book of Job offers a biblical reason to be hopeful about unearned suffering, since God's purposes are beyond our comprehension. Rather than limit the power of God, King appealed to a divine purpose beyond human comprehension. Thus, in this way he shifted his focus to divine transcendence, rather than immanence. This is an approach firmly rooted in King's black church roots. Again we recall King Sr.'s advice to young M.L. at the death of his maternal grandmother. Informed by his own black church roots, Daddy King appealed to divine transcendence and mystery, counseling his son, "God has His own plan and His own way."[76] Deeply impacted by his father's words, King, Jr. developed a healthy respect for hopeful mystery. King never intended his redemptive suffering theodicy as an intellectually comprehensive explanation for all evil. Beyond philosophies there must be a faith that in all things God has a redemptive plan—especially when life appears bleak and confusing. King would maintain this deep respect for mystery throughout his career.

Secondly, King appealed to the "suffering servant" in Isaiah as an explanation for unearned pain. King explains that the servant's pain was vicarious, not directly due to anything he has done. It was also redemptive, in that the knowledge of God is spread to the Gentiles through the unearned suffering of the servant. King explains, "those unbelievers seeing that this suffering servant is innocent will become conscious of their sins and repent and thereby be redeemed."[77] King notes that the New

Testament identifies the servant with Jesus Christ, and thereby offers a hopeful solution to the problem of evil through the cross of Christ. Therefore, King reaffirms his commitment to the cross as the paradigmatic revelation of unearned suffering which brings redemptive transformation. There is a pedagogical purpose through the sufferings of Christ. Though unearned suffering is in many ways mysterious, this offers hope that the sufferings of the innocent are not meaningless. King also noted that the New Testament teaching on immortality offers hope that injustices experienced in this life will be corrected in the life to come.[78] King received this theodical lesson from the death of his maternal grandmother. In his *Autobiography of Religious Development*, he recalled that after his grandmother died he began to seriously consider the doctrine of immortality for the first time. After his parents explained it to him, he says, "I was assured that somehow my grandmother still lived. I guess this is why today I am such a strong believer in personal immortality."[79] More than intellectual answers, this early experience with theodicy gave King a deep appreciation for the faith aspect of theodicy, setting him on a trajectory to address the question as pastor and theologian more so than philosopher. For King, the answers to theodicy are rooted in faith in God's incomprehensible good purposes, faith in Christ as redemptive sufferer, and faith in life after death. He notes that "We can say in conclusion that the Bible teaches that the ultimate problem of suffering is in faith and fellowship with God. In such a setting the individual does not necessarily have an intellectual solution, but he transcends the problem."[80] According to King, God's presence and faith in his redemptive purposes raise the faithful above such intellectual inquiries.

Therefore, King not only embraced mystery within his theodicy, but he also included a real note of mysticism which would carry him through some of his darkest moments of doubt. Having been reared in a church tradition friendly towards the idea of immediate divine encounters and influenced by the likes of the great mystic Howard Thurman, King readily affirmed the reality of mystical experiences.[81] Thurman defined mysticism as, "The response of the individual to a personal encounter with God within his own spirit."[82] King held that such immediate experiences with God were an important, meaningful, and useful part of religious life.[83] He appealed to such personal encounters when philosophical answers to theodicy wouldn't suffice. His insistence that fellowship with God can help a person transcend the intellectual problem of evil reveals King's dependence on mystical experiences to address tensions too complex for philosophical inquiry. Direct experience with God carries the mystic through suffering, and gives them a perspective otherwise inaccessible through intellectual inquiry. A personal encounter with God can bring comfort and resolution to painful circumstances, even where such experiences are in some ways ineffable. This is the dimension of theodicy to which King would appeal in his famous "vision in the kitchen," as David Garrow calls it. Feeling the pressure of persecution for his leadership in the fledgling Montgomery Bus Boycott, King could not find comfort in intellectual solutions to the problem of suffering. Rather a mysterious inner voice pointed him towards the omnipotent God worshipped in the black church, the God who could "make a way out of no way."[84] This mystical experience renewed King's faith in the God who was able to protect, sustain, and deliver him amidst deep trials. Second, the voice offered reassurance of God's presence during his struggles. He was comforted by the idea that as he fought for justice and truth, God would be with him. King often included this story in sermons delivered in black churches, which most often readily embrace such mystical encounters. King's retelling of the story normally reached its crescendo as King repeated that Jesus would never leave him alone, no never alone.

King's "vision in the kitchen" does not represent a complete repudiation of the theodicy he had developed up to that point in his academic writings. Rather, it shows that King did not appeal to academic those sources as comprehensive. The ultimate answers to theodicy arise as a matter of faith in the mysterious purposes of God and the presence of God. Referring to the "vision in the kitchen," Smith, Kirby, and Burrow suggest that during the Civil Rights Movement, King's formal philosophical approach to theodicy gave way to his religious experiences. While this is basically true, I would nuance the position a bit by contending that in his formal writings on theodicy, King deliberately made space for the kinds of religious experiences he had in the kitchen vision.[85] So that King's kitchen experience reaffirmed the basic approach he adopted throughout his seminary and graduate school days—a thoughtful redemptive suffering analysis which readily acknowledged the limits of philosophical inquiry into theodicy, and the deep need for personal encounters with God where such inquiries left off. For King, a mystical experience reaffirmed his faith in the power and presence of the God that he learned about at Ebenezer and articulated even in his qualifying exams on the bible.

CONCLUSION

With this, we have seen that King's basic redemptive suffering theodicy remained intact through his years at Boston. Through a particular focus on the doctrine of God, at Boston, King carefully and selectively synthesized a wide array of protestant liberal theodical concepts which were in-step with his fundamental black church sensibilities. Through encountering McTaggart, King refocused his definition of divine omnipotence in ways that would meet the practical realities of black suffering. Hocking's ideal absolutism helped King firmly ground his theodical hope in God as creator and in the fundamental character of the universe itself—an optimism he inherited in his upbringing. Hegel's dialectic also gave King metaphysical grounding for the theodical outlook that historical progress occurs through struggle. Although King deeply engaged Brightman's finitism and had deep sympathies with it, his view ultimately resembled the absolutism of Bowne and DeWolf—versions of personalism which affirmed divine omnipotence in ways which engender unqualified trust in God's incomprehensible purposes for oppressed people.

Overall, this project examines the roots and implications of King's redemptive suffering theodicy. Part 1 of our study considered the roots of King's theodicy, seeking to understand the varied factors that came together to forge King's unique theodical perspective. Before we turn to the implications of King's theodicy and place him in conversation with his modern womanist and black humanist critics, it would be helpful to offer a recap of where we have been.

Chapter 1 looked at the family and cultural roots of King's theodicy. There, I traced the redemptive suffering theme through a line of black cultural icons including David Walker, Alexander Crummell, and W.E.B. DuBois right down to King, showing that redemptive suffering themes like black messianism are deeply imbedded within the black communal consciousness. Additionally, I looked at King's family lineage, showing how the message of redemptive suffering came to him from his paternal grandmother Delia Lindsay through Daddy King. Experiences such as the sudden death of his maternal grandmother, Jennie Celeste Williams, provided opportunities for the young King to wrestle deeply with the issue of theodicy. These early experiences helped fashion his fundamental theological orientation toward the issue of theodicy.

Chapter 2 examined at the black church roots of King's theodicy. Out of the many possible angles, I chose to focus on the pastoral, musical, and prayer tradition of the black church as influences on King's theodicy. I traced redemptive suffering as a theme through the pastoral ministries of Willis Williams, A.D. Williams, Daddy King, down to King, Jr., showing how each figure had a particular concern to address the problem of black suffering. The question of theodicy also appears prominently in Negro spirituals like "Didn't My Lord Deliver Daniel," "There is a Balm in Gilead," "I Been 'Buked" and hymns like "We'll Understand It Better By and By." Finally, the prayer tradition of the black church also provided a rich context for deep theodical reflection and articulation as well.

Chapter 3 dealt with King's early engagement with protestant liberalism. I argued that King's theodicy represents a true synthesis of the liberal ideas he encountered at Crozer with the "homespun" ideas he acquired from his family, church, and cultural influences. Morehouse influences such as George Kelsey and Benjamin Mays gave King a model for the critical engagement of the evangelical liberalism he encountered at Crozer. Rather than reject the faith of his youth, I contend that Kelsey taught King to use Liberalism in order to enhance the basic theological ideas he'd already received at Ebenezer. Therefore, when King arrived at Crozer, he was ready to apply the best of the critical methods he encountered to address the issue of black suffering, while rejecting aspects of the liberal tradition that didn't fit with the black experience or traditional religious sensibilities. Every major theodical development King made during his Crozer years has some "homespun" root.

King's Boston years reflect the same general pattern, as he appropriated sources that would help him develop a theodicy that could be practically applied to the lives of the black masses he would serve. As he broached the problem of evil in the graduate school classrooms, King leaned heavily upon hopeful mystery, repeatedly emphasizing the importance of the religious, rather than intellectual, answers to theodicy. This left space for the kinds of experiences typified by his famous "vision in the kitchen." This demonstrates the basic theodical continuity King would maintain throughout his career. King essentially held that the omni-benevolent and omnipotent personal God uses human engagement with unearned suffering to bring about redemptive transformation according His mysterious and all-encompassing purpose revealed at the cross. This theodical outlook reflects an eclectic blend of homespun ideas inherited from his family, church, and cultural roots and the protestant liberal sources he encountered in seminary and graduate studies. With this understanding of the various roots, influences, and core content King's theodicy we are finally ready for Part 2 of our study. Now we will consider whether King's concept can effectively address contemporary forms of black suffering. For that, we begin with the black humanist critique.

NOTES

1. Coretta Scott King, *My Life with Martin Luther King, Jr.*, Revised (New York: Puffin, 1994), 56.

2. Clayborne Carson, "Introduction," in *The Papers of Martin Luther King, Jr.: Volume 2: Rediscovering Precious Values July 1951–November 1955*, ed. Peter Holloran, Ralph Luker, and Penny A Russell, vol. 2 (Berkeley: University of California Press, 1992), 10; Martin Luther King, Jr., "Loving Your Enemies (Atlanta, 1952)," in *The Papers of Martin Luther King, Jr.: Volume 6: Advocate of the Social Gospel September 1948–March 1963*, ed. Clayborne Carson et al. (Berkeley: University of California Press, 1992), 128.

3. Rufus Burrow, Jr., "The Doctrine of Unearned Suffering," *Encounter* 63, no. 1–2 (December 1, 2002): 70.

4. Martin Luther King, Jr., "A Comparison and Evaluation of the Philosophical Views Set Forth in J.M.E. McTaggart's *Some Dogmas of Religion*, and William E Hocking's *The Meaning of God in Human Experience* with Those Set Forth in Edgar Brightman's Course on 'Philosophy of Religion,'" in *The Papers of Martin Luther King, Jr.: Volume 2: Rediscovering Precious Values July 1951–November 1955*, ed. Clayborne Carson et al. (Berkeley: University of California Press, 1992), 83.

5. Rufus Burrow, Jr., *Personalism: A Critical Introduction* (St. Louis, Mo.: Chalice Press, 1999), 159.

6. Ibid., 37.

7. J.M.E. McTaggart, "An Ontological Idealism," in *Contemporary British Philosophy*, ed. J.H. Muirhead (New York: Macmillan, 1924), 251.

8. Martin Luther King, Jr., "The Personalism of J.M.E. McTaggart Under Criticism," in *The Papers of Martin Luther King, Jr.: Volume 2: Rediscovering Precious Values July 1951–November 1955*, ed. Clayborne Carson et al. (Berkeley: University of California Press, 1992), 65.

9. Burrow, Jr., *Personalism*, 37.

10. King, Jr., "The Personalism of J.M.E. McTaggart Under Criticism," 66–67.

11. J.M.E. McTaggart, *Some Dogmas of Religion* (London: Edward Arnold, 1906), 203–204. Although he rejected theism, McTaggart admitted that theistic finitism is the most plausible form of theism to resolve the question of theodicy. Ibid., 219; King, Jr., "A Comparison and Evaluation of McTaggart, Brightman, and Hocking," 85; Burrow, Jr., *Personalism*, 36.

12. Martin Luther King, Jr., "A Comparison and Evaluation of the Philosophical Views Set Forth in J.M.E. McTaggart's *Some Dogmas of Religion*, and William E Hocking's *The Meaning of God in Human Experience* with Those Set Forth in Edgar Brightman's Course on 'Philosophy of Religion,'" in *The Papers of Martin Luther King, Jr.: Volume 2: Rediscovering Precious Values July 1951–November 1955*, ed. Clayborne Carson et al. (Berkeley: University of California Press, 1992), 83.

13. King, Jr., "The Personalism of J.M.E. McTaggart Under Criticism," 68.

14. Ibid.

15. King, Jr., "A Comparison and Evaluation of McTaggart, Brightman, and Hocking," 83.

16. Burrow, Jr., *Personalism*, 157.

17. Ibid.

18. Ibid., 159.

19. Martin Luther King, Jr., "Religion's Answer to the Problem of Evil," in *The Papers of Martin Luther King, Jr.: Volume I: Called to Serve, January 1929–June 1951*, vol. 1, First, The Papers of Martin Luther King, Jr. (Berkeley: University of California Press, 1992), 426. King first broached theistic finitism in an essay entitled "A Conception and Impression of Religion Drawn from Dr. Brightman's Book Entitled *A Philosophy of Religion*," written for George Washington Davis' Philosophy of Religion course at Crozer. Although King briefly described Brightman's theory there, he offers no real assessment of it. The essay does however represent King's first sustained academic engagement with Brightman. Martin Luther King, Jr., "A Conception and Impression of Religion Drawn from Dr. Brightman's Book Entitled A Philosophy of Religion," in *The Papers of Martin Luther King, Jr.: Volume I: Called to Serve, January 1929–June 1951*, ed. Clayborne Carson, Ralph Luker, and Penny A Russell (Berkeley, California: University of California Press, 1992), 414–415.

20. King, Jr., "A Comparison and Evaluation of McTaggart, Brightman, and Hocking," 83.

21. Ibid.

22. Ibid., 84.

23. Ibid., 85.

24. Brightman himself didn't think he was proposing a weak God. Rather, he insisted that God is supremely valuable, able to bring good out of evil, and ultimately triumphant over every circumstance. In *The Problem of God*, he explained, "This conception of God means that we think of him as the one who can bring good out of evil. If he is supremely value, he cannot allow any evil that will permanently frustrate his purpose. He may delay, but he cannot fail. Whatever the origin of evil may be, and however awful it may be, God is the one who can never be baffled by any evil . . . in any given situation, we may suppose, God can achieve certain goods through man's co-operation; if man does not co-operate, then different goods will have to be achieved by God in a different way. But no situation is finally evil. Beyond every obstacle there lies a possible achievement, out of every evil a possible good may grow. This is the meaning of faith in God." Edgar S. Brightman, *The Problem of God* (New York: Abingdon Press, 1930), 122; Cited in Rufus Burrow, Jr., *God and Human Dignity: The Personalism, Theology, and Ethics of Martin Luther King, Jr.* (Notre Dame: University of Notre Dame Press, 2006), 92–93.

25. William E. Hocking, *The Meaning of God in Human Experience* (New Haven: Yale University Press, 1912), 134; King, Jr., "A Comparison and Evaluation of McTaggart, Brightman, and Hocking," 85.

26. King, Jr., "A Comparison and Evaluation of McTaggart, Brightman, and Hocking," 85.

27. Hocking explained, "No man can be an optimist, then, without going behind the superficial returns. The character of the world upon which he bases his judgment must be a real character, as opposed to apparent character your optimist must be something of a metaphysician, something of a seer." Hocking, *The Meaning of God in Human Experience*, 168.

28. King, Jr., "A Comparison and Evaluation of McTaggart, Brightman, and Hocking," 85.

29. Hocking, *The Meaning of God in Human Experience*, 224.

30. Martin Luther King, Jr., "An Autobiography of Religious Development," in *The Papers of Martin Luther King, Jr.: Volume I: Called to Serve, January 1929–June 1951*, vol. 1, First Edition, The Papers of Martin Luther King, Jr. (Berkeley: University of California Press, 1992), 361.

31. Martin Luther King, Jr., "Application for Admission to Crozer Theological Seminary," in *The Papers of Martin Luther King, Jr.: Volume I: Called to Serve, January 1929–June 1951*, ed. Clayborne Carson and Ralph E. Luker (Berkeley, California: University of California Press, 1992), 144.

32. Hocking, *The Meaning of God in Human Experience*, 224, 330; King, Jr., "A Comparison and Evaluation of McTaggart, Brightman, and Hocking," 85–86.

33. Hocking, *The Meaning of God in Human Experience*, 331.

34. Benjamin E. Mays, *The Negro's God as Reflected in His Literature* (New York: Russel & Russel, 1938), 21.

35. King, Jr., "Autobiography of Religious Development."

36. Martin Luther King, Jr., "Rediscovering Lost Values," in *A Knock at Midnight: Inspiration from the Great Sermons of Reverend Martin Luther King, Jr.*, ed. Clayborne Carson and Peter Holloran (New York: Warner Books, 1998). Thomas Carlye's famous quote "No lie can live forever" appears in his famous book *The French Revolution: A History* where he says that faith consists in the belief that all delusions are destined for destruction. Thomas Carlyle, *The French Revolution: A History* (The Modern Library, 1934), pt. 1 Book 5, chpt. 5. William Cullen Bryant's famous phrase "Truth, crushed to earth will rise again" appears in his poem "The Battle-field" where it signifies the hope that goodness shall ultimately triumph even though it suffers temporary defeats. William Cullen Bryant, "The Battle-Field," in *Yale Book of American Verse*, ed. Thomas Raynesford Lounsbury (New Haven: Yale University Press, 1912), v. 33.

37. This does not mean that evils are really goods seen from an earthly perspective. Rather it means that the divine perspective reveals that evils are only temporary residents in a world that is fundamentally good. It also means that God is with God's people ensuring helping them resist evil through revealing the divine perspective on evil.

38. In a paper written on Karl Barth's doctrine of God, King reaffirmed his commitment to divine immanence. According to King, God is ever present expressing his creative genius through the essential goodness of the world. Martin Luther King, Jr., "Karl Barth's Conception of God," in *The Papers of Martin Luther King, Jr.: Volume 2: Rediscovering Precious Values July 1951–November 1955*, ed. Clayborne Carson et al. (Berkeley: University of California Press, 1992), 104.

39. Martin Luther King, Jr., "Final Examination Answers, Philosophy of Religion," in *The Papers of Martin Luther King, Jr.: Volume 2: Rediscovering Precious Values July 1951–November 1955*, ed. Clayborne Carson et al. (Berkeley: University of California Press, 1992), 109.

40. King, Jr., "Final Examination Answers, Personalism," 111.

41. Jimmy L. Kirby and Rufus Burrow, "Conceptions of God in the Thinking of Martin Luther King, Jr and Edgar S Brightman," *Encounter* 60, no. 3 (June 1, 1999): 292; Edgar Sheffield Brightman, "The Given and Its Critics," *Religion in Life* 1, no. 1 (December 1, 1932): 137.

42. Edgar S. Brightman, "The Essence of Christianity," *Crozer Quarterly* 18 (April 1941): 119.

43. Kirby and Burrow, "Conceptions of God in the Thinking of Martin Luther King, Jr and Edgar S Brightman," 288–289.

44. Lewis V. Baldwin, *There Is a Balm in Gilead: The Cultural Roots of Martin Luther King, Jr* (Minneapolis: Fortress Press, 1991), 26–27.

45. Smith and Zepp, *Search for the Beloved Community*, 124.

46. John J. Ansbro, *Martin Luther King, Jr.: The Making of a Mind*, 1st ed. (Maryknoll: Orbis Books, 1984), 120.

47. Heraclitus, "Heraclitus," in *The Presocratics*, ed. Philip Ellis Wheelwright (New York: The Odyssey Press, 1966), 71.

48. Ibid., 77.

49. Martin Luther King, Jr., "Pilgrimage to Nonviolence," in *Stride Toward Freedom: The Montgomery Story* (San Francisco: HarperCollins, 1987), 100.

50. Ansbro, *The Making of a Mind*, 122.

51. Ibid.

52. Hegel's dialectic helped King reconcile the truths of opposing viewpoints while avoiding the excesses of any particular view. He applied this principle to his analysis of a wide array of subjects including liberalism and neo-orthodoxy, individual and collective responsibility in the Kingdom of God, opposing views of anthropology, and race relations just to name a few. Martin Luther King, Jr., *Strength to Love* (New York: Harper and Row, 1963), 88, 99, 136; Smith and Zepp, *Search for the Beloved Community*, 126–127.

53. King, Jr., "Pilgrimage to Nonviolence," 101. Daddy King and A.D. Williams also upheld tis idea, however there is no evidence that they learned it from Hegel. Hegel offered King philosophical categories to help develop this principle that he originally learned from his father and maternal grandfather.

54. Martin Luther King, Jr., "Facing the Challenge of a New Age," in *The Papers of Martin Luther King, Jr.: Birth of a New Age, December 1955–December 1956*, ed. Carson Clayborne et al. (Berkeley, California: University of California Press, 1997), 451.

55. Smith and Zepp, Search for the Beloved Community, 127.

56. Kirby and Burrow, "Conceptions of God in the Thinking of Martin Luther King, Jr and Edgar S Brightman," 295.

57. Ibid., 294.

58. King, Jr., "Religion's Answer to the Problem of Evil," 428.

59. Ibid., 432; Kirby and Burrow, "Conceptions of God in the Thinking of Martin Luther King, Jr and Edgar S Brightman," 297. Harold DeWolf also left substantial space for mystery in his theodicy. L. Harold DeWolf, *Theology of the Living Church*, Revised Edition (New York: Harper and Row, 1953), 143.

60. Kirby and Burrow, "Conceptions of God in the Thinking of Martin Luther King, Jr and Edgar S Brightman," 284.

61. Martin Luther King, Jr., "A Comparison of the Conceptions of God in the Thinking of Paul Tillich and Henry Nelson Wieman," (Ph.D. dissertation, Boston University, 1955) in *The Papers of Martin Luther King, Jr.: Rediscovering*

Precious Values, July 1951–1955, ed. Clayborne Carson et al., vol. 2 (Berkeley, California: University of California Press, 1992), 529–530.

62. Kirby and Burrow, "Conceptions of God in the Thinking of Martin Luther King, Jr and Edgar S Brightman," 293.

63. King, Jr., "A Comparison of the Conceptions of God in the Thinking of Paul Tillich and Henry Nelson Wieman," 530.

64. Ibid.

65. Ibid., 530–531.

66. Ibid., 531; DeWolf, Living Church, 133–135.

67. DeWolf, Living Church, 133–134.

68. Ibid., 134.

69. Ibid.

70. Ibid.

71. Ibid., 136.

72. Ibid., 134–135.

73. Ibid., 136–137.

74. Martin Luther King, Jr., "The Significant Contributions of Jeremiah to Religious Thought," in *The Papers of Martin Luther King, Jr.: Volume I: Called to Serve, January 1929–June 1951* (Berkeley, California: University of California Press, 1992), 189–193; King, Jr., "Religion's Answer to the Problem of Evil," 432–433.

75. Martin Luther King, "Qualifying Examination Answers: Theology of the Bible," in *The Papers of Martin Luther King, Jr.: Volume 2: Rediscovering Precious Values July 1951–November 1955*, ed. Clayborne Carson et al. (Berkeley: University of California Press, 1992), 207–208. This does not indicate that King viewed suffering itself as a good. King simply means that there may be some incomprehensibly great purpose behind God allowing natural evils to occur.

76. Martin Luther King, Sr., *Daddy King: An Autobiography*, 1st ed. (New York: William Morrow & Co, 1980), 109; Mays, *The Negro's God as Reflected in His Literature*, 153.

77. King, "Qualifying Examination Answers: Theology of the Bible," 208.

78. Ibid.

79. King, Jr., "Autobiography of Religious Development," 362.

80. King, "Qualifying Examination Answers: Theology of the Bible," 208.

81. See especially Cynthia Carsten Wentz, "Martin Luther King, Jr, and the American Mystical Tradition," *Sewanee Theological Review* 38, no. 2 (January 1, 1995): 105–113.

82. Howard Thurman, *Mysticism and the Experience of Love* (Wallingford, PA: Pendle Hill, 1961), 3, 6.

83. King, Jr., "Final Examination Answers, Philosophy of Religion," 108.

84. David J. Garrow, *Bearing the Cross: Martin Luther King, Jr., and the Southern Christian Leadership Conference* (New York: William Morrow & Co, 1986), 57–58; See also Baldwin, *There Is a Balm in Gilead*, 189.

85. Ervin Smith, *The Ethics of Martin Luther King, Jr.* (New York: Edwin Mellen Press, 1981), 27; Kirby and Burrow, "Conceptions of God in the Thinking of Martin Luther King, Jr. and Edgar S. Brightman," 297.

2

Critics and Contemporary Relevance of King's Theodicy

5

THE BLACK HUMANISTS

INTRODUCTION

Despite its popularity within the black community, the redemptive suffering tradition has almost always had its critics. Some worried that assigning redemptive purposes to black suffering would undermine black dignity. Others feared the tradition promoted social passivity by justifying oppression as part of the divine will and casting the responsibility for liberation to divine, rather than human agency. As early as the late nineteenth century, abolitionist Martin Delany and journalist T. Thomas Fortune denied that God had any redemptive purpose associated with the enslavement of blacks or that any good could come from it.[1] By the early twentieth century, church historian Carter G. Woodson and even Morehouse president Benjamin Mays suggested that an overemphasis on the absolute power and sovereignty of God might undermine active resistance to oppression.[2] Mays explains, "Though the idea may have enabled the Negro to struggle for his needs, it has also helped to make him satisfied and complacent."[3] Belief in a redemptive plan at work in suffering has often saved blacks from frustration and despair, sustained them in the hour of deepest need, and kept them committed to religious practices such as prayer.[4] However, the idea may also promote an unhealthy otherworldliness which cultivates complacency and undermines resistance to oppression in the here and now. "Believing this about God," he says, "the Negro, in many instances, has stood and suffered much without striking back, and without trying aggressively to realize to the full his needs in this world."[5]

THE HUMANIST CRITIQUE PART I: WILLIAM R. JONES

The most sustained challenge to the redemptive suffering tradition would come nearly a half century later, from black humanist William R. Jones. In 1973, Jones published his landmark work *Is God a White Racist?*, which questioned whether black suffering could be adequately addressed within the framework of traditional beliefs about divine goodness and power.[6] Inspired by Algerian-French philosopher Albert Camus, Jones suggested that statements of theodicy support oppressive structures by promoting quietism.[7] By quietism, Jones did not mean "do nothingism." Rather, for Jones, quietism means to act in such a way as to preserve the oppressive *status quo*. Jones explains that assigning a positive value to suffering dictates that oppression be endured and embraced, that the social *status quo* be preserved. Redemptive suffering theodicies "rob suffering of its pernicious flavor" by attempting to exonerate God's purposes and governance in the face of unearned human suffering. Therefore, says Jones, they are particularly adept at propping up oppression. Jones mainly critiques King's theodicy because it allegedly promotes quietism through assigning suffering a salvific quality.[8] As blacks think of their suffering as somehow redemptive, willed by God, and destined to be rectified at the eschaton, they are less likely to seek to eliminate it in the here and now. If blacks continue to believe that their suffering has positive value, he wonders how they will ever justify positive action against it.

Additionally, Jones questioned whether blacks should assume that God is for them in the face of protracted communal suffering. He held that the sufferings of the black community are "multievidential"—that is, they may just as easily be interpreted to support divine malevolence as its opposite, divine benevolence.[9] Jones explains, "any given occurrence of human suffering harmonizes equally well with antithetical positions, divine favor or disfavor, God's grace or God's curse. Consequently, in the face of human suffering, whatever its character, we must entertain the possibility that it is an expression of divine hostility."[10] Therefore, he alleges that the overabundance of suffering in the black experience forces a serious consideration of divine racism as a possible interpretation of the painful facts. If traditional theodicies continue to insist on God's absolute sovereignty and omnipotence, they must admit that God is able to prevent black suffering and yet unwilling to do so. According to Jones, this at least holds out the possibility that black suffering is the result of divine malevolence, racism towards blacks.[11] Jones alleges that traditional redemptive suffering theodicies don't take this possibility seriously enough.[12]

Moreover, Jones considered King's theodicy as particularly problematic because it indirectly identified the black community with the "suffering servant" biblical motif.[13] Jones argues that the resurrection vindicated the suffering servant (Christ) as God's righteous chosen servant. Jones contends that if the suffering servant theme correctly applies to African Americans, there needs to be some corresponding exaltation-type event that proves that blacks are the objects of divine favor despite signs to the contrary. In the absence of such evidence, Jones suggests that King's theodicy could imply that blacks are objects of the divine curse or somehow culpable for their own oppression.[14]

Jones insisted that traditional theodicies must reconsider the sovereignty and power of God in relation to history. In response, he proposed a "humanocentric theism," an alternative theism which affirms the "functional ultimacy" of humanity in determining its own destiny.[15] By eliminating the idea of divine sovereignty over human history and destiny, he believed he could relieve the philosophical and emotional tension created by the reality of black suffering and successfully maintain divine benevolence. Moreover, Jones believed that this version of theism would compel blacks to resist oppression as they acknowledge that human liberation only comes through human effort and agency. According to Jones, black theists are better served by holding that God limited God's self by endowing humanity with the freedom and responsibility to create its own destiny, a functional ultimacy. God works to persuade his free creatures but does not coerce them to make positive choices. Racism is solely a matter of human misdoings, a consequence of our stubborn rejection of God's gentle voice. There is no plan behind it and no redemptive purpose in it. Human suffering (particularly black suffering) is ultimately and solely caused by human choices and must be alleviated by human choices.[16] Jones offered a limited God theodicy as a remedy to the quietism allegedly supported by King's redemptive suffering theodicy.

THE HUMANIST CRITIQUE PART 2: ANTHONY PINN

Jones' seminal challenge to the redemptive suffering concept paved the way for Anthony Pinn's atheistic humanist critique.[17] Starting with the early seventeenth century, Pinn has taken aim at the entire redemptive suffering tradition in its varied forms, including King's version. He describes redemptive suffering as the general belief that suffering is a moral evil that God manipulates for redemptive purposes. Suffering in the here and now strengthens African Americans morally and spiritually for the ultimate fulfillment of a divine teleological design. Sometimes this includes the reorganization of Africa or the betterment of American society. Pinn places King into the latter category since, according to Pinn, he held that "suffering will afflict the American conscience and foster an end to racial discrimination."[18]

Pinn rejects redemptive suffering as detrimental to black liberation because, he says, such beliefs undermine human responsibility. He maintains that there is nothing beneficial about enduring suffering. Much like William Jones, Anthony Pinn suspects that redemptive suffering theodicies promote quietism and, in turn, preserve the structures of black oppression.[19] He explains,

> These [redemptive suffering] arguments are unacceptable because they counteract efforts at liberation by finding something of value in black suffering. In essence, these arguments go against social transformation activity. Redemptive suffering and liberation are diametrically opposed ideas; they suggest ways of being in the world that, in effect, nullify each other. One cannot embrace suffering as redemptive . . . and effectively speak of liberation.[20]

Pinn could have hardly expressed his disdain for redemptive suffering more forcefully than this. Not only does he find the idea unhelpful in achieving black liberation, he suspects it counteracts liberation. And so, one cannot consistently and effectively hold liberation and redemptive suffering together. The person that effectively strives for liberation must do so in spite of any acceptance of redemptive suffering. According to Pinn, King's effectiveness in the freedom struggle occurred independent of and despite his adherence to the "unfortunate" doctrine of redemptive suffering. King's redemptive suffering theodicy actually promotes oppression, as a prop to keep the oppressed from resisting and to keep them complacent, acquiescent, and continually enslaved.

Surprisingly, Pinn suggests that William Jones' humanocentric theodicy ultimately falls prey to the same quietistic pitfall as King's because according to his scheme, in the end humanity looks to God as a co-worker in achieving liberation. Pinn characterized Jones' humanocentric theism as a "weak humanism" since it holds that humans must work with God to achieve liberation. Pinn suspects that the very belief in a sovereign and powerfully active God undermines human efforts at liberation, even when that God is conceived as a limited co-worker at liberation. Therefore, Pinn advances what he calls a "strong humanism" in which there is "no God concept to contend with in addressing moral evil."[21] By denying the existence of God, Pinn hopes to eliminate the belief that God in any way approves of human suffering or that such suffering has any redemptive benefit or potentially redemptive benefit. According to Pinn, these views devalue human life, destroy human quality of life, and prevent the oppressed from striving for their own freedom. Without the possibility of divine assistance, Pinn says, the oppressed are free to enact their own social liberation. "Humanity has complete control over its destiny and therefore, one cannot hide behind God and plead that non-action is a divine command."[22] To promote sufficient social engagement, blacks must assume the full responsibility for their own liberation without seeking any external source of assistance.

According to Pinn, the reality of black suffering must be the prevailing factor and interpretive lens for any black theodical discourse. His form of humanism prioritizes the experience of human suffering as having more value than any allegiances to Christian tradition or doctrine. Such commitments, he says, already make compromises with the human suffering by seeking to find some good divine purpose in it. Therefore, Pinn insists that a truly liberating approach to suffering must include a radical critique of the existence of God, resist the "theological pothole" of redemptive suffering, and emphasize human responsibility and power to achieve its own liberation.[23]

Pinn's early argument against redemptive suffering runs like this.[24] (1) Since suffering is inherently evil, any goods derived from experiences with suffering are extrinsic and secondary, rather than basic. Here, Pinn assumes that theodical assertions should be based upon their correspondence to human experience, in this case black suffering. According to

Pinn, an adequate theodicy should not place theological categories above the reality of black suffering itself. "Truth" he says, "is experienced."[25] Black suffering is the primary and fundamental reality that should dominate the discussion of theodicy, rather than any secondary benefit derived from it. (2) The secondary good that blacks receive from unearned suffering is actualized by and credited to an outside force, in this case to God, rather than blacks themselves. (3) Black liberation means that the same God who oppressed blacks by allowing their unearned suffering must now be their savior. The oppressive God concept itself must be dispensed with to achieve full black liberation. (4) Blacks must take up full responsibility for their own liberation. Humans created the problem of black suffering and humans must solve it.[26] Pinn wonders how strongly blacks will fight for social change while looking for signs of God's presence and waiting for Him to intervene. He concludes, "Humanity is far better off fighting with the tools it has—a desire for transformation, human creativity, physical strength, and untapped collective potential."[27] Simply put, redemptive suffering theodicies like King's undermine black liberation by enticing the oppressed to wait for God to do for them what they can and should do for themselves.

More recently, Pinn softened his tone towards King's thought, admitting that King's concern for human freedom and dignity helped spur civil rights activism.[28] In an article entitled "Martin Luther King, Jr.'s God, Humanist sensibilities and Moral Evil," Pinn attempted to combine King's personalism with his own black humanism in order propose a theodicy that does not "collapse" into redemptive suffering.[29] There Pinn suggested that King opened up possibilities to view God as well-intentioned but misguided and prone to divine missteps. Pinn holds up this limited God concept, allegedly inspired by aspects of King, as a solution to the theodical dilemma. He supposes that this theological turn would successfully avoid casting suffering as somehow positive, since human suffering would then result from God's unfortunate miscalculations rather than God's redemptive purposes.

Drawing on King's theodical engagement with theistic finitism, Pinn suggests that King reconsidered the traditional understanding of God's power in relation to history. He rightly notes that King understood omnipotence as sufficient power to accomplish the most noble purposes in cooperation with created persons.[30] However, Pinn wrongly insists that

King's view of omnipotence admits divine missteps, shifts in perspectives, plans, and direction. He explains,

> Even King notes that God is the best example of personality, action, and faithfulness. Nonetheless for King, this involves the best of these traits, not the perfection of these traits. In a word, God—even as matchless in character and capability—may shift perspective, change direction, and 'repent' for decisions made without losing status as best knower and doer, as the ultimate source of our understanding of freedom and the framework for our sense of relationship and community.[31]

Pinn continues to describe the reconceived God that is supposedly opened through King's theology.

> It is not the motivation or commitment of this God that is questioned; rather it is recognition that this God's activities are incomplete. This God's work is incomplete or flawed, in part because this God's liberative work is experimental—changing and reactive—demonstrating commitment and concern, but guaranteeing little. This God interacts with people in ways involving self correction, changed plans, and paths. God according to this scheme is deeply attached and committed to the welfare of humanity—but at times penultimate events that fail to suggest an ultimate and positive resolution ... Moral evil is not simply free will out of control, current circumstances also arise from miscalculation on God's part.[32]

Pinn's description appears fundamentally out-of-step with King's doctrine of God. For King, God is not simply the best example of personality, action, and faithfulness. He maintained that God is the "perfection that far surpasses that of human persons, who are but faint images of essential personhood."[33] King was a theistic absolutist, who carefully maintained a view of God as perfect being, with sufficient power to achieve God's noble purposes. King nuanced his articulation of divine omnipotence in order to avoid affirming philosophical absurdities, but this did not put him out-of-step with traditional black church understandings of omnipotence. He readily affirmed that God can actualize the good and realize his purposes without the kind of missteps and blunders that Pinn proposes. King explained, "If God is truly God and warrants man's ultimate devotion, he must not only have an infinite concern for the good but an infinite power to actualize the good. This is the truth expressed in the somewhat misleading doctrine of the divine omnipotence."[34] King critiqued Brightman's version of theistic finitism (in seminary and graduate school papers) and Henry Nelson Wieman (in his dissertation) on exactly this point, their failure to affirm God's infinite power to realize God's purposes.[35] King staunchly insisted that God is able to do whatever God wants to do according to God's divine character and purpose.

Since the black church tradition has often been concerned with practical liberation, rather than abstract philosophical speculations, King's doctrine of divine omnipotence would have resonated. He held out the practical hope and comfort that comes from the *guarantee* that God would accomplish his will through blacks' engagement with their suffering. King occasionally used language consistent with Brightman's theistic finitism.[36] However, he ultimately embraced a theistic absolutism informed by the black church tradition and more like Borden Bowne and Harold DeWolf's than Brightman.[37] Furthermore, King held that having good purposes without the power to actualize them (the way Pinn suggests) is empty. He explains, "Moral perfection would be an empty possession apart from a corresponding and sustaining power."[38] King's beliefs about the perfection of God seems to preclude the kind of self-correcting deity that Pinn proposes as a solution to theodicy. King regarded divine imperfection (especially the kind that couldn't guarantee deliverance) as unworthy of human devotion. In the end, Pinn's conciliatory efforts at actually don't bring him any closer to King's theodicy since Pinn's version of deity would likely have been unrecognizable and unacceptable to King himself.

By way of recap, we have seen that King's redemptive suffering theodicy has been criticized by the black humanists William R. Jones and Anthony Pinn for allegedly promoting quietism by casting black suffering as having some redemptive or potentially redemptive quality. They allege that as blacks think of their suffering as willed by God for some redemptive purpose, they more likely to become complacent within it and less likely to vigorously strive to see it ended. Both Jones and Pinn want blacks to prioritize the experience of black suffering rather than prior theological commitments as the interpretive lens through which to approach theodicy. Jones insists that this will force a serious consideration of the charge of divine racism or even black culpability for oppression (victim-blaming) since black suffering may be interpreted in multiple ways. In order to avoid this charge, redemptive suffering advocates would need to produce some evidence that God will redeem their suffering. In the absence of such evidence, he proposes a version of theistic finitism which makes humans co-workers with God. This places the burden of human suffering solely on the backs of sinful humanity, since, in this conception, God is believed to be unable to prevent human suffering. It also avoids quietism since it insists that God needs human cooperation to realize the good, he purposes.

Pinn carries Jones' critique much further, insisting that redemptive suffering and liberation are diametrically opposed ideas. Suffering is an evil which must never be spoken of as producing any benefit, lest it undercut human efforts at achieving social liberation. According to Pinn, humanists could cite countless examples in which the church, crippled by its belief in redemptive suffering, has failed to engage important social ills.[39] Furthermore, he alleges that even theism itself undermines human initiative by promising external help to humanity and casts suffering in a favorable light. He wonders how the oppressed will ever strive for their own freedom while seeking the divine hand in oppression and waiting for God to rescue them from it. He insists that to avoid quietism, the oppressed must think of themselves as having complete control over their own destiny, without any dependence upon God whatsoever. Only then will they effectively use the resources at their disposal to pursue freedom.

Having laid out their basic arguments, we now consider whether King's theodicy does in fact undermine social activism the way Jones and Pinn allege.[40] Using the black experience, Pinn's very own criterion for theological inquiry, we can show that King's theodicy was a tremendous force for social activism and reform.[41] The Birmingham Campaign of 1963 highlights the way King's theodicy practically functioned to encourage non-violent protests and demonstrations. Next, I will examine how King's theodicy even avoids potential quietistic abuses by emphasizing the need to transform non-redemptive suffering into something positive through non-violent resistance. Finally, I will show that King's theodicy used a goal oriented understanding of divine omnipotence to promote continued participation in the freedom struggle.

AVOIDING QUIETISM PART 1: KING'S THEODICY AND THE PROVING GROUND OF BLACK EXPERIENCE

From his earliest days as a theologian, Martin King was deeply concerned about the practical implications of his theology for the black social situation. For King, the experience of the oppressed provided an important criterion by which to assess the usefulness of his theodicy.[42] As he used redemptive suffering to explain the deaths of the four young martyrs of the Sixteenth Street Baptist Church bombing, he appealed to experience to substantiate his theodicy. He noted, "God still has a way of wringing good out of evil. History has proven over and over again that unmerited suffering is redemptive."[43] Therefore, King took the "proving ground" of experience, particularly the experience of the oppressed, very seriously.

Before he ever applied it to the freedom movement in America, King already learned about the efficacy of redemptive suffering through Gandhi's experience in India. In a 1950 lecture delivered by Howard University President Mordecai Wyatt Johnson, King discovered how Mohondas Gandhi used redemptive suffering as a powerful motivation for non-violent social change. Intrigued by the possibilities for the black social situation, King scoured Gandhi's books to learn more about his non-violent methodology.[44] He was especially attracted to the concept of *satyagraha*, the "truth-force" or "soul-force" at the heart of Gandhi's non-violent resistance.[45] He found that redemptive suffering was one of the three basic assumptions behind *satyagraha*. Gandhi held that "the sight of suffering by the masses could melt the heart of the aggressor and induce him to desist from his course of violence."[46] So, for Gandhi, the belief in redemptive suffering was a part of the motivation for non-violent social action.[47] Rather than promote the oppressive status quo, his belief in redemptive suffering helped propel Gandhi's successful non-violent campaign against British imperialism. For King, this proved the efficacy of redemptive suffering as a motivation for social action. Gandhi's example also showed King that it could work in the public arena and on the social, rather than merely personal, level.

With Gandhi's experience backing his theodical convictions, King applied redemptive suffering to the black experience as a motivating force for social reform. Redemptive suffering became one of the chief catalysts for the non-violent direct action of the freedom movement. In 1961, King explained, "Another thing that stands at the center of this movement is another idea: that suffering can be a most creative and powerful social force .... The nonviolent say that suffering becomes a powerful social force when you willingly accept that violence on yourself, so that self-suffering stands at the center of the nonviolent movement and the individuals involved are able to suffer in a creative manner, feeling that unearned suffering is redemptive, and that suffering may serve to transform the social situation."[48] According to King, redemptive suffering inspired the freedom fighters to resist oppression non-violently. It stood at the center of the freedom movement, as a primary driving force. This means that redemptive suffering helped inspire one of the greatest movements for social change in the black experience. Inspired by the hope that unearned suffering is redemptive, scores of blacks participated in non-violent social protests, often putting themselves directly in harm's way.

Although numerous examples could be used, the Birmingham campaign of 1963 highlights the way King's redemptive suffering theodicy helped propel tremendous social engagement and transformation. Encouraged by King's message of redemptive suffering, thousands of black children skipped school (some climbing out of windows and over gates) and gathered at the Sixteenth Street Baptist Church in Birmingham for the expressed purpose of protesting and being arrested in defiance of the city's recent injunction barring civil rights protests. They intended to fill the Birmingham jails to capacity driven by the hope that God would use their suffering to bring transformation to the city. By the end of the first day of protest, 900 young people had been arrested, so many that buses needed to be called in to haul them off. By the next day, the demonstration was even larger. More than 2,500 young people turned out to march and willingly be arrested. They were so revved up that King and his staffers had trouble restraining them. But this day Eugene "Bull" Connor, Birmingham's Commissioner for Public Safety, blocked the young protesters. Accompanied by police officers and the fire department, Connor ordered them to return to the church. Stephen Oates explains what happened next. "When the demonstrators refused to return to the church, Connor bellowed, 'Let 'em have it.' With scores of reporters and TV cameramen recording what happened, the firemen turned on their hoses, which exploded with a noise like a machine-gun fire and sent columns of water crashing into children and adults alike, knocking them down. Ripping their clothes, smashing them against the sides of buildings, sweeping them back into the street, driving them crying and bloodied into the park."[49] The scene was so moving even a number of firemen were seen crying as they aimed hoses at the protestors.[50] There was national shame and outrage as newspapers all over the country and the world carried front page reports and photographs of the carnage in Birmingham. When the news reached the White House, President Kennedy explained that the race-driven violence he saw in the papers made him "sick."[51] However, the violence of that day didn't deter the young protesters themselves. Inspired by the hope of redemptive suffering, the next day's protest was even larger and even more dramatic than the day before. As the marchers went out to face Bull Connor's forces again, they were compelled by King's words about redemptive suffering trumpeted over a sound system.[52]

> My friends, we must keep on believing that unearned suffering is redemptive. We must say to our white brothers and sisters who try to keep us down: We will match your capacity to inflict suffering with our capacity to endure suffering. We will meet your physical force with soul force. We will not hate you. And yet we cannot in all good conscience obey your evil laws. Do to us what you will . . . We will wear you down by our capacity to suffer. In winning the victory, we will not only win our freedom. We will so appeal to your heart and your conscience that we will win you in the process. And our victory will be a double victory. We will win our freedom, and we will win the individuals who have been perpetrators of the evil system that has existed so long.[53]

The Birmingham movement demonstrates the power of redemptive suffering as a motivation to confront oppression and injustice. This message was so potent that thousands of teenagers and children (some as young as four years old) forced their way into the protest. They willingly went to dark Birmingham jails (often repeatedly) and bravely confronted vicious German Shepherds, police Billie clubs, and water hoses. Amazingly, the threat and even the experience of suffering violence was not as powerful as the hope that their suffering could bring redemptive transformation to their city. The more Bull Connor inflicted the protestors with suffering, the more people became involved and the greater their motivation to continue. They felt called to engage suffering as a form of non-violent resistance in order to dramatize and overcome the daily sufferings of oppressed blacks all over the South. Rather than undermine the social engagement of Birmingham's black citizenry, redemptive suffering empowered it in a historic way. Civil Rights experiences, like the Birmingham campaign, directly contradict Jones and Pinn's allegations against King's theodicy. They serve as experiential proof of the power of redemptive suffering to provoke social engagement rather than undermine it.

Pinn questions the wisdom of an approach that sees suffering as potentially redemptive and then willingly places black people in a position to suffer as a result.[54] By admitting that suffering can be a mechanism for transformation, Pinn says, King does not tenaciously safeguard black bodies from unmerited sufferings.[55] However, King didn't use redemptive suffering to create new sufferings in the hope that they would bring change. He aimed to protect human dignity and bodies in the long term by allowing concealed hostilities to rise to the surface.[56] King recognized that blacks were already suffering profoundly. Non-violent direct action merely exposed that suffering, dramatizing it in a way that could bring conviction to the oppressor. "If you confront a man who has been cruelly misusing you, and say 'Punish me if you will, I do not deserve it, but I will accept it so that the world will know that I am right and you are wrong,' then you wield a powerful and just weapon. This man, your oppressor, is automatically morally defeated, and if he has any conscience, he is ashamed."[57] He believed that God would use these exposed sufferings of the oppressed to help create the beloved community and bring about social reform in America. In the end, the unearned sufferings of the Birmingham protestors helped overthrow local segregation ordinances in Birmingham, inspired landmark civil rights legislation, and shift the nation's opinion about the evils of segregation. Therefore, in practice, King's theodicy served as a powerful motivation to confront injustice.

AVOIDING QUIETISM PART 2: KING'S THEODICY AND HUMAN RESPONSIBILITY

Although King's theodicy was effective in practice, we must also determine whether it is as susceptible to quietism in theory as the humanists allege. Could King's theodicy easily lead to social acquiescence? King himself considered social acquiescence to be an immoral and cowardly response to oppression. He explained, "To accept passively an unjust system is to cooperate with that system; thereby the oppressed become as evil as the oppressor. . . . It [acquiescence] is the way of the coward."[58] With such a strong disdain for social passivity, we would expect him to make sure his theodicy avoids it. Moreover, King regularly encountered blacks who criticized his direct action in favor of a more passive gradualist approach to injustice. If it were particularly susceptible to quietism, redemptive suffering might easily have been co-opted by King's critics to promote gradualism. On the other hand, King frequently encountered black militants who thought redemptive suffering made blacks acquiescent and played right into the hands of white oppressors. If redemptive suffering actually promoted quietism, the militants would be proved right. King carefully crafted his theodicy in a way that promotes the human responsibility to engage suffering in order to realize social transformation.

King distinguished between redemptive and non-redemptive sufferings in order to stress the need to transform oppressive suffering into a force for social transformation.[59] King freely admitted that not all suffering is redemptive and that the violent also use suffering as a powerful social force to keep the subjugated oppressed. In fact, if not redemptively engaged, suffering could become a tremendously negative social force to foster even more oppression. King explained,

> Now it is very interesting at this point to notice that both violence and nonviolence agree that suffering can be a very powerful social force. But there is this difference: violence says that suffering can be a powerful social force by inflicting that suffering on somebody else: so this is what we do in war, this is what we do in the whole violent thrust of the violent movement. It believes that you can achieve some end by inflicting that suffering on another. The nonviolent say that suffering becomes a powerful social force when you willingly accept that violence on yourself . . .[60]

By distinguishing between redemptive and non-redemptive suffering King's theodicy places a distinct responsibility upon the oppressed to help transform their situations of oppression into something liberating. The oppressed are not called to passively endure suffering, they are called to actively engage it—and through non-violent direct action, to turn suffering on its head. King maintained that suffering "*becomes* a powerful social force [emphasis mine]" only as one willingly engages it. King insisted that suffering has multiple possibilities, either for good or for ill. This challenges the oppressed to creatively use their suffering in a way that would promote a redemptive outcome. In an article for the *Christian Century*, King revealed how his personal trials taught him about the multiple possibilities of responding to suffering and how he had the moral obligation to seek to transform his sufferings into a positive force. After detailing many of the hardships he endured as a result of his civil rights activism, he explained,

> My personal trials have also taught me the value of unmerited suffering. As my sufferings mounted I soon realized there were two ways that I could respond to my situation: either to react with bitterness or to seek to transform the suffering into a creative force. I decided to follow the latter course. Recognizing the necessity for suffering I tried to make of it a virtue. If only to save myself from bitterness, I have attempted to see my personal ordeals as an opportunity to transform myself and heal the people in the tragic situation that now obtains. I have lived the last few years with the conviction that unearned suffering is redemptive.[61]

Here, King admits at least two possible responses to suffering.[62] He could respond with bitterness or attempt to transform suffering into a "creative force." Faced with these choices, the oppressed have a moral obligation to promote redemptive transformation rather than more bitterness and hatred. For him, suffering presents an opportunity that the oppressed may use to help to bring transformation to themselves and to the oppressor alike. The oppressed do not choose to suffer. But given the reality of sufferings thrust upon them, they can choose how to respond. In fact, they have a moral responsibility to respond creatively, that is, in a way that helps create redemptive personal and social transformation. Rather than undermine human responsibility, King's theodicy stressed it. God has not called the oppressed to passively endure sufferings in the hopes that someday they will serve some pedagogical and redemptive purpose. Rather, according to King, God calls human creatures to active engagement with the tragic situations that obtain in the world to help bring healing. In language which clearly emphasizes human responsibility, King mentions suffering as an opportunity to bring transformation and healing, choosing to transform his situation into something redemptive, and making suffering into a virtue. For him, suffering provided an opportunity that needed to be actively engaged in order to yield results. Suffering is not redemptive *per se*. Because non-redemptive suffering must be transformed in order to become redemptive, King's theodicy encouraged the oppressed to resist their oppression by engaging in creative suffering.

In King's context, this took the form of noncooperation, the righteous refusal to support injustice by obeying unjust laws. Following Henry David Thoreau and M.K. Gandhi, King insisted that noncooperation with evil was just as much a moral obligation as cooperation with good. Given the brutal realities of the segregated South, King knew that this noncooperation would incite racially motivated violence against the peaceful protestors. But despite the suffering the freedom fighters likely would endure, he insisted that they could not in good conscience participate in the system of segregation. This suffering, if willingly accepted, could help transform the hearts and minds of the oppressed and oppressors alike. The daily sufferings encountered by blacks in the South would be brought to a dramatic head through their peaceful refusal to cooperate with the unjust system of segregation. However, this suffering, if used non-violently would work for the cause of liberation by exposing the brutality of southern racism and the justice of the cause of the freedom fighters. The short term redemptive suffering endured by protestors was a small sacrifice in the broader effort to help eliminate the non-redemptive suffering daily experienced by the oppressed masses. Therefore, King's theodicy consistently promoted the elimination of suffering by using short-term localized redemptive suffering as a force to eradicate longstanding systemic non-redemptive suffering. By viewing suffering as providing an opportunity for redemptive engagement with a moral obligation attached, King's theodicy consistently promoted social liberation.

The humanists are right to want the oppressed to participate in their own liberation. However, they are wrong to suggest that King's theodicy undermines this participation, since King encouraged black social activism through the effective use of redemptive suffering. By distinguishing between redemptive and non-redemptive suffering, King encouraged the oppressed to strive for freedom by seeking to transform non-redemptive suffering into something liberative. Not only does suffering provide an opportunity to bring social and personal transformation through redemptive suffering, the oppressed have a moral obligation to avoid bitterness

THE BLACK HUMANISTS

and make their suffering into a virtue. Therefore, from the human side, King's theodicy avoids the pitfall of quietism. Although some blacks were exposed to short term unearned suffering during protests, this redemptive suffering was a powerful means to assuage the broader unearned suffering inherent to the system of segregation.

The question remains as to whether speaking of suffering as redemptive undermines liberation by coaxing the oppressed to become complacent in their oppression or even amenable towards it. Pinn alleges that if the oppressed don't view suffering as entirely evil, they won't vigorously seek to eliminate it. This is a powerful point, and one with which King himself would mostly agree. He tenaciously strove to help complacent blacks become dissatisfied their race-based social suffering. Although King spoke of race-based sufferings as an opportunity, he also referred to them as the "tragic situation that now obtains." King never spoke of suffering as an acceptable or preferred state of affairs. Following his Boston University mentor Harold DeWolf, King maintained that God intends humans to be perplexed by the existence of pain and moved to help relieve it, as much as possible, wherever it is found.[63] In *Theology of the Living Church,* DeWolf wrote, "We must not think there is a complete solution to the problem of evil while any neighbor anywhere is in distress which we could ameliorate. It is probably God's own purpose that we must be perplexed and plagued, intellectually as well as practically, by the very existence of pain and trouble as long as we need them."[64] King essentially held this position. Although he admitted that suffering is somehow needful, King held that God wills humans to strive to end suffering in themselves and their neighbors. For him, the divine purposes for pain and trouble are served "only so long as we cannot be at peace with them in ourselves or others."[65] Therefore the oppressed must seek to end suffering in all its varied forms. So King's theodicy does not undermine efforts to eradicate suffering. God's redemptive purposes in suffering include God's will that we should seek to end suffering.

AVOIDING QUIETISM PART 3: KING'S THEODICY AND DIVINE OMNIPOTENCE

Pinn is also concerned that the doctrine of divine omnipotence undermines black responsibility and active participation in liberation. As the oppressed wait for outside (divine) intervention, they become complacent and use less ingenuity in achieving their own freedom. However, King's theodicy did not promote omnipotence at the expense of human activity. For King, omnipotence was the practical hope that God can realize God's purposes precisely in and through human effort. King didn't understand divine omnipotence in terms of sheer power, able to crush any and every obstacle in its path.[66] Rather, he meant God's ability to achieve his ultimate moral purposes and realize concrete good through human freedom and, at times, even through pain.[67] He held that God created human beings for freedom and that God would work through human freedom to achieve moral purposes. These moral purposes can use both cooperation and non-cooperation to advance. "Almost anything that happens to may be woven into the purposes of God . . . . The cross, which was willed by wicked men, was woven by God into the tapestry of world redemption."[68] This illustrates the point that although human beings may will and act in evil ways, God is able to work through freely chosen activities to bring about his redemptive purposes.

King articulated this powerfully in *Stride Toward Freedom* where he detailed the events surrounding the Montgomery Bus Boycott. There, he explained that the violent methods the opposition freely chose to suppress the movement repeatedly propelled the movement forward. For instance, the arrest of Rosa Parks served as the catalyst for the bus boycott. Attempts to suppress the upcoming boycott through reports in newspapers and over television and radio airwaves only further publicized the event, allowing the protest to achieve a level of exposure and participation among black citizens that would have been impossible with the movement's meager resources. Intimidation tactics such as arrests, house bombings, and harassment only further solidified the black community and engendered broad sympathy for the movement.[69] King saw God powerfully acting in and through freely chosen events to realize his purpose.

King's theodicy does not imply that blacks should wait for God to supernaturally intervene on their behalf. Rather it suggests that God is already powerfully at work in and through human activity and in and through painful events to advance the cause of justice and goodness. In his 1963 sermon entitled "The Answer to a Perplexing Question," King took up the matter of how evil is cast out of the world, whether by God alone or by human beings alone. He suggested that neither of these responses is correct. God will not cast out evil while human beings sit complacently by the wayside, neither can humanity cast evil out of the world by its own power. Rather, he said, "both man and God made one in a marvelous unity of purpose through an overflowing love as the free gift of Himself on the part of God and by perfect obedience and receptivity on the part of man, can transform the old into the new and drive out the deadly cancer of sin. The principle which opens the door for God to work through man is faith."[70] As human beings actively resist evil in faith in God's loving purposes and power, they become conduits through which the divine power works to bring transformation. God has chosen to work through human faith and effort.[71] King says that this is a divine gift and yet, it is a gift that requires human activity for its efficacy. Therefore, King's doctrine of omnipotence avoided the pitfall of inducing complacency while at the same time engendering the kind of hope that could empower perseverance.

King's theodicy stresses human freedom, responsibility, and action while also affirming divine omnipotence as a motivation to continue social engagement. For King, the doctrine of omnipotence holds out the hopeful promise that the goal of freedom, justice, and the beloved community will be achieved one day. In King's absolutist conception, the realization of this goal is never in doubt. God is able to realize his purpose through the faith-filled actions of free creatures that make sinful choices. According to King, God works through "sharing and cooperative endeavors with persons," rather than domination.[72] King believed that God's matchless power, working through human activity, would bring eventual success to the struggle for freedom. Redemptive suffering is an affirmation of the inevitability of this success. Rather than cause King to rest on his laurels, this belief served as a powerful motivation continue the struggle for freedom. In fact, John Ansboro suggested that without his absolutist understanding of divine power, King most likely would not have persevered in the struggle and the outcome of the freedom movement would have been quite different.[73]

Ansboro may well be right. January 27, 1956, around midnight, as King thought about his personal trials, human frailty, and the improbability of victory, he was driven to the brink of despair. He lost both his courage and his will to continue fighting. He prayed,

> I am down here trying to take a stand for what I believe is right. But now I am afraid. The people are looking to me for leadership, and if I

stand before them without strength and courage, they too will falter. I am at the end of my powers. I have nothing left. I've come to the point where I can't face it [my sufferings] alone.[74]

Fearful and weak, King had come to the end of his own internal resources. He was ready to walk away from the movement altogether. And yet this reaffirmation of God's power and presence motivated him to continue his participation in the struggle for freedom. King's belief in God's ability to "make a way out of no way," empowered him to continue his leadership in the Montgomery Bus Boycott. He continued,

> And it seemed to me that I could hear an inner voice saying to me, "Martin Luther, stand up for righteousness. Stand up for justice. Stand up for truth. And lo I will be with you, even until the end of the world. . . ." I heard the voice of Jesus saying still to fight on.[75]

King would draw motivation and strength from this pivotal moment repeatedly throughout his civil rights career. God's matchless power didn't become the excuse for him to become passive in the movement. It was a motivating force to continue the fight for freedom. King believed that the omnipotent God was with him as he actively stood up for truth and righteousness. The vision began with three successive commands to continue his civil rights involvement. God's matchless redemptive power would be at work as he did so, guaranteeing that his efforts would not be in vain, and that ultimately, the freedom struggle would reach its teleological goal of the beloved community.[76]

While recognizing both the tragedy of oppression and enduring hope for the oppressed, King's theodicy encourages and empowers the oppressed to resist their suffering non-violently—to see themselves as cooperating with the omnipotent God, and thereby to avoid despair, no matter how bleak their situation may appear. By recognizing the omnipotence of God, King's theodicy offers hope where options are limited and sufferings are inescapable. It offers the hope that the oppressed can resist oppression by non-violently engaging their suffering, and that such resistance is deeply meaningful. The black church has long held that God will not do for the oppressed what God has given them the power to do for themselves, but that God will do for the oppressed what they cannot do for themselves.[77] Although God normally works through human agency, the black church has mostly taught that God is not limited by human weakness. Since God has the power to do for people what they cannot do for themselves, human failures don't imperil God's redemptive plan. God is able to bring about God's plan, even where human powers find their limit. King's theodicy reflects the best of this tradition.

Redemptive suffering holds out the hope that God is at work through the non-violent resistance of God's people guaranteeing that their struggle participates, however modestly, in the coming of the Kingdom of God, the realization of the beloved community. God will lovingly provide strength, guidance, and hope to the oppressed and guarantee that their efforts are not ultimately in vain. They struggle with the theodical hope of omnipotence, the confidence that they are participating in a victorious cause. Far from encouraging social acquiescence and passivity, this hope empowers the oppressed to continue the struggle, to creatively engage suffering, turning it into a force for freedom.

CONCLUSION

This chapter has demonstrated that Martin Luther King Jr.'s redemptive suffering theodicy successfully avoids the pitfall of quietism alleged by black humanists William R. Jones and Anthony Pinn. The humanists maintain that redemptive suffering theodicies induce an attitude of social resignation and acquiescence in the oppressed through the suggestion that suffering is somehow redemptive, and that victims should passively wait for divine intervention in painful circumstances. Rather than promote social passivity, King's theodicy promotes and guides non-violent direct Christian action through its emphasis on redemptive engagement with pernicious suffering in light of divine omnipotence.

Using the Birmingham campaign of 1963, we saw how King's theodicy practically functioned to promote non-violent direct action, rather than acquiescence or retaliation. King's theodicy resisted even the potential of quietism by strongly emphasizing the human responsibility to engage suffering non-violently in order to help transform it into something redemptive. According to King, suffering held out multiple possibilities for engagement. The oppressed have the responsibility to actively and creatively respond in love rather than bitterness. By carefully distinguishing between non-redemptive and redemptive suffering, King was also able to take evil seriously while simultaneously holding out the responsibility and hope that non-redemptive suffering could and should be turned on its head. Finally, King's doctrine of divine omnipotence encouraged social action through being decisively teleologically oriented. Through emphasizing God's ability to realize God's good purpose in concrete ways and God's intention to work in and through the efforts of the oppressed to bring it about, King's theodicy offered a powerful hope that motivated continued participation in the freedom struggle. The black church has long held that God would "make a way out of no way," but that God would do it in and through God's people of faith. Almighty God doesn't bring social deliverance while God's people sit idly by the wayside. King's theodicy represents the best of this longstanding tradition, emphasizing human participation in the redemptive mission of God in a way that encourages social activism.

NOTES

1. Anthony B Pinn, "Introduction," in *Moral Evil and Redemptive Suffering: A History of Theodicy in African-American Religious Thought* (Gainesville, FL: University Press of Florida, 2002), 12.

2. Benjamin E. Mays, *The Negro's God as Reflected in His Literature* (New York: Russel & Russel, 1938), 184, 213. Having already adopted a rudimentary form of his redemptive suffering theodicy (including black messianism) by the time he entered Morehouse, King would almost certainly have taken Benjamin Mays' challenge against it to heart. As we have noted, King viewed Mays as a mentor and perhaps the model Christian minister, in many ways patterning himself after Mays. After reading Mays' critique of the worst abuses of black messianism, he would have been keen to avoid the quietistic pitfall that Mays pointed out. As we will see, King deliberately formulated and deployed his theodicy during the freedom movement as an instrument precisely to avoid quietism.

3. Ibid., 153.
4. Ibid., 14, 153.
5. Ibid., 24–25.
6. Pinn, "Introduction," 14.
7. William R. Jones, *Is God a White Racist?: A Preamble to Black Theology* (Garden City, NY: Doubleday, 1973), 42. Jones mainly follows Camus' arguments in *The Plague* and to a lesser extent, *The Rebel*. Albert Camus, *The Plague*, trans. Stuart Gilbert (New York: Vintage Books, 1991, 1948). Albert

Camus, *The Rebel: An Essay on Man in Revolt*, trans. Alfred A. Knopf (New York: Vintage Books, 1991, 1956).

8. Jones, *Is God a White Racist?: A Preamble to Black Theology*, 80–81. Jones takes direct aim at Joseph R. Washington, whose version of black theology includes a redemptive suffering concept which resembles King's. However, Jones goes out of his way to say that his critique of Jones would also apply to King's theodicy. He explains, "The criticism of Washington, with only slight modification is also applicable to any black theologian who adopts the theodicy of vicarious suffering, including Martin Luther King for example."

9. Ibid., 6–8.

10. Ibid., 9.

11. The basic form of this argument was most famously proposed by Scottish philosopher David Hume. David Hume, "Concerning Natural Religion," in *The English Philosophers from Bacon to Hill*, ed. Edwin A. Burtt (New York: Random House, 1967), 741; Victor Anderson, "Faith on Earth," in *Creative Exchange: A Constructive Theology of African American Religious Experience* (Minneapolis: Fortress Press, 2008), 86–87.

12. He reasons that under normal circumstances morally, responsible persons are expected to alleviate suffering when it is within their power to do so. Traditional theisms need historical evidence to support their unwavering faith in God's benevolence towards blacks, some tangible proof that God has good reasons for allowing so much black suffering, reasons which include the good of the victims themselves.

13. Martin Luther King, Jr., *Stride Toward Freedom: The Montgomery Story* (HarperCollins, 1987), 224; Lewis V. Baldwin, *There Is a Balm in Gilead: The Cultural Roots of Martin Luther King, Jr* (Minneapolis: Fortress Press, 1991), 234–236.

14. Jones, *Is God a White Racist?: A Preamble to Black Theology*, 15–20. Jones assumes that an exaltation event is the only way blacks could be sure that the suffering servant motif correctly applies to them. But perhaps the resurrection is not the only way God distinguished the suffering servant as being favored and chosen. According to Isaiah 53:9 as interpreted in 1 Peter 2:22–23, one of the distinctive signs of the suffering servant as being chosen and favored by God, is the distinctive way he responded to suffering, i.e., non-violently and without retaliation. King held that blacks, as a racial group, had been endowed with a special proclivity to respond to suffering non-violently. Alongside an exaltation event, the history of non-violent engagement with suffering could be seen as evidence that blacks had been uniquely called to help transform America through non-violent direct action. Cornel West, Prophesy Deliverance: *An Afro-American Revolutionary Christianity* (Philadelphia: Westminster Press, 1982), 74–75.

15. Jones, *Is God a White Racist?: A Preamble to Black Theology*, 187.

16. Ibid., 194–197.

17. Anthony B. Pinn, *Why, Lord?: Suffering and Evil in Black Theology* (Continuum, 1999), 16; Anthony B. Pinn, *Varieties of African American Religious Experience* (Minneapolis, MN: Fortress Press, 1998).

18. Anthony B. Pinn, *Why, Lord?*, 17.

19. Ibid., 17–18; Pinn, *Varieties of African American Religious Experience*; Pinn, "Introduction"; Anthony B. Pinn, *Understanding & Transforming the Black Church* (Eugene, OR: Cascade Books, 2010).

20. Anthony B. Pinn, *Why, Lord?*, 17–18.

21. Pinn, "Introduction," 15; Anthony B. Pinn, *Why, Lord?*, 141.

22. Anthony B. Pinn, *Why, Lord?*, 157.

23. Ibid., 18; Anderson, "Faith on Earth," 95.

24. I am indebted to Victor Anderson for this concise outline of Pinn's basic argument. See Anderson, "Faith on Earth," 96–97.

25. Anthony B. Pinn, *Why, Lord?*, 18.

26. Pinn, *Varieties of African American Religious Experience*, 185.

27. Anthony B. Pinn, *Why, Lord?*, 158.

28. Anthony B. Pinn, "Martin Luther King Jr.'s God, Humanist Sensibilities, and Moral Evil," *Theology Today* 65, no. 1 (April 1, 2008): 60.

29. Ibid., 57.

30. Ibid., 59–60. Pinn got his description of King's view of omnipotence directly from Rufus Burrow, Jr., *God and Human Dignity: The Personalism, Theology, and Ethics of Martin Luther King, Jr.* (Notre Dame: University of Notre Dame Press, 2006), 106, 111–113.

31. Pinn, "Martin Luther King Jr.'s God, Humanist Sensibilities, and Moral Evil," 62.

32. Ibid., 64–65.

33. Rufus Burrow, Jr., "Personalism, the Objective Moral Order, and Moral Law in the Work of Martin Luther King, Jr.," in *The Legacy of Martin Luther King, Jr.: The Boundaries of Law, Politics, and Religion*, ed. Lewis V Baldwin (Notre Dame, IN: University of Notre Dame Press, 2002), 221. Ironically, this is the very same article Pinn cites in order to substantiate his erroneous claim that King denied divine perfection.

34. Martin Luther King, Jr., "A Comparison of The Conception of God in the Thinking of Henry Nelson Wieman and Paul Tillich," in *The Papers of Martin Luther King, Jr.: Volume 2: Rediscovering Precious Values July 1951–November 1955* (Berkeley, California: University of California Press, 1992), 525; Jimmy L. Kirby and Rufus Burrow, "Conceptions of God in the Thinking of Martin Luther King, Jr and Edgar S Brightman," *Encounter* 60, no. 3 (June 1, 1999): 293.

35. King thought Brightman's concept created a dualism in the nature of God itself and endangered faith in God as supreme. He also thought Wieman minimized the power of God.

36. Even as they admit that King used language consistent with finitism, Rufus Burrow and Jimmy Kirby say forthrightly "Martin Luther King, Jr. was not a theistic finitist." Kirby and Burrow, "Conceptions of God in the Thinking of Martin Luther King, Jr and Edgar S Brightman," 299.

37. Even though Brightman thought that God is limited by the "free choices of others and by restrictions within his own nature [i.e., 'the Given']," it is unclear whether even Brightman's concept leaves any opening for the kind of theism Pinn proposes. Brightman didn't think of his God as weak or hapless, the way Pinn's "strong humanism" would suggest. Rather, Brightman thought of God as able to overcome the hindrances within His own nature. Edgar S. Brightman, *The Problem of God* (New York: Abingdon Press, 1930), 113; Kirby and Burrow, "Conceptions of God in the Thinking of Martin Luther King, Jr and Edgar S Brightman," 291.

38. King, Jr., "A Comparison of Wieman and Tillich," 526.

39. Pinn, *Varieties of African American Religious Experience*, 184.

40. Although Pinn has acknowledged the church's role in promoting social transformation during the Civil Rights movement, he attributes this activism to King's anthropology rather than his theodicy. Pinn suggests that King's doctrine of "somebodyness" highlighted human dignity and saw the state of black human bodies as the benchmark of God's liberative activity. This led to a renewed determination to achieve liberation, not King's "unfortunate" instance upon redemptive suffering See Pinn, "Martin Luther King Jr.'s God, Humanist Sensibilities, and Moral Evil," 58–61.

41. This line of argument is based in large part on Dwight Hopkin's review of Why, Lord. Dwight N. Hopkins, "Why Lord?: Suffering and Evil in Black Theology," *African American Review* 31, no. 3 (1997): 515–516. There, he contends that the most progressive social change organizations and movements within the black experience have come from the black church and other theistic sources. On other hand, he alleges that non-theistic sources have yet to sustain any major movement for social reform within the black community.

42. During an email correspondence, Rufus Burrow Jr, noted that King's emphasis on the experience of the oppressed as the proving ground for theodical claims "essentially anticipated liberation theology." This is a major point that needs to be explored further. Rufus Burrow, Jr., "Comments on Edmondson Dissertation Chapter 5," March 2014.

43. Martin Luther King, Jr., "Eulogy for the Martyred Children," in *I Have a Dream: Writings and Speeches That Changed the World, Special 75th Anniversary Edition*, 1st ed. (San Francisco: HarperOne, 1992), 116.

44. William D. Watley, *Roots of Resistance: The Nonviolent Ethic of Martin Luther King, Jr* (Valley Forge: Judson Press, 1985), 48–49. Watley's timeline may be problematic. At present, King scholars are not certain how closely King read the half-a-dozen books on Gandhi he purchased after hearing Mordecai Johnson's lecture. He was known for taking upwards of fifteen hours a term at Crozer which would have left little time for extra-curricular studies of this sort. Although he learned about Gandhian non-violence during his seminary days, he may not have read more deeply until he met Bayard Rustin, and later Glenn Smiley. Rustin and Smiley gave King several more books on Gandhian non-violence and helped sharpen his ideas about it. Burrow, Jr., "Comments on Edmondson Dissertation Chapter 5"; Clayborne Carson, Tenisha H. Armstrong, and Susan Englander, *The Martin Luther King, Jr., Encyclopedia*, ed. Susan A. Carson and Erin K. Cook (London: Greenwood Press, 2008), 308–309.

45. M.K. Gandhi, *Non-Violent Resistance (Satyagraha)* (Mineola, NY: Dover, 2001), 3.

46. Ibid., 362.

47. E. Stanley Jones, *Mahatma Gandhi: An Interpretation* (New York: Abington-Cokesbury Press, 1948), 88.

48. Martin Luther King, Jr., "Love, Law, and Civil Disobedience," in *A Testament of Hope: The Essential Writings and Speeches of Martin Luther King, Jr.*, ed. James M. Washington (San Francisco: Harper and Row, 1986), 47.

49. Stephen B. Oates, *Let the Trumpet Sound: A Life of Martin Luther King, Jr.*, Reprint (New York: Harper Perennial, 1994), 234.

50. By the fourth day of protests, the Birmingham Fire Fighters refused Bull Connor's orders to turn their hoses on protestors.

51. Oates, *Let the Trumpet Sound*, 235.

52. Ibid., 236.

53. Martin Luther King, Jr., "Some Things We Must Do," in *The Papers of Martin Luther King, Jr.: Symbol of the Movement January 1957–December 1958*, ed. Carson Clayborne et al. (Berkeley: University of California Press, 2000), 341–342. King adopted this passage from the E. Stanley Jones description of Gandhi's non-violent strategy. Jones, *Mahatma Gandhi: An Interpretation*, 88.

54. King faced this criticism throughout his career, often by other church leaders like Joseph Jackson, the head National Baptist Convention. However, redemptive suffering's most famous critic was the black militant Malcolm X. James H. Cone, *Martin & Malcolm & America: A Dream or a Nightmare* (Maryknoll: Orbis, 2001), 146–147.

55. Pinn, "Martin Luther King Jr.'s God, Humanist Sensibilities, and Moral Evil," 61.

56. Smith and Zepp, *Search for the Beloved Community*, 50.

57. Martin Luther King, Jr., "Playboy Interview With Martin Luther King, Jr.," in *A Testament of Hope: The Essential Writings and Speeches of Martin Luther King, Jr.* (New York, NY: HarperCollins, 1991), 348. Deeply aware of the sinfulness of the human heart, King added this important qualifier "if he has any conscience." King did not think every oppressor would be transformed by the creative suffering of the oppressed. For instance, there is no evidence that Bull Conner and Jim Clark were affected by non-violent direct action. King held that a person had to have enough moral sensibility to appreciate the value of the sufferings they beheld. Burrow, Jr., "Comments on Edmondson Dissertation Chapter 5."

58. Martin Luther King, Jr., *Stride Toward Freedom*, 212.

59. Distinguishing between redemptive and non-redemptive suffering also allowed King to take evil suffering seriously, calling it for what it is. King's theodicy does not suggest that the non-redemptive suffering foisted onto the oppressed is really good in disguise.

60. King, Jr., "Love, Law, and Civil Disobedience," 47.

61. Martin Luther King, Jr., "Suffering and Faith," *Christian Century* 101, no. 77 (April 1960): 510.

62. Normally, King mentioned resignation as a potential third response to suffering. Resignation or acquiescence, passively accepts suffering with the belief that the suffering is deserved. Since resignation agrees with the oppressor about the inherent inferiority of the oppressed, it does not insist on resistance to oppression. Martin Luther King, Jr., *Stride Toward Freedom*, 212.

63. John J Ansbro, *Martin Luther King, Jr.: The Making of a Mind* (Maryknoll, N.Y.: Orbis Books, 1984), 59.

64. L. Harold DeWolf, *Theology of the Living Church*, Revised Edition (New York: Harper and Row, 1953), 143; Ansbro, *The Making of a Mind*, 59.

65. DeWolf, *Living Church*, 143.

66. Martin Luther King, Jr., "Religion's Answer to the Problem of Evil," in *The Papers of Martin Luther King, Jr.: Volume I: Called to Serve, January 1929–June 1951*, First, vol. 1, The Papers of Martin Luther King, Jr. (Berkeley: University of California Press, 1992), 428; Burrow, Jr., *God and Human Dignity*, 100.

67. Burrow, Jr., *God and Human Dignity*, 100; Edgar Sheffield Brightman, *The Finding of God* (New York: The Abingdon Press, 1931), 189.

68. Martin Luther King, Jr., "Shattered Dreams," in *The Papers of Martin Luther King, Jr., Volume VI: Advocate of the Social Gospel, September 1948–March 1963*, ed. Clayborne Carson et al. (Berkeley: University of California Press, 2007), 521.

69. Martin Luther King, Jr., *Stride Toward Freedom*, 135–150; Ansbro, *The Making of a Mind*, 125–126.

70. Martin Luther King, Jr., "The Answer to a Perplexing Question," in *The Papers of Martin Luther King, Jr., Volume VI: Advocate of the Social Gospel, September 1948–March 1963*, ed. Clayborne Carson, Gerald L. Smith, and Tenisha Armstrong (Berkeley: University of California Press, 2007), 552.

71. Burrow, Jr., *God and Human Dignity*, 101.

72. Ibid., 122.

73. Ansbro, *The Making of a Mind*, 59.

74. Martin Luther King, Jr., *Stride Toward Freedom*, 134.

75. David J. Garrow, *Bearing the Cross: Martin Luther King, Jr., and the Southern Christian Leadership Conference* (New York: William Morrow & Co, 1986), 57–58. Martin Luther King, Jr., "Pilgrimage to Nonviolence," in *Stride Toward Freedom: The Montgomery Story* (San Francisco: HarperCollins, 1987), 134–135. Baldwin, *Balm in Gilead*, 187–188. Martin Luther King, Jr., *"Thou, Dear God": Prayers That Open Hearts and Spirits*, ed. Lewis V. Baldwin (Boston: Beacon Press, 2012), 76.

76. The allusion to Matthew 28:20 (KJV) makes clear that King saw his civil rights activity as participating in God's redemptive purposes.

77. Mays, *The Negro's God as Reflected in His Literature*, 92; Burrow, Jr., *God and Human Dignity*, 114.

6

THE WOMANISTS

INTRODUCTION

Throughout American history, the exploitation of black women has often gone unaddressed due to the idea that their suffering provided certain benefits to their oppressors. This begs the question of whether black women can safely embrace the idea of redemptive suffering without also adopting a dangerous martyr mentality which condones their suffering as sacred.[1] Womanist theologians[2] such as Delores Williams and Jacquelyn Grant suspect that Martin Luther King Jr's theodicy falls prey to this oppressive dynamic by casting black women's suffering in a redemptive light.[3] Following Joanne Carlson Brown and Rebecca Parker, Williams alleges that King's theodicy valorizes suffering and makes black women acquiescent in the face of their own oppression. Redemptive suffering, she says, prioritizes the redemption of the oppressor over the dignity, self-esteem, and overall well-being of the oppressed. Taking aim at the entire cruci-centric tradition that King typifies, Williams completely rejects the cross as God's central revelation of redemptive suffering.[4] Although Jacquelyn Grant acknowledges the usefulness of the redemptive suffering tradition as a survival strategy, she says it stops short of encouraging true liberation for black women. Within the context of black women's socio-political and economic disempowerment, she suggests that King's frequently used imagery of suffering servant becomes more sinful than redemptive.[5]

King's sexist attitudes and behaviors also present a potential obstacle to applying his theodicy to women's liberation. Gender-related issues represent a conspicuous gap in King's theological corpus. Despite his famed commitment to ending the three great evils of racism, poverty, and militarism, King did not readily apply his theology to eradicating sexism. Consequently, King didn't think extensively about how redemptive suffering might have uniquely impacted the lives and experiences of black women. Since he didn't speak on these issues directly, it is more difficult to discern whether King's theodicy has sufficient resources to overcome the potential setbacks posed by his modern Womanist critics. King not only neglected women's issues, but, as scholars have increasingly noted, he harbored the same chauvinistic tendencies predominant among the black preacher circles he frequented. Although King was generally cordial and gracious towards female colleagues, he failed to treat women leaders with the same level of respect as their male counterparts in the Civil Rights movement. King's strained relationship with famed SCLC leader and human rights activist, Ella Baker demonstrates this unsettling habit. Although he praised the considerable efforts of female civil rights giants like Baker, Diane Nash, and Rosa Parks, King did not encourage their participation at the highest levels of the movement. Although women were on the front lines of the freedom movement, their hard work often went unrecognized and underappreciated while their male counterparts received most of the public acclaim. King also participated in this sexist dynamic. However, Womanists theologians have tended to appropriate Kingian concepts without feeling the need to explain away his sexism.

Feeling that King's sexist behaviors were at odds with his theological ideas and ethical ideals, Womanists such as Joanne Marie Terrell and Katie Cannon simply use King's theodicy without apology.[6] Terrell described redemptive suffering as a powerful and uplifting theodicy for women if it renders suffering meaningful through "moral and creative" agency and serves a pedagogical purpose.[7] Katie Cannon argues that King's emphasis on agape and the beloved community helps black women reclaim their rightful sense of dignity and self-worth. According to Cannon, these ideas provide "conceptual elements for enhancing the moral agency of Black women." Far from inducing social passivity, King's approach to suffering promotes sustained and focused social action.

This chapter argues that King's redemptive suffering theodicy promotes true liberation for women of color. Rather than prioritize the transformation of oppressors at the expense of the oppressed or acculturate them to accept unjust suffering passively, King's theodicy emphasizes cross-centered agapic engagement with oppression towards the end of realizing personal dignity, resistance to oppression, and the realization of the beloved community. After laying out Williams and Grant's main arguments, I will make my case by demonstrating that King's theodicy prioritizes the redemption of the oppressed and promotes their dignity and esteem precisely through appealing to the cross. Despite the dark and painful history of black female exploitation through surrogacy in the United States, the cross still communicates a liberating message in the face of oppression. Instead of valorizing suffering and thereby undermining personal esteem, King's theodicy empowers the victims of oppression through connecting their sufferings with the sufferings of Christ and calling them to take up their calling to engage their sufferings to promote liberation. Black women have borne an additional burden of gender-based oppression in ways that I (as a black male living in a sexist society) can never fully understand. So I remain uniquely indebted to the wisdom of womanist voices about how to effectively apply this aspect of King's thought to their struggle. In this chapter, I take my cues from how womanist themselves, (writing from black women's perspectives) use King's theodicy to promote liberation.

THE WOMANIST CRITIQUE PART 1: DELORES WILLIAMS

Delores Williams' criticisms of Martin Luther King's theodicy trace back to her rejection of the cross as the central Christian symbol of redemptive suffering. As Williams read Korean feminist Chung Hyun Kyung's *Struggle to Be the Sun Again*, she became increasingly uneasy about the connection between redemptive suffering, the cross, and the ongoing oppression of women.[8] Chung explained that Korean women's oppression has been aggravated by the doctrine of atonement handed to them by fundamentalist Western missionaries. With Christ as the ultimate example of redemptive suffering, Korean women have often been encouraged to accept their own social suffering peacefully and passively.[9] With this in mind, Williams began to question seriously the high redemptive value

Christianity places on suffering and its practical impact on women.[10] At least since the time of Constantine, the cross has been among the chief signs of Jesus' life and redemptive ministry. However, Williams wonders how beneficial this is. Whatever the cross communicates about salvation, she insists that it also remains a constant reminder of violence foisted upon the innocent. Williams suggests that the cross represents a violent murder and the risk that reformers take if they would successfully challenge the *status quo*, nothing more. Therefore, to speak of the cross as a symbol of redemption only reinforces the dangerous message that good can come from violence.[11] Williams explains that the cross and Jesus crucifixion are "symbols of violence and innocent suffering." She continues, "Neither violence nor suffering is good, nor should we attach positive value to them."[12] In an essay about black women's experiences of surrogacy and Christian images of redemption, Williams says forthrightly, "There is nothing of God in the blood of the cross . . . as Christians, black women cannot forget the cross. But neither can they glorify it. To do so is to make their exploitation sacred. To do so is to glorify sin."[13] If the central image of our faith depicts violence and suffering, Williams wonders how Christians can possibly avoid condoning and perpetuating violence, especially violence against women. With such a disdain for redemptive suffering and the cross as the foundational symbol of Christianity, it follows that Delores Williams would take issue with Martin Luther King's thoroughly cruci-centric, redemptive suffering theodicy.

Along with feminists Rebecca Parker and Joanne Carlson Brown, Williams alleges that King's theodicy foster's social passivity and acquiescence. She explains, "Their [Parker and Brown's] critique of Martin Luther King, Jr's idea of the value of suffering of the oppressed in the oppressed-oppressor confrontations accords with my assumption that African-American Christian women can, through their religion and leaders, be led passively to accept their own oppression and suffering—if the women are taught that suffering is redemptive."[14] Parker and Brown leveled this landmark critique in an essay entitled "For God so Loved the World?" where they surveyed twentieth-century responses critical of traditional atonement theories. One popular approach describes the suffering of the righteous as ushering in the dawn of a new age. According to this scheme, suffering is an essential and inevitable part of the process of redemption. Therefore, violence against the vanguards of a new age should be expected and accepted non-violently. This acceptance witnesses against the purveyors of violence and enobles the victims. In sum, for these theologians, "suffering is a positive and necessary part of social transformation."[15] Parker and Brown place King in this category since he accepted the inevitability of violence directed against the freedom movement and stressed the responsibility of its participants to "bear the violence in order to transform the situation."[16] While Parker and Brown's assessment is partly correct, they overlook some important distinctions. King certainly didn't view suffering as being inherently positive or virtuous *per se*, rather he spoke of seeking to transform his sufferings into something virtuous. According to King, suffering is non-redemptive in and of itself, but it can be made into something redemptive—if handled in the proper way.[17] Blacks weren't called on merely to bear suffering passively, but in view of God's redemptive purposes to engage suffering actively, in a way that made the brutality of racism and the righteousness of the freedom movement obvious. The sufferings of civil rights protestors were dramatic instances of the daily sufferings experienced by blacks all over the South. King held that Blacks had a responsibility to engage this daily suffering in a non-violent and creative way. His focus remained on the responsibility of redemptive engagement with suffering, rather than the suffering itself.

Despite overgeneralizing King's approach to suffering, Parker and Brown rightly pinpoint the cruci-centric nature of King's theodicy. They liken King's approach to the so-called "moral influence" theory of the atonement, which traces its roots to medieval thinker Abelard and became popular among twentieth-century protestant liberals.[18] According to this theory, the unearned sufferings of the cross of Christ represent the redemptive revelation of God's love which transforms the hearts of the wicked.[19] Likewise, the unearned sufferings of the oppressed can be used to transform the hearts of the perpetrators of violence. Brown and Parker view this approach as especially problematic because it, "asks people to suffer for the sake of helping evildoers see their ways."[20] They suggest that this places concern for the salvation of the oppressor over concern for the well-being of the oppressed and "makes victims the servants of the evildoers' salvation."[21]

Delores Williams essentially echoes this argument from Parker and Brown as well, applying it within her own black Womanist framework.[22] Williams rejects King's theodicy as an adequate response to black women's questions about redemption and surrogacy.[23] In *Sisters in the Wilder-*

ness, Williams explains that black women have endured physical and sexual exploitation through surrogacy, being forced to assume various roles that would ordinarily belong to others. During the antebellum period black women were often forced to fill hard labor roles that society deemed appropriate for men only. At other times, they were made to fill nurturing roles, household management roles, and even sexual roles in the place of slave owner's wives. Due to socio-political and economic oppression, these destructive social-role dynamics have continued to find expression even after emancipation.[24] Black women's surrogacy experience in America has consistently placed the concerns of their oppressors ahead of their own. According to Williams, King's theodicy may easily serve to perpetuate this sinful dynamic by calling on the oppressed to suffer for the sake of seeing their oppressors transformed.[25]

Finally, Williams dismisses King's use of redemptive suffering as a foundation for social action as "ancient" and "antiquated," an old Civil Rights strategy unfit to address today's unique challenges.[26] She admits that redemptive suffering was effective at prodding "the white moral conscience" during the abolitionist movement in America, when the prevailing issue was chattel slavery. However, Williams holds that redemptive suffering stands little chance of ameliorating modern social ills like economic disparities and white privilege. In general, she has very little confidence in appeals to the moral conscience of the nation to address the multifaceted and widespread oppression within the black community. She suggests that White America is much more motivated by the potential of financial loss than any appeals to moral conscience. Therefore, Williams recommends the economic boycott as a much more effective and proven strategy to promote liberation. Using redemptive suffering to address such problems she says, is "about as effective as a cup of water on a forest fire."[27]

Having characterized appeals to redemptive suffering as anachronistic, Williams insists that black women must appropriate theological symbols from their own experiences to help promote liberation. Medieval theologians like Abelard and Anselm used the language and sociopolitical categories of their day to make sense of the cross of Christ. Rather than use the language and sociopolitical categories of medieval European or even ancient thinkers, Williams suggests that black women should use the language and sociopolitical thought from their own world to understand Jesus and the cross. She notes, "Whether we talk about Jesus in relation to atonement theory or Christology, we womanists must be guided more by black Christian women's voices, faith, and experience, than anything that was decided centuries ago at Chalcedon."[28] For Williams, this means womanists must seek to liberate redemption from the "sacred aura" placed around the cross by the patriarchal responses to Jesus' death.[29] She maintains that black women today must reject any positive valuation of suffering (whether Christ's or their own) as a means to bring about redemption.[30] She asserts that Jesus conquered sin through his life rather than his death. For Williams, the cross represents the defilement of a human body, the degrading of Christ's glorious ministerial vision, and the culmination of human sin—not the conquering of it. However, Jesus' life (especially during his temptations in the wilderness) represents the conquering of sinful temptations through resistance. Therefore, Williams calls on black women to look to the life of Jesus for motivation to resist sin and oppression, not his death. Jesus' life and resurrection, she says, offers black women the "ministerial vision" necessary to show them how to live in proper relationship with themselves and the world.[31] According to her, any black woman who would adopt King's description of the cross as the definitive answer to the problem of evil and as the foundation for non-violent social action would be guilty of a dangerous anachronism. In sum, Williams alleges that by centralizing the cross, King's theodicy unwittingly condones violence against women, prioritizes the oppressor's salvation at the expense of their victims' dignity, and lacks the resources to meet the modern challenges faced by black America.

KING, THE CROSS, AND BLACK WOMEN'S LIBERATION

Just as Williams alleges, the moral influence theory of the cross stands at the center of King's theodicy.[32] However, this is exactly what helped King avoid the surrogacy theme that Delores Williams finds so problematic. King also found the idea of surrogacy deeply problematic, seeking to avoid it in his approach to the cross, and in turn, his cruci-centric theodicy. Following personalists like A.C. Knudson, King categorically rejected atonement theories that include the idea of substitution.[33] He held merit and guilt to be inalienable from personality and unable to be abstracted from the concrete realities of life. Therefore, he maintained that merit and guilt are incapable of being transferred from one person to another. King also considered the idea of substitutionary atonement to be out-of-step with Christian morality and ethics.[34] Quoting Knudson, King explained, "no person can morally be punished in place of another."[35] For King, the cross did not represent suffering *in the place of* another (i.e., surrogacy), but suffering *for the sake of* another (i.e., sacrificial service). King believed the cross represented the definitive revelation of divine agapic love and righteousness, God's willingness to sacrifice *for the sake of* those who were undeserving as well as God's "power to overcome sin and evil through suffering."[36] Despite King's atonement dichotomy, many theologies have successfully held the moral influence theory of the atonement (which emphasizes Christ as prophet) without abandoning substitutionary theories (which emphasize Christ as priest). However, I would suggest that even these more multi-faceted approaches to the cross must never apply the language of substitution beyond Christ's unique and unrepeatable atoning sacrifice. Therefore, even those who hold substitution as a central theme of the atonement can remain in step with King's theodicy, provided they don't apply this aspect of the atonement to victims of oppression.

While avoiding the theme of surrogacy, King's theodicy still centralizes the cross to preserve the hope that God is at work through the painful circumstances of the oppressed for the cause of freedom. God works through non-violent sacrificial love to achieve liberation for the oppressed. Even if they should suffer violence in their cause, God does not forsake the oppressed or waste their experiences. Rather, God makes the suffering of the oppressed redemptive, working towards the cause of their freedom. According to King, the cross is history's greatest proof of this, providing the hope of liberation for the oppressed and a powerful motivation for freedom fighters to resist the natural tendency to meet oppression with retaliatory violence. Therefore, King's theodicy encourages black women to strive for their own liberation through creative resistance in the hope that, even if they should suffer for their cause, God would use these circumstances for their good.

King's moral influence approach to the cross also avoided glorifying violence. King dedicated much of his life to ending unjust suffering and violence.[37] Yet, he centralized a horrifically violent event as the definitive revelation of God's agapic love and righteousness. Despite its violence, King maintained his commitment to the cross because the cross reveals the end of unjust suffering and violence and the triumph of liberation. As Lewis Baldwin explains, "The cross of Christ was for King, the black theologian, a symbol of suffering and salvation, of subjugation and liberation."[38] The cross reveals God's power to end the sinful oppression through non-violent sacrificial love that is willing to endure suffering and, if need be, even death.

According to King, the violence of the cross revealed Jesus' steadfast commitment to confronting evil, seeking the highest ethical good and loving sacrificially even at the expense of his own life.[39] Horrific though it was, the violence of Calvary only further revealed the true depth of Jesus' risk for the sake of justice, the true depth of his convictions and commitment to confront evil, and the true depth of suffering he was willing to undergo for the sake of justice and the salvation his people. According to King, the violence of the cross displayed the true nature of Christ's "dangerous" and "excessive" altruism. He explained, "He [Jesus] died in excruciating pain which was an expression of his willingness to engage in the most dangerous altruism . . . . His altruism was willing to travel dangerous roads in that he was willing to relinquish fame, fortune and even life itself for a cause he knew was right. His altruism was excessive, for he chose to die on Calvary, history's most magnificent expression of obedience to the unenforceable."[40] Without the suffering of the cross, the true nature of Jesus' risk would not have been clear. The violence of the cross showed that Jesus' love undertook the greatest risks for liberation. A cross-centered commitment to liberation must be willing to take real substantial risks for liberation. Suffering endured often makes it certain that the danger was real and that the willingness to take substantial risks was real. The violence of the cross revealed the magnitude of the danger that Jesus willingly undertook for the sake of his people, the true nature of his "dangerous altruism."[41]

Additionally, the depth of Jesus' suffering of the cross revealed the depth of his love, what King called his "excessive altruism." As the magnitude of Christ's sufferings became clear so did the depth of his love; there was no length that he was not willing to go to rescue his people. If Jesus had not suffered the horrors of the cross, the true abundance of God's love for us would have gone unrevealed. Following Harry Emerson Fosdick, King describes the cross as history's "greatest display of obedience to the unenforceable." By the unenforceable, King meant "the inner attitudes, genuine person to person relations, and expressions of compassion which law books cannot regulate and jails cannot rectify."[42] By choosing to suffer such a horrific death for the sake of his people, Jesus reveals compassion and love which society does not have the capacity to enforce. Jesus was willing to endure the worst for the cause of love and truth and resist evil till the very end.

The cross also revealed Jesus' radical commitment to justice and liberation, his extremism for love and justice. King explained, "In that dramatic scene on Calvary's hill three men were crucified. We must never forget that all three men were crucified for the same crime—the crime of extremism. Two were extremists for immorality, and thus fell below their environment. The other, Jesus Christ, was an extremist for love, truth, and goodness, and thereby rose above his environment."[43] According to King, Christ was crucified precisely because of his extremism for love. Having risen so far above his "environment" in his commitment to love and truth, this world rejected him in the most brutal way. Exemplified at the cross, this rejection only further reveals the radical extent to which Jesus' life rose above the sinful world he inhabited. Therefore, rather than glorify suffering or violence *per se*, the cross reveals Jesus' willingness to take substantial risks for love and justice, to suffer and even die for love and justice, and his radical commitment to love and justice.[44]

By centralizing the cross, King's theodicy also emphasizes the dignity of humanity through a focus on agapic love. At its core, the freedom struggle was a struggle for human dignity. King believed that one of the worst legacies of racism was the false sense of inferiority that it foisted upon African Americans. He viewed the cross and the transformative agapic direct action that it inspires as powerful weapons against this false message. As we have repeatedly seen, King considered the cross the divine revelation of agapic love. For King *agape* is inextricably tied to human dignity as the central energizing force that transforms a people otherwise robbed of its sense of self-worth and endows them with a new sense of "somebodyness," a new self-appreciation and self-respect.[45] By centralizing the cross, King was centralizing a powerful force for restoring human dignity. During the freedom struggle, King insisted that cross-inspired agapic direct action created "in the mind of the negro a new image of himself." He continued, "It has literally exalted the person of the Negro in the South in the face of daily confrontations that scream at him that he is inferior or less than because of the accident of his birth."[46] King envisioned agapic action as producing a fundamental transformation in the way one views herself. The agapic love of the cross, transforms the oppressed into non-violent resisters whose sufferings mean that they too bear in their body the marks of Christ.

King's theodicy does not glory in self-suffering in a way which would undermine human dignity. In "Suffering and Faith," King openly disparaged the kind of "martyr complex" Delores Williams fears women would adopt should they embrace King's theodicy. Although King did not glory in suffering *per se*, he did not refuse it as a means to bring transformation to himself and others. Rather than glorify personal suffering, King would only call attention to his considerable trials insofar as they shaped his thinking in certain ways. From his trials, King learned that God would strengthen his determination to confront injustice and use his creative moral agency to bring a redemptive benefit to himself and others. King did not focus on the suffering itself, but the way in which he engaged it and its usefulness as a means to bring certain kinds of redemptive transformation. For King, the cross was the definitive revelation of these truths. He noted,

> I have lived these last few years with the conviction that unearned suffering is redemptive. There are some who still find the cross a stumbling block, and others consider it foolishness, but I am more convinced than ever that it is the power of God unto individual and social salvation. So like the Apostle Paul, I can humbly yet proudly say, 'I bear in my body the marks of the Lord Jesus.'[47]

Here, King seems mindful of critics who viewed the cross as an unhelpful image for people in subjugation. Yet, for King, the cross held out the hope of social and individual salvation. He saw his personal sufferings as somehow participating in the sufferings of Christ, of being the kind of sufferings that result from a life lived in sacrificial service to others and in conflict with injustice. King's quote from Galatians 6:17 implies that he believed the sufferings in his life in some way reflected the sacrificial service of Jesus, and in so doing could be pedagogical not only for himself, but for others as well. Convinced by the power of God's revelation at the cross, King committed himself to agapic love, confronting evil, and seeking the highest in human ideals regardless of the personal costs, all while avoiding a martyr mentality which glorified self-suffering.[48]

Moving beyond the particularities of the black male experience, King's theodicy embraces and espouses liberation for African American women. Although King himself did not directly apply his theodicy to black women's unique experiences of oppression, he laid the theological groundwork to address such issues. With a profound concern for liberation, King's theodicy views the cross as a powerful motivating force for black women to vigorously resist oppression rather than acquiesce to it. Precisely by centralizing the cross, King's theodicy calls African American women to hope in God's power to work through their creative resistance and to follow Jesus' example of risk-taking, deep, sacrificial commitment to love and justice. But is this theodical message of the cross safe to communicate to black women who live within a context of deep subjugation? This section will look at Joanne Marie Terrell's black womanist application of these key themes from King's theodicy.

A WOMANIST RESPONSE TO WILLIAMS: JOANNE MARIE TERRELL

In *Power in the Blood?*, Joanne Marie Terrell surveys King's theodical treatment of the cross and, in turn, appropriates it as a helpful resource for black women's liberation. She notes that, in keeping with the black church tradition, King combined a focus on the cross with a theodical concern for the redemption of the community.[49] But this theodical appropriation of the cross did not lead to social acquiescence or passivism.[50] She rightly suggests that for King, God's *agapic* love revealed at the cross bespeaks a way to use one's moral and creative agency to "confront the earthly powers." This revelation lay at the very heart of the entire nonviolent movement.[51] Inspired by the cross, King directly confronted the system of segregation using non-violence, which he often called the weapon of love. Terrell holds that King's commitment to non-violent direct action fundamentally reshaped the way in which African Americans understood suffering and sacrifice. She explains, "Through his ability to persuade many blacks (and whites) to practice nonviolent, direct action techniques in the battle against systemic racism, King, with the masses, bodily reinterpreted the hermeneutics of sacrifice as it pertained to the human agency of the despised community, in the process reorienting the way black and white Christians of today ground their understanding of the nature and work of Christ." In other words, through his nonviolent example King taught America how to engage suffering in a creative and redemptive way and so better understand a unique dimension of the cross itself. Therefore, Terrell associates King's theodical appropriation of the cross with promoting social action rather than acquiescence, actively using one's moral agency rather than moral passivity. King's theodicy suggests that such sacrifices may serve as a "redemptive force" to help end the oppression of sexism.

Terrell maintains that King's cruci-centric theodicy particularly resonates with the black experience. She explains, "The cross in the African American experience *is* theodicy [emphasis Terrell's]."[52] Generally speaking, black Christians readily identify with the experience of the cross because they too suffer unjustly. However, according to Terrell, the cross has a peculiar resonance with African American women who seek to make meaning out of their personal sufferings.[53] It is precisely the terrible violence of the cross which reaches down into the "nitty gritty" dimensions of black women's daily realities, which makes it an indispensable theodical revelation. Terrell explains, "Although I despised the melodrama captured in the depiction of Jesus crucified, I could not avoid contemplating the suffering God because here was a mirror to my world."[54] The cross made meaning out of her own experiences of physical and emotional abuse and her mother's tragic death at the hands of a jealous lover. It helped give her hope that "God still has a way of wringing good out of evil."[55] These words seem fit to address the current struggle against sexism, and the sacrifices of so many women who have suffered under its violence. It also served as a redemptive revelation of God's "*with-us-ness*" in these violent experiences and a hope that God works even through such experiences.[56] For Terrell, the redemptive suffering revealed at the cross meant that her suffering and her mother's death were not in vain. For black women like Terrell, the cross represents not only eschatological hope for tomorrow, but a teleological promise for today, that God intends something redemptive from great sacrifices made while confronting evil.[57] Terrell suggests that Black women's sacrifices can bring personal and societal transformation, going so far as to call them "sacramental" and "atoning."[58] Terrell goes on to explain that the cross reveals sacrificial love and the cost of confronting evil in service to a higher cause, the very same ideas that King himself found so compelling, and which undergirded his cruci-centric theodicy.[59]

Terrell insists that these beliefs far outweigh any rhetorical baggage surrounding the imagery of surrogacy. She notes, "Although I may never be required to give up my life for the sake of my ultimate claims, the peculiar efficacy of my mother's sacrifice as well as the Christian story prevent me from discarding the idea altogether, particularly the notion of sacrifice as the surrender or destruction of something prized or desirable for the sake of something with higher claim, a potentially salvific notion with communal dimensions that got lost in the rhetorical impetus of the language of surrogacy."[60] Since the cross typifies the commitment to undergo tremendous self-sacrifice for the sake of a higher claim, Terrell refuses to dismiss it. She identifies her mother's experience with the cross and calls the countless women who died resisting injustice and oppression empowered witnesses, rather than acquiescent victims. Their examples can be liberative if they teach other women and also influence them to exercise their own creative moral agency in order to resist oppression.

With this moving example, Terrell pinpoints how King's cruci-centric theodicy addresses the liberation of black women, even those who have and are suffering under the terrible scourge of domestic violence and emotional abuse. If understood correctly, King's redemptive suffering theodicy would honor the sacrifices of women such as Joanne Terrell's mother by identifying them with the crucified Christ, casting them as courageous witnesses rather than acquiescent victims, their sufferings as inspiring lessons rather than meaningless tragedies.

King insisted that unjust suffering must be engaged in a way that brings pedagogical benefits.[61] This seems to be precisely what Terrell, as a womanist, is calling for. She explains, "My mother's ultimate sacrifice and those of countless other black women, who suffer abuse and die at the hands of patriarchal, violence driven persons; whose deaths go unreported and under-reported, unprosecuted and under-prosecuted—are potentially liberating for women if we learn from their experiences, if we see how they exercised or did not exercise their moral and creative agency."[62] Like King, Terrell points to the pedagogical nature of redemptive suffering which she considers it to be applicable to black women's experiences of oppression. She suggests that the lives of black women who suffer violence are witnesses who speak to other women (and I would add men as well). They must teach other black women how to properly exercise their own creative agency to effectively resist and escape such terrible oppression. If women don't learn from their personal experiences and the experiences of others, they cut themselves off from the wisdom of these experiences. They may remain caught in an oppressive system without any clear strategy to resist. [63] This pedagogical purpose does not end with individual women. It also implies a concern to address the entire oppressive system which produces violence against black women.[64] Their sufferings demand an account not only of their abusers, but also of the systems that produced their abusers. And so, they call us all to consider how to use our moral agency to impact the sexist systems that help produce and support abusers.

King's theodicy also implies that black women who suffer violence may still be empowered witnesses. No matter the circumstance, black women always have some ability to exercise their moral agency. Although they may be victimized, that is not the totality of their identity. They are still moral agents who can choose to engage their suffering in a creative way or not. This means the pervasive violence in black women's lives is not utterly determinative *per se*. It may be necessary, but it is not ultimate.[65] It only provides the context, the raw material through which moral agents may work with God to engage a sinful world in a redemptive way.[66] Though suffering may be inevitable and necessary, they may choose to "transform it into a creative force" to "make of it a virtue" and use it to bring transformation to themselves and others.[67] Therefore, King's theodicy describes sufferers as empowered witnesses who have the ability to creatively resist, and to help bring transformation to someone else. Gripped by the sacrifice of Christ and her mother who also resisted oppression to the point of death, Terrell learned something valuable about the power of love and commitment to a higher cause. Although she was caught in the bondage of physical and emotional abuse, Terrell's mother used her moral agency to prioritize the life of her daughter above anything else. She remained steadfast in this commitment, even to the point of death. The cross and her mother's sacrifice helped teach Terrell more than mere strategy; it taught her about love, and this love transformed her. She explains, "Secretly I despised Jesus, my mother and myself because I resented what seemed to be needless suffering. And yet I loved us all because I willed it and because somehow I knew I was loved."[68] This is the most powerful lesson which King's theodicy ascribes to the sufferer, the transformative lesson of agape. By identifying their sufferings with Christ, King's theodicy correctly lifts up black women's sufferings as so many transformative displays of agapic love.

By ascribing redemptive significance to black women's sufferings, King's theodicy also prioritizes the dignity of sufferers over the violent intent and actions their abusers. Unwilling to view them merely as unfortunate victims, King's theodicy affirms the dignity of women who have suffered the very worst forms of abuse.[69] The preservation of human dignity is a central theme throughout King's theological corpus, serving as one of the main reasons he embraced the philosophy of personalism.[70] Although King did not reflect extensively on black women's experiences, Katie Cannon insists that "a strong affirmation of the dignity of all black people," is emergent in his theology.[71] His theodicy maintains this trend by affirming the absolute dignity of women oppressed by violence.[72] While condemning the violence that victims suffer in their confrontation with evil, King's theodicy valorizes sacrifices and steadfast commitment to resist injustice at great personal cost. It calls us to think of them as heroines, martyrs, and witnesses, rather than as mere victims. This is exactly how King referred to Addie Mae Collins, Carol Denise McNair, and Cynthia Diane Wesley, three of the four children killed September 15, 1963, in the infamous 16th Street Baptist Church bombing. In his famous "Eulogy for the Martyred Children" King explained, "They are the martyred heroines of a holy crusade for freedom and human dignity. So they have something to say to us in their death."[73] King's language pointed his audience past the violence of the perpetrators to the courage and dignity of the little girls. Even "one of the most vicious crimes ever perpetrated against humanity" could not erase the dignity of the young victims. Rather, the cross they bore only served to highlight their personal dignity and the broader cause for human dignity.[74] This theodical lesson must be applied to women who have suffered and died bearing the cross of violence. It affirms the truth that sufferers are more than only that. Because of the cross, they can in fact be redeemed. Terrell notes that "when black women can see the truth of this revelation self-love becomes imminently possible."[75]

Moved by the sacrificial love of Christ, King's theodicy also calls black women to use their moral agency to resist oppression and abuse in the faith that God is with them in their struggle, and if need be in their suffering.[76] Using the cross, King emphasized the call to resist injustice standing ready to surrender something costly for the sake of something or someone else with a higher claim. For King, this was not an abstract theological speculation. The revelation at the cross demands concrete practical action. It calls the followers of Christ to be willing to suffer for their beliefs by putting them into practice. Baldwin explains, "King held that the task of truly moral and committed persons involved suffering with Christ for human redemption and transformation."[77] King's theodicy called him to follow Christ in engaging the suffering of his people in a creative way in order to bring about redemptive transformation.[78] Indeed King distinguished himself from theologians like Reinhold Niebuhr through his confidence that agapic love could be practiced in reality.[79] Therefore, his theodicy calls for practical action, rather than passive acquiescence or non-action.[80] King's theodicy implies that the sufferings of black women are liberative not only because they instruct, but because they call for liberating action. King said about the young martyrs, "Their death says to us that we must work passionately and unrelentingly for the realization of the American dream."[81] For him suffering is redemptive in the sense that it summons to action. As women and men consider the examples of women who have suffered the indignities of oppression, they also must be summoned to action. King's theodicy calls us to work "passionately and unrelentingly" to help realize a society without the scourge of sexism and domestic violence.

THE WOMANIST CRITIQUE PART 2: JACQUELYN GRANT

Although Jacquelyn Grant describes King's theodicy as a suitable strategy to make meaning out of hopeless situations, she insists that redemptive suffering lacked sufficient resources to promote real and lasting freedom. In "The Sin of Servanthood," Grant explains that by viewing suffering as redemptive, black folks essentially denied their oppressor's claim to legitimate authority. It was a way of confessing God's sovereign and redemptive claim over the oppressor and the oppressed, even in their situations of oppression. She notes, "Their speaking titles as Lord and Master with regard to Jesus and God meant that the lords and masters of the white world were illegitimate."[82] Grant describes this as a helpful strategy that allowed black folks to continue surviving by providing comfort and hope under the strain of bleak circumstances.[83] Hope notwithstanding, when King called black people (particularly black women) to suffer for the sake of transforming America, Grant implies that he was also calling them to subordinate themselves beneath the salvation of their oppressors. She notes "Martin Luther King, Jr's notion of 'suffering servant' explains how Black people and Black women were able to make sense out of, and possibly bring hope out of apparently hopeless life situation. Whereas both of these interpretations are helpful as a part of the survival strategies for Black people, they are unable to provide true liberation."[84] In order for freedom to occur, she says, this hope must be accompanied by certain psychological, political, and social conditions to help nurture the process.

For Grant, attaining this freedom means particularly eliminating "servant" language which reinforces the sinful mentality of subordination. Although it kept black women from sinking into despair, the language of servanthood would have reinforced the kind of psychological subordination that would have contravened lasting liberation by masking oppressive realities rather than eliminating them. By valorizing the position of servitude, Grant holds the suffering servant motif undermines black women's resistance to oppression. "True service," she says, "may mean relinquishing the dubious honor of servanthood . . . . for women of color, the sin is not the lack of service, but too much service. The liberation of servants means that women will no longer shoulder the responsibility of service."[85] Instead of servants, Grant contends that the black women should embrace the imagery of disciples, which she suggests would avoid reinforcing camouflaging oppressive realities. She suggests that this discipleship should also avoid relational images like covenant and reconciliation. She insists that conciliatory images inevitably put black women back into subordinate roles with other covenant parties without substantive action for liberation and justice. In sum, Jacquelyn Grant holds that King's theodicy camouflaged and reinforced oppressive realities by applying the language of suffering servant to black women.[86]

WOMANIST RESPONSES TO GRANT: KAREN BAKER-FLETCHER AND KATIE CANNON

This section will attempt to show that King's theodicy sought to foster the very psychological, political, and social conditions that Grant rightly suggests must accompany freedom. Rather than implying social subordination, King's servanthood language promoted a sense of self-dignity and determination to fight oppression. First, we will look at King's actual use of the suffering servant language and motif, to learn if he explicitly and directly applied it to black people in the way Grant alleges. Finally, we will consider Karen Baker-Fletcher and Katie Cannon's womanist appropriations of King's theodical themes to promote liberation.

Jacquelyn Grant's misgivings about King's suffering servant language and imagery likely follow black humanist William R. Jones' critique of King's theodicy.[87] Jones also characterized King as holding a suffering servant theodicy, likening King's thought to Joseph Washington's direct identification of blacks as contemporary suffering servants *à la* Isaiah 53 in *The Politics of God*.[88] To support his claim, Jones only offers a vague reference to King's book *Stride Toward Freedom*.[89] Absent of any page numbers, it is difficult to know exactly which passages Jones had in mind. The black messianic vision King articulated in *Stride* certainly included the idea that African Americans had been especially chosen and used by God as an appeal to the nation, and that their love, goodwill, and non-violence would be used to that end.[90] But this stops well short of applying suffering servant language to the black community like Joseph Washington.[91] While King articulated a substantial black messianic vision, commitment to Christian service, and a willingness to suffer and die for his ideals, in *Stride Toward Freedom* he seems to have avoided the servant imagery and language that Grant finds so problematic.[92]

Throughout his career, King's direct comments about Isaiah 53 were surprisingly scant, appearing almost exclusively in his seminary writings.[93] For instance, at Crozer, he identified the prophet Jeremiah as the "supreme example" of the suffering servant.[94] Later, at Boston University, King directly identified the suffering servant as Jesus Christ. He explained, "The suffering servant passage in the 53rd chapter of Isaiah could well be applied to Jesus. In a real sense he is the only one who fulfills this prophesy."[95] He preferred the servant be interpreted as an individual rather than a community, exclusively as Jesus Christ rather than the broader people of God.[96] Rather than cite any of these sources, Grant directly cites King's 1961 *Christian Century* article "Suffering and Faith" to support her claim that King referred to blacks as suffering servants. However, King never directly or indirectly identifies blacks as servants to their oppressors in the article. In fact, servant imagery only appears in the article once, specifically in reference to the Christian's service to Christ. King explained, "I have learned now that the Master's burden is light precisely when we take his yoke upon us."[97] However, Grant does not directly take issue with servanthood language referring to the Christian's subordination to Christ, only in reference to subordination to oppressors.[98]

In the article, King does suggest that his sufferings "served" his own discipleship process. They helped shape his thinking, draw him closer to God, provide an opportunity for transformation, and "heal the people involved in the tragic situation which now obtains."[99] As we have seen in previous chapters, the lessons King learned and the transformation he experienced through engaging suffering only served to sharpen and strengthen his resolve to oppose oppression. They guarded him from bitterness, brought him closer to God, and reaffirmed his commitment to viewing the cross as the power of God for social and individual salvation.[100] King focused on how the suffering experience itself primarily serves the transformation, liberation, and positive self-image of the oppressed.

Rather than servant of his oppressor's salvation, we might say that King was servant to the redemptive formation of the beloved community. King's concern for the liberation of the oppressor acknowledged that the oppressed could not truly be liberated without regard to the healing of the entire society.[101] Agape, the force at work through redemptive suffering, aims to create and sustain the beloved community, a society modeled after the Kingdom of God in which everyone would live together as sisters and brothers.[102] As the oppressed engage their suffering agapically, they look toward more than their own personal liberation, but toward the creation of the beloved community. King explained, "Agape is love seeking to preserve and created community. It is insistence on community even when one seeks to break it . . . In the final analysis, agape means a recognition of the fact that all of life is interrelated. All humanity is involved in a single process, and all men are brothers."[103] This idea of life being interrelated means that the oppressed cannot fully enjoy liberation apart from any concern for the state and fate of their oppressors. They are not servants of their oppressors' salvation, but liberation without reconciliation and mutual agapic love is lacking something substantial. Therefore, King's theodicy does not hold out hope for the individual liberation wholly apart from the oppressor.

This does not thrust the oppressed back into relationships of unhealthy subordination. Instead, it means living in a society in which both parties seek to live in mutual agapic love. Through agapic love, segregationists needed to be liberated from the bondage of hatred and their own false

THE WOMANISTS

sense of superiority. To King's mind, this would help segregationists not only recognize the dignity of the oppressed, but also rediscover their own human dignity. King noted, "So long as the Negro is treated as a means to an end, so long as he is seen as anything other than a person of sacred worth, the image of God is abused in him and consequently and proportionately lost by those who inflict the abuse."[104] In oppressing their victim, King held that abusers are acting beneath their own human dignity. This situation could be rectified through an agapic love which lifts the dignity of the oppressed and oppressor together. He concluded, "nonviolence exalts the personality of the segregator as well as the segregated."[105]

Through this broad vision of liberation for all and the interrelatedness of human life, King's theodicy avoids the subordination of black women while promoting the conditions for black women to fully enjoy liberation. Garth Baker-Fletcher maintains that King offers an important corrective for abuse-victims who think of remaining in abusive relationships as "imitating Christ." He explains that King's reformulation of God's love as teleological (rather than just self-sacrificial) guards against an unhealthy focus on suffering *per se*. As we have discussed in previous chapters, it is not suffering in and of itself that brings about redemptive transformation. It is the creative agapic engagement with suffering. The focus on the beloved community guards against valorizing suffering in an unhealthy way. It also helps to engender courage to risk self-harm for the sake of a teleological goal, the beloved community. In this case, the emphasis is on the teleological goal and the courage inculcated through one's commitment to it, rather than the sacrifice itself.[106]

The communal focus of King's theodicy also highlights the kind of covenantal relationships and community in which they are called to live. In her *Black Womanist Ethics*, Katie Cannon highlights this idea exactly. She lists King's theodical ideas of agape, the beloved community, and the interrelatedness of human life as being particularly useful to help black women analyze the character of situations of injustice and promote social action. She explains, "As members of the 'beloved community,' Black women are responsible, along with others who care for collecting the facts to determine whether injustice exists, whether a law, an historical situation, existing social relations elevate or debase human beingness.... Ethical living requires an intolerance of civil arrangements that result in the horrors of racism, gender discrimination, economic exploitation and widespread cruelty. The interdependency of the 'beloved community' projects a 'constructive equality of oneness.'"[107] The theodical principle of agape helps unmask unjust relationships, exposing them for what they truly are. Agape looks toward the formation of the beloved community, a society of love, justice, and mutual dignity. Black women cannot settle for anything less than agape within their marriages, churches, schools, and society.

Cannon also explains that King's "solidaristic approach to human existence" helped galvanize the masses behind the cause for liberation.[108] He didn't seek to demonize or humiliate his opponent. Rather he readily affirmed the mutuality and interrelatedness of all people. "Whatever affects one directly affects all indirectly."[109] This helped people from across the racial, cultural, and socio-economic spectrum view themselves as having a stake in freedom movement and to contribute real resources towards it. Only when black males, white males, white women, and everyone else within our society realizes their own dignity by learning to treat black women with agapic love and dignity will the psychological, social, and economic conditions necessary for wholistic black women's liberation truly be realized.

CONCLUSION

This chapter has demonstrated that King's redemptive suffering theodicy meets the challenge of is womanist critics Delores Williams and Jacquelyn Grant. While avoiding the language of surrogacy that Williams decries, King's theodicy promotes true liberation for black women through applying the moral influence approach to the cross which calls them to learn from and resist experiences of oppression as empowered moral agents. By identifying victims with Christ, King's theodicy also casts black women who suffered while resisting oppression as empowered witnesses, rather than as mere victims. King's theodicy also avoids the servanthood language that Grant decries. Rather than subordinate black women as servants to their oppressor's salvation, King's theodicy calls for serving humanity through helping to create the beloved community in which love, justice, and mutual dignity are realized in practical ways. King viewed redemptive suffering as healing the entire "tragic situation" of racism and oppression "which now obtains." For King, redemptive suffering didn't mask social oppression. Rather, through teleological emphasis on the beloved community, it exposed and healed oppression, creating the psychological, political, and economic conditions Grant says must accompany liberation.

In my final chapter, I will turn towards King's theodicy and the modern context of the black church. I will examine popular engagements with King's redemptive suffering theodicy, especially in the work of Cheryl Kirk-Duggan and James Cone. I intend to examine how King's theodicy ranks among popular theodicies in use today, and demonstrate that King's theodicy provides one of the most powerful tools for the black church to help support its great theodical heritage and witness. Finally, I will apply King's theodicy to some of the contemporary challenges the black church faces. As Katie Cannon eloquently concluded in *Black Womanist Ethics*, I hope to show that King's theodical ideas provide the "moral resources for the great struggle that *still lies ahead* [emphasis Cannon's]."[110]

NOTES

1. Karen V. Guth, "Reconstructing Nonviolence: The Political Theology of Martin Luther King Jr. after Feminism and Womanism," *Journal of the Society of Christian Ethics* 32, no. 1 (March 1, 2012): 75–76, 78–79; Rufus Burrow, Jr., "The Doctrine of Unearned Suffering," *Encounter* 63, no. 1–2 (December 1, 2002): 65.

2. Womanist theologians approach their theological task with particular attention to the beliefs, perspectives, culture, experiences, values, empowerment, and liberation of Black women. Generally speaking, Womanism seeks the liberation of all women, especially women of color. Therefore, Womanists such as Williams and Grant are especially concerned with redemptive suffering's viability (or lack thereof) as a tool for women's liberation. Alice Walker, *In Search of Our Mothers' Gardens: Womanist Prose* (Orlando: Harcourt, 2004), xi–xii; Delores Williams, "A Womanist Perspective on Sin," in *A Troubling in My Soul: Womanist Perspectives on Evil and Suffering*, ed. Emilie Maureen Townes (Maryknoll, N.Y.: Orbis Books, 1993), 130–147.

3. Rachel Muers, "Bonhoeffer, King, and Feminism: Problems and Possibilities," in *Bonhoeffer and King: Their Legacies and Import for Christian Social Thought*, ed. Willis Jenkins and Jennifer M. McBride (Minneapolis: Fortress Press, 2010), 35. There is some debate about exactly how much influence King has exercised on Womanist thinking. For instance, Karen Guth laments, "there is little feminist or womanist engagement with his [King's] thought." Guth, "Re-

constructing Nonviolence," 75. However, Katie Cannon's *Black Womanist Ethics* (Eugene, OR: Wipf & Stock, 2006). And Emilie Towne's "Notes on Appropriation and Reciprocity: Prompts from Bonhoeffer and King's Communitarian Ethic," in *Bonhoeffer and King: Their Legacies and Import for Christian Social Thought*, ed. Willis Jenkins and Jennifer M. McBride (Minneapolis: Fortress Press, 2010). Represent notable exceptions, demonstrating how Womanists have deeply engaged and appropriated King's thought. Katie Cannon in particular

4. Delores Williams, (Maryknoll, N.Y.: Orbis Books, 1993), 199–200; Joanne Carlson Brown and Rebecca Parker, "For God So Loved the World?" in *Christianity, Patriarchy, and Abuse: A Feminist Critique*, ed. Joanne Carlson Brown and Carole R. Bohn (Pilgrim Press, 1989), 19–20.

5. Jacquelyn Grant, "The Sin of Servanthood," in *A Troubling in My Soul: Womanist Perspectives on Evil and Suffering*, ed. Emilie Maureen Townes (Maryknoll, NY: Orbis Books, 1993), 212–214.

6. Muers, "Bonhoeffer, King, and Feminism: Problems and Possibilities," 35. In *Black Womanist Ethics,* womanist Katie Cannon engages King extensively, applying his theology to gender-related issues. However, she never mentions his personal attitudes towards women as a significant barrier to her project. In fact, her book concludes with this thought. "Black women today must embrace the formal features of the theological ethics of Thurman and King because they provide moral resources for the great struggle that *still lies ahead* [emphasis Cannon's]." Cannon, *Black Womanist Ethics*, 174. Guth, "Reconstructing Nonviolence," 75; Muers, "Bonhoeffer, King, and Feminism: Problems and Possibilities," 34–35. David J Garrow, *Bearing the Cross: Martin Luther King, Jr., and the Southern Christian Leadership Conference* (New York: Perennial Classics, 2004), 141, 374–376, 655; Rufus Burrow, Jr., *God and Human Dignity: The Personalism, Theology, and Ethics of Martin Luther King, Jr.* (Notre Dame: University of Notre Dame Press, 2006), 148–149; Lewis V. Baldwin, *There Is a Balm in Gilead: The Cultural Roots of Martin Luther King, Jr* (Minneapolis: Fortress Press, 1991), 269–270; Lewis V Baldwin and Amiri YaSin Al-Hadid, *Between Cross and Crescent: Christian and Muslim Perspectives on Malcolm and Martin* (Gainesville: University Press of Florida, 2002), 3, 6, 168, 170. Rufus Burrow, Jr has especially noted King's theological inconsistency on gender issues, explaining that King's chauvinistic behavior was fundamentally out of step with the philosophy of Personalism.

7. JoAnne Marie Terrell, *Power in the Blood?* (Maryknoll, N.Y.: Orbis, 1998), 143.

8. Delores Williams, "A Crucifixion Double Cross? The Violence of Our Images May Do More Harm Than Good," *Other Side* 29, no. 5 (September 1, 1993): 25.

9. Hyun Kyung Chung, *Struggle to Be the Sun Again: Introducing Asian Women's Theology* (Maryknoll, N.Y.: Orbis Books, 1990), 53–54; Williams, "A Crucifixion Double Cross?" 25. The Korean women in Chung's book take a much more positive view of redemptive suffering than Delores Williams. Their preferred image of Christ is suffering servant, and, as we shall see, these women of color view the cross of Christ as liberating precisely because it exemplifies redemptive suffering.

10. Williams, "A Crucifixion Double Cross?" 25.

11. Ibid., 26.

12. Ibid., 27.

13. Delores Williams, "Black Women's Surrogacy Experience and the Christian Notion of Redemption," in *After Patriarchy: Feminist Transformations of the World Religions*, ed. Paula M Cooey, William R. Eakin, and Jay B. McDaniel (Maryknoll, N.Y.: Orbis Books, 1991), 12–13.

14. Williams, *Sisters in the Wilderness: The Challenge of Womanist God-Talk*, 200. Given the nature of the last chapter, I will not address this criticism of King's theodicy in detail. In general, I would respond to the Womanist concerns about King's theodicy promoting social passivity the same way I responded to the Black humanist concerns. King's theodicy resists the charge of quietism by strongly emphasizing the human responsibility to engage suffering non-violently in order to help transform it into something redemptive. King's theodicy also emphasized God's power to realize God's purposes in concrete ways, therefore providing the oppressed with sufficient hope to continue struggling for their liberation. Finally, King's theodicy functioned in practical ways to motivate the oppressed to resist their oppression. Although this could be shown in numerous ways, one quote from King's famous "I have a Dream Speech" captures the foundational place of redemptive suffering in encouraging the social action, at least of the civil rights movement. After offering the eschatological imagery of Amos 5:24, King said, "I am not unmindful that some of you have come here out of excessive trials and tribulation . . . . You have been the veterans of creative suffering. Continue to work with the faith that unearned suffering is redemptive." Martin Luther King, Jr., "I Have a Dream (1963)," in *A Testament of Hope: The Essential Writings and Speeches of Martin Luther King, Jr.* (San Francisco: Harper SanFrancisco, 1991), 219. Rather than social resignation, this demonstrates the central place of King's theodicy in motivating and guiding non-violent direct action.

15. Brown and Parker, "Christianity, Patriarchy, and Abuse," 21.

16. Ibid., 20.

17. Martin Luther King, Jr., "Suffering and Faith," *Christian Century* 101, no. 77 (April 1960): 510.

18. King strongly favored the moral influence theory as the best theory of the atonement. Martin Luther King, Jr., "A View of the Cross Possessing Biblical and Spiritual Justification," in *The Papers of Martin Luther King, Jr.: Volume I: Called to Serve, January 1929–June 1951*, ed. Clayborne Carson, Ralph Luker, and Penny A Russell (Berkeley, California: University of California Press, 1992), 266–267; Martin Luther King, Jr., "Final Examination Answers, Religious Teachings of the Old Testament," in *The Papers of Martin Luther King Jr., Rediscovering Precious Values: July 1951–November 1955*, ed. Clayborne Carson and Ralph E Luker (Berkeley, California: University of California Press, 1994), 170.

19. Alan Richardson, *Creeds In The Making* (Student Christian Movement Press, n.d.), 21.

20. Brown and Parker, "Christianity, Patriarchy, and Abuse," 20.

21. Ibid. Interestingly enough, Williams does commend Abelard's theological method to Womanist theologians. Like Abelard and his contemporary Anselm, Womanist should employ the language and sociopolitical thought of their time to makes sense of Christian principles.

22. Williams, *Sisters in the Wilderness: The Challenge of Womanist God-Talk*, 273. Williams does disagree with Parker and Brown at certain points. For instance, she does not think women should leave the church in order to avoid participating in patriarchal ideas like redemptive suffering. Rather, she advocates that since women makes up a sizable majority of black church membership, they should bring transformation through controlling the church's purse strings.

23. Williams, "Black Women's Surrogacy Experience and the Christian Notion of Redemption," 10.

24. Williams, *Sisters in the Wilderness: The Challenge of Womanist God-Talk*, 60–83.

25. Ibid., 273. Due to lack of scientific studies on the subject, Williams acknowledges that she is unsure whether the black church still places a high value on suffering or whether its female parishioners believe their own sufferings are redemptive. However, she suggests that because most black Christians identify the cross with redemption, they do hold at least some form of suffering to be redemptive.

26. Ibid., 200, 273.

27. Ibid., 273–274. Williams maintains that White America is more moved by economic loss than moral appeals. Therefore, she recommends the boycott as a more effective civil rights strategy than redemptive suffering since it makes no appeals to moral conscience.

28. Ibid., 203.

29. Williams, "Black Women's Surrogacy Experience and the Christian Notion of Redemption," 10–11.

30. Ibid.

31. Ibid., 12–13; Williams, *Sisters in the Wilderness: The Challenge of Womanist God-Talk*, 166–167.

32. King, Jr., "A View of the Cross Possessing Biblical and Spiritual Justification."

33. King described the substitutionary theory of the atonement as the view that "Christ actually took the place of sinners in the sight of God, and as a substitute suffered the punishment that was due to men." Martin Luther King, Jr., "A Comparison of the Theology of Luther with that of Calvin," in *The Papers of Martin Luther King, Jr. Volume II: Rediscovering Precious Values July 1951–November 1955*, ed. Peter H. Holloran and Clayborne Carson (Berkeley: University of California Press, 1994), 189.

34. King also believed that this idea would undermine the ethical life. He suggested "if Christ by his life and death paid the full penalty of sin, there is no valid ground for repentance or moral obedience as a condition of forgiveness." King, Jr., "A View of the Cross Possessing Biblical and Spiritual Justification."

35. Ibid.; King, Jr., "A Comparison of the Theology of Luther with that of Calvin," 189; Albert C Knudson, *Basic Issues in Christian Thought* (New York: Abington-Cokesbury Press, 1950), 144.

36. King, Jr., "A View of the Cross Possessing Biblical and Spiritual Justification"; Lewis V. Baldwin, *To Make the Wounded Whole* (Minneapolis: Fortress Press, 1992), 62.

37. Burrow, Jr., *God and Human Dignity*, 26–27.

38. Baldwin, *To Make the Wounded Whole*, 62.

39. King, Jr., "A View of the Cross Possessing Biblical and Spiritual Justification."

40. Martin Luther King, "Strength to Love," in *The Papers of Martin Luther King, Jr., Volume VI: Advocate of the Social Gospel, September 1948–March 1963*, ed. Tenisha Hart Armstrong et al., First edition (Berkeley: University of California Press, 2007), 486.

41. Karen Baker-Fletcher and Garth Baker-Fletcher, *My Sister, My Brother: Womanist and Xodus God-Talk* (Maryknoll: Orbis, 1997), 79–80. Womanist Karen Bake-Fletcher highlights King's cruci-centric theology as typifying an ethic of risk.

42. Martin Luther King, Jr., "On Being a Good Neighbor," in *The Papers of Martin Luther King, Jr., Volume VI: Advocate of the Social Gospel, September 1948–March 1963*, ed. Clayborne Carson et al. (Berkeley: University of California Press, 2007), 484.

43. Martin Luther King, Jr., *Why We Can't Wait* (New York: Harper and Row, 1964), 88–89.

44. Filipino theologian Lydia Lascano and Korean theologian Choi Man Ja both point these aspects of the cross as particularly liberative for Asian women as well. Chung, *Struggle to Be the Sun Again*, 57.

45. Garth Baker-Fletcher, *Somebodyness: Martin Luther King, Jr. and the Theory of Dignity* (Minneapolis: Fortress Press, 1993), 126, 134–135.

46. Martin Luther King, Jr., "The Ethical Demands for Integration," in *A Testament of Hope: The Essential Writings and Speeches of Martin Luther King, Jr.*, ed. James M. Washington, Reprint edition (San Francisco: HarperOne, 2003), 125.

47. King, Jr., "Suffering and Faith," 510.

48. According to Lewis Baldwin, King's willingness to bear the cross in service to humanity may be the most important aspect of his profound legacy. Lewis V. Baldwin, "Revisioning the Church: Martin Luther King, Jr. as a Model for Reflection," *Theology Today* 65, no. 1 (April 1, 2008): 39.

49. Terrell, *Power in the Blood?*, 79–80.

50. Ibid., 79. Terrell distinguishes King's confidence in the realization of agape in the here and now from Reinhold Niebuhr's doubts. Niebuhr doubted whether even something like non-violent direct action was truly agapic, rather than self-interested. He also seemed to confuse agapic love with non-resistance to evil. King distinguished passive non-resistance from non-violent resistance. In his estimation, non-violent direct action could be a practical expression of agapic love. The cross then became the definitive expression of non-violent direct action and served as a fundamental theme and central symbol within the freedom movement.

51. Ibid.

52. Ibid., 142.

53. According to Chung Hyung Kyung, Asian women also use redemptive suffering approach to the cross both to describe and make meaning out of life's hardships. She notes, "When Asian women live through the hardship of suffering and obedience their family, society, and culture inflict upon them, they need a language that can define the meaning of their experience. The image of the suffering Jesus enables Asian women to see meaning in their own suffering. Jesus suffered for others as Asian women suffer for their families and other community members. As Jesus' suffering was salvific, Asian women are beginning to view their own suffering as redemptive. They are making meaning out of their own suffering through the stories of Jesus' life and death. As Jesus' suffering was life-giving, so Asian women's suffering is being viewed as a source of empowerment for themselves and for others whose experience is defined by oppression. Chung, *Struggle to Be the Sun Again*, 54. This is very similar to the implications of King's theodical use of the cross for black women. Although a further examination of the Korean application of redemptive suffering falls out-

side the purview of this project, it shows that theodical uses of the cross like King's can be helpful in addressing sexist dynamics.

54. Terrell, *Power in the Blood?*, 143.

55. Martin Luther King, Jr., "Eulogy for the Martyred Children," in *I Have a Dream: Writings and Speeches That Changed the World, Special 75th Anniversary Edition*, 1st ed. (San Francisco: HarperOne, 1992), 221.

56. Terrell, *Power in the Blood?*, 125, 142. Lydia Lascano explains that this truth particularly resonates with Filipino women as well. For them, Jesus knows their suffering personally because he suffered similarly. Chung, *Struggle to Be the Sun Again*, 56.

57. Terrell, *Power in the Blood?*, 124–125.

58. Ibid., 143.

59. Ibid.

60. Ibid., 142.

61. King, Jr., "Suffering and Faith." As we apply his thinking to Black women, it is vital to note that King himself applied these lessons within the crucible of deep personal suffering. He spoke of the pedagogical nature of suffering as one who learned much from his own sufferings and hoped that they would be fruitful to teach others.

62. Terrell, *Power in the Blood?*, 142–143.

63. Although King looked to the cross of Christ as the definitive example of non-violent direct action, he also looked to Gandhi as a model for how to effectively apply this approach to the public arena. He said, "Christ furnished the Spirit and motivation while Gandhi furnished the method." Martin Luther King, Jr., "Pilgrimage to Nonviolence," in *Stride Toward Freedom: The Montgomery Story* (San Francisco: HarperCollins, 1987), 38. For King, Gandhi's sufferings were pedagogical, teaching him to how to effectively use his creative agency to resist oppression in the segregated South. This may imply that would imply that black women should especially look to survivors of abuse to learn effective strategies to overcome abuse themselves.

64. King mentioned this lesson as he made sense of the death of three slain little girls. King, Jr., "Eulogy for the Martyred Children."

65. The so-called "necessity" of suffering is one of Brown, Parker, and Williams' chief complaints against King's theodicy. By describing suffering as necessary, they assert that he holds suffering as the only means to bring change, and thus, unwittingly condones the violent circumstances of many black women. Joanne Carlson Brown, *Christianity, Patriarchy, and Abuse: A Feminist Critique* (New York: Pilgrim Press, 1989), 20. However, by describing suffering as a "necessity," King was merely describing the circumstances rather than condoning them. They were necessary, in the sense that these were the circumstances he inherited as an African American in the segregated south and was thrust into by

virtue of his struggle for freedom. Since he found himself within these painful circumstances, he would choose to help transform them into something redemptive rather than corrupting. This seems to make the best sense out of his words. Black women suffer inevitably as a result of their circumstances in America and through fighting for freedom. Even Delores Williams agrees that the cross is reveals the risk and consequences which necessarily follow from confronting the earthly powers. Therefore, if black women would confront the earthly powers, they will suffer. King's black messianic vision would also suggest that African American women have been endowed by God with a peculiar ability (this would include courage, patience, and agapic love) to be able to transform their suffering into something redemptive.

66. This does not mean unjust violence is somehow morally neutral. Unjust violence and suffering are evil, yet the evil of such circumstances does not have the final say. They only provide the context for a redemptive engagement.

67. King, Jr., "Suffering and Faith."

68. Terrell, *Power in the Blood?*, 143.

69. King's theodicy does not deny that victims of abuse are truly *victims* of abuse. However, it insists they are more than just victims. Their moral agency along with God's redemptive intention and activity turn, what otherwise would be a meaningless tragedy into a redemptive witness.

70. Burrow, Jr., *God and Human Dignity*, 126–128.

71. Cannon, *Black Womanist Ethics*, 174. King's sexist attitudes and practices towards women show his life was inconsistent with his theological claims at this point. This inconsistency does not mean that King was a mysoginist. There is no evidence that he was ever intentionally malicious, violent, or verbally or physically abusive towards women. His sexism evinced itself in his unwillingness to advocate women's involvement in positions of authority within the freedom movement and within marriage relationships. Burrow, Jr., *God and Human Dignity*, 140.

72. Burrow, Jr., *God and Human Dignity*, 146. Rufus Burrow argues that King's personalist doctrine of dignity did not fully accommodate women since he did not consistently advocate women's involvement in positions of authority in practice. He notes, "King would be the first to say that abstract dignity means nothing to the en-fleshed human being whose humanity and dignity are ignored. This must be the conclusion regarding women as well." Although Burrow rightly notes that King emphasized concrete action over abstract theological speculation, I argue that King's theodicy does have the resources to affirm the dignity of women in the most concrete ways, even if King himself did not always do so.

73. Martin Luther King, Jr., "Eulogy for the Martyred Children," in *A Testament of Hope: The Essential Writings and Speeches of Martin Luther King, Jr.* (New York, NY: HarperCollins, 1991), 221.

74. The alternative would be to prioritize the violence of the perpetrator as triumphant over the courage and dignity of the sufferer, to view the cross they bore as nothing but a symbol of violence, humiliation, and innocent suffering. However, Terrell and many other women are unable to think their mothers, sisters, and daughters suffered as mere victims. Terrell, *Power in the Blood?*, 142–143.

75. Ibid., 125.

76. I am aware that some would think of this approach to women's oppression as much too passive and potentially submissive to injustice. King's theodical message of non-violent resistance has often confused with passive non-resistance. Faced with similar criticisms during his lifetime, King often clarified the difference between the two. He explained, "True non-violent resistance is not unrealistic submission to evil power. It is rather a courageous confrontation of evil by the power of love, in the faith that it is better to be the recipient of violence than the inflictor of it, since the latter only multiplies the existence of violence and bitterness in the universe, while the former may develop a sense of shame in the opponent, and thereby bring about a sense of shame and a transformation and change of heart. Non-violent resistance does call for love, but it is not a sentimental love. It is a very stern love that would organize itself into collective action to right a wrong by taking on itself suffering." Martin Luther King, Jr., "My Trip to the land of Ghandi," in *The Papers of Martin Luther King, Jr.: Volume V: Threshold of a New Decade: January 1959–December 1960*, ed. Tenisha Armstrong and Clayborne Carson (Berkeley, California: University of California Press, 2005), 234.

77. Baldwin, *To Make the Wounded Whole*, 62.

78. King's theodicy does not call for inciting violence where it does not already exist. Instead, it calls for creatively and non-violently engaging the violence that already exists.

79. Terrell, *Power in the Blood?*, 79.

80. As King put is theodicy to practice, King often decried the moral laxity of the apathetic and the fearful. King, Jr., *Why We Can't Wait*, 88–91.

81. King, Jr., "Eulogy for the Martyred Children."

82. Grant, "The Sin of Servanthood," 213.

83. Ibid.

84. Ibid., 214.

85. Ibid., 215.

86. Ibid., 215, 218.

87. In her article, Grant directly applies Jones' arguments to her critique of redemptive suffering as a theodicy and to servanthood language. Ibid., 209.

88. William R. Jones, *Is God a White Racist?: A Preamble to Black Theology* (Garden City, NY: Doubleday, 1973), 80; Joesph Washington, *The Politics of God: The Future of the Black Churches* (Boston: Beacon Press, 1967), 155.

89. Jones, *Is God a White Racist?: A Preamble to Black Theology*, 216.

90. Martin Luther King, Jr., *Stride Toward Freedom: The Montgomery Story* (HarperCollins, 1987), 224.

91. Roy Melugin and Paul Anderson both argue that King's willingness to love the oppressor and suffer for his beliefs were rooted in the Christian interpretive tradition of Isaiah 53. Roy F. Melugin, "The Book of Isaiah and the Construction of Meaning," in *Writing and Reading the Scroll of Isaiah: Studies of an Interpretative Tradition*, ed. Craig C. Broyles and Craig A. Evans (Leiden: Die Deutsche Bibliothek, 1997), 53; Paul N. Anderson, "The Suffering Servant of Isaiah in Cognitive Critical Perspective: Logotherapy and the Bible," in *Psychological Hermeneutics for Biblical Themes and Texts: A Festschrift in Honour of Wayne G. Rollins*, ed. Harold J. Ellens (New York: T&T Clark International, 2012), 193.

92. This common identification of King with the suffering servant comes more from his legacy than his actual self-assessment. See for instance Craig C. Broyles and Craig A. Evans, *Writing and Reading the Scroll of Isaiah: Studies of an Interpretative Tradition* (Brill, 1997), 53. Scholars such as Lewis Baldwin rightly note that King's life and untimely death exemplify sacrificial service and that this remains one of his most important legacies for the church. For Baldwin, this means that one should be willing to suffer, and if need be, even die for the highest ethical ideals. However, one remains hard-pressed to find King identifying himself or black people with the suffering servant of Isaiah 53. Lewis V Baldwin, *The Voice of Conscience: The Church in the Mind of Martin Luther King, Jr.* (Oxford: Oxford University Press, 2010), 245; Baldwin, "Revisioning the Church," 39.

93. In a historical overview of King's influences, Richard Wills notes that the Black church "readily identified with Jesus as the suffering servant." However, he does not say that King directly identified the black community as suffering servants. Richard W. Wills, *Martin Luther King, Jr., and the Image of God* (Oxford University Press, 2009), 38.

94. Martin Luther King, Jr., "The Significant Contributions of Jeremiah to Religious Thought," in *The Papers of Martin Luther King, Jr.: Volume I: Called to Serve, January 1929–June 1951* (Berkeley, California: University of California Press, 1992), 195.

95. King explained, "There has been much debate as to whether this passage refers to the nation or to an individual. . . . It is my opinion that the passage refers to an individual, and, Jesus more than any other fulfills this description." King,

Jr., "Final Examination Answers, Religious Teachings of the Old Testament," 170.

96. King, Jr., "The Significant Contributions of Jeremiah to Religious Thought," 170.

97. King, Jr., "Suffering and Faith," 510.

98. In fact, Grant refers to herself as a "servant" of Christ noting, "Womanist theology is committed to bringing wholism to Black women. Being a servant of the redeemer means joining in the struggle of the redeemer against oppression, wherever it is found." Grant, "The Sin of Servanthood," 213.

99. King, Jr., "Suffering and Faith," 510.

100. King, Jr., "Suffering and Faith."

101. Burrow, Jr., *God and Human Dignity*, 155. Rufus Burrow, Jr highlights the consistent emphasis that King placed on the individuals in community through his helpful neologism "personal communitarianism."

102. Ibid., 155–160.

103. Martin Luther King, Jr., "An Experiment in Love," in *A Testament of Hope: The Essential Writings and Speeches of Martin Luther King, Jr.*, ed. James M. Washington, Reprint edition (San Francisco: HarperOne, 2003), 20.

104. King, Jr., "The Ethical Demands for Integration," 119.

105. Ibid., 125.

106. Baker-Fletcher and Baker-Fletcher, *My Sister, My Brother*, 52–53.

107. Cannon, *Black Womanist Ethics*, 173.

108. Ibid., 171.

109. Martin Luther King, Jr., "A Christmas Sermon on Peace," *in A Testament of Hope: The Essential Writings and Speeches of Martin Luther King, Jr.*, ed. James M. Washington, Reprint edition (San Francisco: HarperOne, 2003), 254.

110. Cannon, *Black Womanist Ethics*, 174.

CONCLUSION
Contemporary Relevance

INTRODUCTION

This concluding chapter considers the continued relevance of Martin Luther King's theodicy for the contemporary black church and community. With a view towards the cross and the omnipotent God's good purposes in the world, King held that persons have the freedom and responsibility to creatively engage their suffering in order to bring personal and social transformation. King's redemptive suffering approach represents a 250-year-old theodical tradition that helped African Americans redemptively engage the immense suffering of slavery, Jim Crow, and segregation. King adapted and developed this rich black theodical tradition with protestant liberal concepts in order to help address the harsh practical realities of the people he served. Along with cultural resonance, biblical faithfulness, and philosophical coherence, the final test for King's cruci-centric redemptive suffering theodicy must be practical relevance.

King's redemptive suffering theodicy provides resources to help the black church and community address major challenges such as institutionalized racism and intra-communal violence. The longstanding theodical tradition that King inherited remains relevant and viable through his unique developments and appropriations. I will make my case first by examining Womanist theologian Cheryl Kirk-Duggan's treatment of

King's non-violent protest ministry in her book *Refiner's Fire*. Kirk-Duggan highlights some of the limitations she sees in King's redemptive suffering message as he attempted to apply it among the urban ghettos of the North and outside the context of the black church. The issues Kirk-Duggan raises will help frame my discussion of the continued relevance of King's theodicy. I will demonstrate that these supposed limitations don't undermine the usefulness of King's theodicy to meet today's challenges. Next, I will propose some practical ways local churches and the black community can apply King's theodical ideas in their struggle for justice and the realization of the beloved community. Finally, I will offer a brief summary of themes examined in this dissertation along with some concluding remarks.

A QUESTION OF RELEVANCE

Cheryl Kirk-Duggan wonders whether King's redemptive suffering theodicy effectively addressed challenges outside of the segregated south of the mid-twentieth century or challenged audiences outside the context of the black church. She suggests that King himself experienced the limitations of redemptive suffering during the latter stages of the freedom movement as he sought to apply this message to the ghettos of the urban North. In the final years of his life, Kirk-Duggan explains, "King spoke less of redemptive suffering and sacrifice and became filled with anger, tempered by his practice of nonviolence."[1] She suspects that King softened his redemptive suffering rhetoric in the face of growing frustration among blacks who were "tired of being beaten and jailed for trying to exercise their constitutional rights."[2] According to Kirk-Duggan, King felt that despite great social, legislative, and moral victories in the South, the message of redemptive suffering had not thoroughly impacted the self-image of the black masses in the North. After he moved to Chicago, Kirk-Duggan says, King's ministry shifted from "Refining the fires of non-violent direct action in the Southern pulpit to the Northern pool room."[3] He aimed to connect with the masses in an attempt to address their socio-economic concerns. However, Kirk-Duggan suggests that King retreated back to Atlanta after realizing that his redemptive suffering approach was inadequate to address the dynamics of black self-hate and socio-economic oppression in the North.[4] Kirk-Duggan views King's

CONCLUSION

shift in strategy and retreat to the South as proof that his theodicy is ill-equipped to address the unjust economic and social realities that undergird racism today.

Kirk-Duggan also doubts whether King's redemptive suffering message was effective among white American Christians. She notes that King was deeply disappointed at the failure of white clergy and their churches to respond to the theodical vision he cast.[5] Some whites impugned the legitimacy of the movement and especially King's non-violent direct action protests as being unchristian or un-American, whereas others kept largely silent about whatever tacit approval they gave King's message. Kirk-Duggan particularly pinpoints what she calls the dilution of the movement with whites who, though enchanted by the movement, were largely unaware and uninterested in overturning the economic and power dynamics that undergird racial stratification. Kirk-Duggan suggests that King's theodicy could not address the institutionalized injustices that undergird racism. Therefore, scores of whites could join the movement without a strong knowledge of or intention to rectify the mal-distribution of power that bolsters the widespread system of racism in America. "As White churches got involved," she says, "confrontation tactics became diluted, notably in the March on Washington, in August, 1963, when marchers were diverse but did not confront injustice."[6] In her opinion, King's theodicy could not move white sympathizers to put their lives and bodies on the line in the same way as the scores of black church foot soldiers that comprised the main core of the movement. Although redemptive sufferings aims at the transformation of whites as well as blacks, Kirk-Duggan doubts that this transformation would empower whites to display the same levels of agapic love on behalf of blacks. Kirk-Duggan explains, "Between 1965 and 1968, King realized that his messages had not moved Whites to change but did move Blacks to action."[7] Kirk-Duggan calls the alleged inability of redemptive suffering to address the institutionalized dynamics that undergird racism or to effectively move whites to radical action "problematic."[8]

As King reached more non-Christians with the message of nonviolence, Kirk-Duggan says he also struggled against the common idea that nonviolence was merely a powerful social tactic, rather than a cross-centered practical appropriation of redemptive suffering. Kirk-Duggan rightly notes that King's vision of the beloved community with blacks as agents of redemptive change was grounded in black cultural and especially ecclesial sources. For black Americans, King's vision of the beloved community meant dealing with racial tensions through Christian agapic love. For them, the way of the cross was the way to freedom. Therefore, the effectiveness of King's redemptive suffering theodicy as a ground for social action was closely tied to black commitment to Christianity, and more specifically, to faith formed within the context of the southern black church tradition. She explains, "He tied redemptive suffering to non-violent direct action . . . King knew it would be difficult to teach people to think and live in non-violent terms when they had been taught to meet violence with violence, but Christian fulfillment meant stressing neighborly love and existence or non-violent protest. Nonviolence would allow one to exercise the virtues of altruism, civic spirit, and friendliness, which required that one first be open to such a message or have a conversion experience that would create an environment where grace, divine loving activity, and love manifested among humanity might occur."[9] King's non-violent direct action was grounded in a specifically Christian theodical vision, the redemptive purposes of God revealed at the cross of Christ. Without embracing the cross as the definitive divine revelation of redemptive suffering, how could demonstrators maintain their commitment to the way of the cross? And, without hope in the omni-benevolent and omnipotent God who is able to wring good out of evil, how could demonstrators maintain their hope in the face of seemingly insurmountable odds? Before people could participate in non-violent demonstrations they had to consent to a certain set of spiritual disciplines that were closely tied to the Christian faith including 1) meditate daily on the life and teachings of Jesus, 2) walk and talk in the manner of love—for God is love 3) pray daily to be used by God in order that all men might be free.[10] These instructions corresponded with a distinctly Christian vision of freedom which demanded a commitment to agapic love and nonviolence as a way of life rather than a convenient means to social victory. Without the strength and wisdom gleaned from the empowering revelation of the cross of Christ even King doubted whether freedom fighters could stay committed to the theodical practice of non-violent resistance. Without the hope inspired by its theodical foundation, non-violent resistance lacked the resources to fulfill the emotional needs of the oppressed.[11]

In summary, Kirk-Duggan pinpoints certain historical limitations King faced as he carried his redemptive suffering message outside the confines of the southern black church of the mid-twentieth century. According to her, King's theodicy failed to effectively meet the institutionalized plight of the urban poor blacks in the North, to move white Christians in mass to sustained deep sacrifices on behalf of the movement, or to keep non-Christians engaged with the true agapic intent behind nonviolent resistance. Finally, she doubts whether King's theodicy is practical enough to shift the socio-economic disparities at the heart of racism. While I don't completely agree with Kirk-Duggan's historical analysis of King, she raises some important challenges which will help frame my discussion of the continued relevance of King's theodicy.[12] The Chicago campaign of the mid-sixties provides a helpful counter-example to Kirk-Duggan's challenges. Having laid out Kirk-Duggan's basic arguments, I will now use the Chicago Campaign of 1965–1966 to examine whether King's theodicy could be applied to the systemic challenges of blacks in northern ghettos and whether its efficacy was somehow limited to black church audiences.

KING'S THEODICY: ITS RELEVANCE OUTSIDE THE SOUTHERN BLACK CHURCH

Even as he worked and lived in the ghettos of the North, King himself maintained confidence in the power of agapic love to bring redemptive transformation to the socio-economic dynamics that undergirded racism in the 1960s, and I suggest still persist today. For instance, when King threatened to lead a mass interracial march into Cicero, a "virulently antinegro" suburb outside Cook County, Chicago, Mayor Richard Daley quickly agreed to sit down with him and address discriminatory housing practices in Chicago.[13] The so-called "Summit Agreement" called on the city to redouble efforts to enforce its open-housing policy and fair housing ordinance; Chicago's savings and banking associations to lend money to qualified families of all races; and the Chicago chamber of commerce, along with several other labor and business organizations, to work on behalf of fair housing in Chicago. Stephen Oates called the Summit Agreement, "the most comprehensive of any of King's previous accords, including that in Birmingham."[14] King himself viewed the Summit Agreement as proof that redemptive suffering could effectively address the systemic issues of the North. On the day the agreement was reached, he told a crowd gathered at a Baptist church on the West side of Chicago,

"They said nonviolence couldn't work in the North. They said you can't fight city hall; you better go back down South. But if you look at what happened here, it tells you nonviolence can work."[15] While King admitted that the same format of demonstrations and marches would not affect the urban ghetto in the same way as the South, he had renewed confidence in the power of redemptive suffering to address the unjust socio-economic dynamics that perpetuated the plight of the poor. He maintained that redemptive suffering itself had as much power to move the masses in the northern ghettos as anywhere else. He just needed to find an effective way to "transmute the deep rage of the ghetto into a constructive and creative force" and "dramatize the need for jobs and economic advancement for the poor."[16] King settled on a "Poor People's campaign" in which scores of unemployed African Americans and poor people of all races would dramatize their suffering by descending on the nation's capital and camping out in front of government buildings for a lengthy period.[17] For King, the effectiveness of the creative and redemptive suffering was never in doubt. Unwavering in his commitment to the power of agapic love, King applied his theodicy to racial as well as socio-economic injustices. Rather than shed redemptive suffering as Kirk-Duggan suggests, King shifted his strategy in order to more effectively apply redemptive suffering, to creatively and effectively dramatize the suffering of the oppressed. King's civil rights successes in Chicago and the genesis of the Poor People's campaign demonstrate that he believed redemptive suffering could address the systemic injustices that plagued poor blacks in the North.[18]

The Chicago campaign also demonstrated the effectiveness of redemptive suffering outside the confines of the institutional church. In Chicago, when King wasn't preaching in pulpits, organizing, or soliciting support for the cause, he was meeting with gang members, offering them a vision of redemptive suffering. King instructed SCLC staffers to work closely with recruits from Chicago's infamous youth gangs like the Vice Lords, Blackstone Rangers, and Cobras. They would regularly escort certain members of these gangs to the flat King rented in Chicago's West Side in order to meet with him personally. After warmly receiving them over a plate of barbecue, King would listen to them recount their conflicts with the police and with the harsh realities of life in the slums. Their struggle for purpose and identity made them a highly sought after group. Communists groups, the Nation of Islam, and white mobsters were all

CONCLUSION

seeking to recruit them to their causes, with the promise of alleviating their suffering through Marxist social-political ideology, Black Nationalism, or the fast money of organized crime. However, King patiently and empathetically offered them another way.[19] Although they viewed violence as the only viable strategy for survival in an increasingly violent environment, King challenged them to seriously consider the power of non-violent resistance. Stephen Oates explains, "Gently, with great sincerity, King would explain the nature and purpose of nonviolence, asking them to try it as an experiment and put away their guns and knives. If they did, he wanted them to serve as marshals once the marches began."[20] King held nonviolence workshops for these young men and vividly contrasted civil rights victories in Selma with the chaos and suffering of the Watts riots. He pointed out that, in the case of the riots, blacks bore the brunt of the injuries and deaths, and the oppressive structures were still in place. However, the way of nonviolence helped to bring lasting systemic changes and even put Selma's sheriff Jim Clark out of a job.[21] Gradually, many of these young men became convinced by King's redemptive suffering vision. "In time," Oates continued, "some two hundred gang members agreed to give nonviolence a chance and turn out for the demonstrations 'as soon as brother Martin gives the word.'"[22] This highlights the effectiveness of King's redemptive suffering message among non-church audiences. Although redemptive suffering is anchored in a vision of the cross, it had the power to persuade members of the community outside the confines of the institutional church.

Having appealed to the Chicago campaign to address Kirk-Duggan's concerns about the applicability of King's theodicy outside the context of the Southern black church, I will now examine the relevance of his theodicy for the black church and community today. Although King's theodicy does not provide an answer for every problem that plagues the black community, it does provide some practical guidance to help it address some of its deepest challenges. Today, the black church finds itself facing multidimensional challenges like mass incarceration, police brutality, disparities in education and healthcare, mass unemployment and underemployment, increasing fatherlessness, and the scourge of intra-communal violence. Without offering overly facile or glib solutions to these complex challenges, I believe King's theodicy does offer guiding principles for a more effective approach to some of these major concerns.

FOUR PRINCIPLES TO APPLY KING'S THEODICY

Principle #1: Critical Analysis of Human Suffering

First, King's redemptive suffering theodicy calls us to critically analyze the systemic and personal dynamics behind oppression. In order to creatively engage suffering, one must first understand the nature of the suffering that is present. This aspect of King's work often goes underappreciated. King rigorously studied the oppressive dynamics at play within the contexts that he worked. This helped him learn the best way to dramatize the suffering he saw with a view toward unmasking the latent violence codified in dehumanizing laws and the daily indignities suffered by the oppressed.[23] Often times these unjust dynamics can be especially difficult to expose since they have a pernicious way of hiding themselves behind the veneer of normalcy. However, King's theodicy calls for sustained, robust, and honest evaluation of the root causes of these challenges with a view towards dramatizing them in a compelling way. As King's experience in Chicago shows, this can be more difficult than it might at first appear. It is not as easy as organizing mass marches to address every challenge the black community faces. Even King acknowledged that although a march down a street in Selma, Alabama, was revolutionary, a march through the turbulence of the northern ghetto was "scarcely even distracting."[24] It takes keen insight to understand the dynamics of these challenges well enough to creatively engage them in a consistently nonviolent way, to wield the weapon of agapic love in a cruel and often loveless world. Therefore, King viewed fact-finding as one of the four essential steps to any non-violent campaign. Before he entered a city, King sent a fact-finding team to study the complex dynamics and systems of oppression at work in the area. The results from this investigation would help King decide on the best way to creatively engage the oppressive forces and social suffering he found. However, each community had its own unique dynamics. King knew he could not blindly repeat the same strategy in city after city. He needed to adapt his approach to find the best way to apply the force of creative suffering.[25]

    Without a deep understanding of the broader cultural and socio-economic dynamics at play within an oppressive situation, it becomes difficult to ensure redemptive rather than destructive engagement. In "The Crisis in Contemporary Religion," Cornel West explains that moralistic

CONCLUSION

acts are often conflated with moral acts. He notes that moralistic acts flow out of "sheer sentimental concern," like pity. However, moral acts, he says, flow from "an understanding of the context in which the action takes place and of the impact of the action on the problem. In short," he says, "moralistic acts rest upon a narrow, parochial anti-intellectualism that sees only pitiful individuals, whereas moral action is based on a broad, robust prophetism that highlights systemic social analysis of the circumstances under which tragic persons struggle."[26] West recognizes that overly simplistic approaches to suffering that neglect the sophisticated dynamics at play will not likely yield true redemptive outcomes.

With its emphasis on agapic engagement and the responsibility of free agents, King's theodicy offers a powerful safeguard against the misguided interventions of bare sentimentalism. King's theodicy uniquely recognizes the responsibility of free moral agents to use the epistemic resources at their disposal to engage their situation redemptively. Therefore King's approach helps guard against the common tendency to perform the kind of moralistic acts that are misguided and superficial. Informed by King's theodicy, Christians and the church must be willing to interact with the best information available as it seeks to think, speak, and lovingly act theodically. The moralistic acts that West has in mind often neglect the complex and pernicious systemic forces that crush people precisely because they are rooted in sentimentalism, rather than agapic love. Sentimentalism has little interest in deep, systemic, and lasting justice for the oppressed and therefore it does not give itself to understand the contexts in which people struggle. Unfortunately, overly simplistic and myopic actions often exacerbate suffering in the long term even while alleviating some measure of it in the short term. True, redemptive engagement means seeking and interpreting the best information with a view towards addressing suffering in a more holistic way.

A crucial part of understanding the suffering of the oppressed involves seriously listening to the oppressed and entering into their experience. This was precisely why King moved into the slums of Chicago, frequented pool halls, and befriended prominent gang members during the Chicago campaign. King's willingness to meet with gang members of Chicago proved critical to understanding the suffering that he sought to engage. In order to understand the complex dynamics that converged in the North and in order to empathize with the people trapped in those circumstances, King needed to spend time living in the ghetto, to use the epistemological resource of experience. Indeed, free moral agents are responsible to use the epistemological resources available to ensure that it may be able to engage suffering in a redemptive way, including the resource of experience.

John Perkins and his Christian Community Development Association (CCDA) provide notable examples of what a Kingian theodical analysis might look like in practice today. While working among the poor in rural Mississippi, Perkins developed his famous principle of relocation as a means of community development. Through relocation into the impoverished communities where the poor often suffer, people can gain a better understanding of the oppression they face. They hold that experience living among the poor provides invaluable resources for redemptive engagement and that the best messengers of the gospel among the poor are people who intimately understand their experiences.[27] Therefore, Perkins' relocation principle seems right in step with a Kingian theodical vision and creative-redemptive strategy to engage oppression. The CCDA designates three kinds of people intentionally living in impoverished communities with a view toward redemptive engagement. "Relocators" are people who were not born among the poor but who move in among them to learn from the poor with a view towards promoting justice. "Returners" are people who grew up among the poor, yet who intentionally relocated back among the poor in order to more closely align their personal interests with the interests of the poor. Finally, the "Remainers" are those who grew up among the poor and have chosen to stay among the poor in order to fight oppression from within the community itself.[28] Although I believe each of these strategies are consistent with a Kingian approach to creative suffering, King's personal experience in Chicago might best be described as an exercise in relocation. His willingness to immerse himself in the experience of the northern ghettos helped him more effectively reach the poor with the message of redemptive suffering and resist oversimplifying the complex factors that cause their suffering.

However, redemptive engagement with suffering may demand more than simply living around the poor, but living among them as one of them. Recognizing the host of privileges that relocators bring to the table, relocators may need to deliberately forsake many of their privileges in order to more fully align with the poor and understand their suffering. For instance, King not only lived around the poor, he deliberately lived among the poor, in their dilapidated housing. He also made a point of eating their unhealthy food, sending his children to play in their barren playgrounds, and engaging in their forms of entertainment. In short, King personally took on the pains and struggles and suffering he sought to help alleviate. A genuinely redemptive engagement with oppression may demand solidarity with the suffering in more ways than we might initially expect. The recent water crisis in poverty-stricken majority black Flint Michigan serves as a notable example of how this principle may be applied. After city officials changed Flint's water to supply from the treated Detroit River to the untreated corrosive Flint River, aging pipes began leaching lead into the city's water supply. It's estimated that between 6,000–12,000 children have been exposed to Flint's lead-contaminated drinking water, a public health crisis of catastrophic proportions. When it was discovered that Michigan Governor Rick Snyder and other officials routinely dismissed complaints from Flint residents for months before finally admitting the crisis, outraged demonstrators took to the streets with the protest chant "Drink the Water Rick! Drink the Water Rick!"[29] This reflects the protestor's Kingian belief that officials will respond only as they personally feel the burden of oppression.

Principle #2: Affirm Human Dignity

Second, King's theodicy calls for a thorough affirmation of the indestructible dignity and empowerment of the oppressed which demands that we see them as more than merely victims. Although oppressive dynamics continue to be foisted upon members of the black community, King's theodicy keeps victims of oppression from being completely defined by their victimization. King's theodicy maintains that persons are responsible to engage their suffering creatively. While blacks are not responsible for their own oppression, they are responsible for how they choose to respond to it. They can choose to engage suffering creatively and self-sacrificially, empowered by agapic love and in view of God's good purposes, or they can choose to retaliate in bitterness or remain passive in despair. Either way, they are free moral agents who are responsible to act redemptively rather than destructively. This outlook also guards against externalizing all the responsibility for black freedom and dignity to whites. In other words, blacks don't need to wait until whites acknowledge their fundamental worth or grant them liberties before they live as free persons. Although oppressive dynamics can tempt blacks with a sense of inferiority, they remain free moral agents, empowered by God to engage their suffering in creative ways. As God's image bearers, the fundamental dignity of blacks has never been diminished in the slightest, even by historic and contemporary forms of systemic oppression. Dignity was a thing inherent to humanity. However, King also believed it was something to be fought for through agapic protest. Agape fostered a transformed sense of self-respect and dignity through participation in God's redemptive purposes personally and socially. By creatively engaging social suffering, moral agents could use moral means to achieve the equal rights which would also foster their sense of dignity.[30]

King's theodical focus on dignity would also provide a much-needed counterbalance to the negative images and stereotypes so prevalent in American society. Since slavery, blacks (particularly young black males) have been consistently stereotyped as threatening, impulsive, and especially predisposed towards criminal behavior. Not only do these stereotypes inform unjust practices like racial profiling and police brutality, they also bombard blacks themselves, diminishing their own sense of self-worth.[31] As we have seen, King's theodicy was informed by a kind of black messianic vision, a belief that God had chosen and providentially fit African Americans with the patience, fortitude, and moral sensibilities to help humanize America. The black church has consistently emphasized the dignity and full humanity of blacks against the prevailing messages of the broader culture. It was a place where God told us who we were and whose we were, and in which black personhood was celebrated and valued through the cultural religious expressions. King's theodical emphasis on dignity would remind particularly young black males that they are not the criminal brutes that American society often says they are. Rather, they are God's image bearers who have the freedom and responsibility to make something of the painful circumstances that they have given; to engage their circumstances in a virtuous manner. African Americans needn't look any further than fifty years ago to rediscover the rich theodical heritage that identifies them as strong, patient, and unwavering in the face of tremendous suffering.

The freedom, dignity, and empowerment that King's theodicy claims for oppressed persons also highlights their moral responsibility to live virtuous personal lives as well as to fight systemic injustices. It calls young black males who are tempted to personally participate in immoral and destructive dynamics to resist these temptations. During the Chicago

CONCLUSION

campaign, King personally lived among and met directly with gang members to encourage them towards this end. He understood that black-on-black crime would not stop until oppressive economic systems were addressed *and* blacks resisted the temptation to carry out violence against one another. Mass incarceration will not stop until the U.S. criminal justice system stops over-sentencing for petty crimes poor black males are likely to commit *and* young black males stop committing those petty crimes. Any viable approach to black suffering must address both institutional oppression and personal responsibility. Approaches which emphasize personal responsibility at the expense of acknowledging systemic oppression or which emphasizes systemic oppression at the expense of personal responsibility are inadequate since they either don't acknowledge the truth about black suffering or the truth about black freedom and dignity as persons made in the image of God. Emphasizing personal responsibility without a view towards eliminating systemic oppression is dishonest about how longstanding widespread institutionalized forces contribute to socio-economic disparities and black suffering. On the other hand, acknowledging systemic factors without personal responsibility identifies oppressed peoples as helpless victims who are unable to enjoy freedom until the oppressor grants it to them. This will only lead to bitterness, despair, and a denial of the personal responsibility and empowerment to address these issues. King's theodicy highlights both systemic and personal dynamics of oppression.

Principle #3: Creative and Redemptive Engagement with Suffering

Third, King's redemptive suffering theodicy calls us *to act* creatively, dramatically, and redemptively. King insisted that anyone confronted with suffering must engage that suffering creatively to help transform both the oppressed and the oppressor. As we have already discussed in previous chapters, this precludes both violence and passivity in the face of oppression. It insists on the third way of non-violent action.[32] This creative engagement often meant that the sufferings of the oppressed must be dramatized in a compelling way. Unearned suffering could not be redemptive if it remained unseen or routinely ignored. Therefore, one of King's main goals was to dramatize suffering in a way that could not be ignored, to make the injustice of an oppressive situation undeniable to any honest onlooker.[33] King's mass protests were an intensified way to dramatize daily indignities that had become normalized.[34] These public dramas provided the kind of public scene that simply could not be ignored. King's march from Selma to Montgomery for equal voting rights illustrates this point. Sunday March 7, 1965, as King and fellow demonstrators attempted to cross the Edmund Pettis Bridge, Sheriff Jim Clark and his deputies brutally attacked them with tear gas, batons, and whips. The nation, and even the White House, were stunned as images of "Bloody Sunday" streamed across network television airwaves. Although King hoped for a peaceful protest, the events of that day exposed the entire nation to the brutality of segregation.

King applied this principle in the North as well. As he marched through southwest Chicago's Marquette Park in 1966, he was struck in the head with a stone. He was among 30 freedom fighters injured that day from a hail of rocks, bottles, and firecrackers thrown by angry whites. When asked why he put himself at risk, King noted, "I have to do this—to expose myself—to bring this hate into the open."[35] King staged protests which deliberately put himself in harm's way because of his commitment to exposing hate. Indeed, part of the genius of the civil rights movement was its uncanny ability to consistently and creatively dramatize the suffering of the oppressed in a compelling way. A Kingian response to social suffering involves bringing the misery of the oppressed into the light of public scrutiny through creative engagement and, as Cornel West noted, to "let suffering speak, let victims be visible, and let social misery be put on the agenda of those with power."[36]

James Cone's *The Cross and the Lynching Tree* provides an interesting contemporary example of dramatizing black suffering in a way that loosely resonates with a Kingian approach. Although Cone's redemptive suffering theodicy is grounded in the basic tenets of black theology, like King, he understands the value of dramatizing suffering in a transformative way. By comparing the cross to the lynching tree, Cone invites American Christians to reexamine the painful history of lynching in America in order to encourage a redemptive transformation. Cone's theodicy almost completely hinges on God's solidarity with the oppressed. By reasserting the shear horror of lynching as an American atrocity, Cone dramatizes oppression so that we may know that through the cross, God demonstrates solidarity with the most degraded and shamed victims in American history. Cone holds that, "Because the faithful can experience

CONCLUSION

the reality of divine presence, they can endure suffering and transform it into an event of liberation."[37] For Cone, God's solidarity with the oppressed motivates us to strive for liberation. He aims to let the suffering of the over 5,000 lynched victims in America speak in a compelling way.[38] Cone's aim is not merely historical. Rather, he seeks to call attention to the "ongoing legacy of white supremacy in America."[39] He suggests that the hatred which lay behind these historic atrocities has not yet disappeared. Cone maintains that these sentiments still help define our way of life and will continue to do so unless we revisit this suffering through the lynching tree, the "quintessential emblem of black suffering."[40] For Cone, the lynching tree provides the most compelling symbol of American oppression and the negation of salvation hope by white supremacy.[41] Therefore, he promotes liberation and transformation through dramatizing the historical and contemporary suffering of blacks using the most compelling image possible, the brutalized bodies of black men, women, and children hanging from the lynching tree.

A Kingian approach to redemptive drama differs from Cone's in its emphasis on agapic resistance. While acknowledging divine solidarity, King's theodical drama also emphasized God's omnipotent power working through the non-violent resistance of the oppressed. Therefore, King specifically dramatized suffering through free agapic engagement with it. God was at work through the weapon of love to end oppression. Instead of focusing on the passive experience of suffering, I believe a more consistently Kingian approach would emphasize courageous faith-filled resistance, the way in which so many lynching victims went to the gallows confessing their unwavering hope in Christ, praying, preaching, and singing the historic hymns of the Christian church.[42] A Kingian approach would cast the cross and the lynching tree, not merely as symbols of suffering and solidarity, but also as symbols of agapic resistance, its victims heralded as courageous martyrs. King's theodicy places the lynching tree in even closer relation to the cross than Cone's theodicy will allow, since it would more directly focus on the way in which victims engaged the worst of circumstances to provide a powerful and compelling testimony, even to their murderers. Not their brutalization, but their faithful resistance, displays the hope of salvation. This, I submit, refocuses our attention where it rightly belongs, on the drama of the faith-filled actions of freedom fighters rather than the hate-filled actions of their oppressors.

King's theodicy also calls for self-giving sacrificial engagement with oppression. The evil of violence must be overcome with the good of loving non-violent resistance. This was one of the most distinctive elements of King's theodical engagement with oppression and the one which appeared the most impractical to consistently implement.[43] However, in an increasingly violent world, it can difficult to implement consistently non-violent measures. In a recent article, Rufus Burrow, Jr. wonders about the practicality of a consistently non-violent approach to the epidemic of intra-communal violence among black males. With a transparency and realism reminiscent of Reinhold Niebuhr, Burrow admits,

> Although King understood the need to adapt nonviolence to the specific community, my sense is that unlike what I think the present state of affairs requires, he would insist on thoroughly non-violent means. Remember, Martin Luther King, Jr. believed fundamentally that the universe is constructed such that the world works best when human beings appeal to non-violent means of addressing social problems. Although I believe this in principle, I am not at all certain of its reasonableness in every concrete situation. We humans are too greedy, selfish, and proud; These traits manifest themselves exponentially in our group relations. Such facts make it difficult for me to understand how nonviolence is necessarily the most realistic approach in every situation, especially the borderline situation.[44]

Few scholars know as much about philosophical roots and practical implications of King's theology than Rufus Burrow, Jr. Yet, as he considers the complexities of black-on-black crime today, even he struggled to offer a solution completely consistent with King's theodical vision. He continues,

> Nevertheless we can be sure that because nonviolence was more than a method or strategy for King, there is no circumstance in which he would advocate violence. And yet, though he would be repulsed by any suggestion that young black males who perpetuate violence should be subjected to violence as a means of removing them from the scene, more and more it seems to me that if the black community is to ever get the violence and homicides stopped it may be necessary temporarily to invoke violence against the perpetrators before it will be possible to introduce non-violent methods.[45]

CONCLUSION

Such comments prove exactly how difficult it can be to remain consistently non-violent in the face of persons who appear to only understand the language of violence. Burrow's comments are particularly aimed at what he calls borderline situations, that is, ethical emergencies that are especially beyond the rule of law. The borderline situation raises the question of the practicality and reasonableness of redemptive suffering in extreme ethical emergencies.

However, King's overall philosophy of nonviolence offers sufficient nuances to be effective even in ethical emergencies. For instance, King's non-violent tactics affirmed the proper place of law enforcement in helping to support the aims of redemptive suffering in an ethical crisis in Little Rock, Arkansas, in 1957. On September 25, 1957, King wrote President Eisenhower praising his deployment of 1200 federal troops to Little Rock, Arkansas, to ensure the safe integration of Central High against the threat of mob violence in the area.[46] King noted, "In the long run, justice finally must spring from a new moral climate. Yet spiritual forces cannot emerge in a situation of mob violence."[47] This comment seems to offer some evidence that King believed in the proper role of restraining force in extreme ethical emergencies. Furthermore, this restraining force actually helped further the aims of nonviolence. The very next day, King wrote a letter urging the black citizens of Little Rock to "adhere rigorously to a way of nonviolence at this time." He then encouraged them, saying, "nonviolence is the only way to a lasting solution of the problem. You must meet physical force with soul force." Finally, King offered this theodical word of hope, "If the white mobs of Little Rock choose to be un-Christian and disgraceful in their barbaric acts, you must continue to be Christian and dignified in yours. . . . The moral conscience of millions of white Americans is with you. Keep struggling with this faith and the tragic midnight of anarchy and mob rule which encompasses your city at this time will be transformed into the glowing daybreak of freedom and justice."[48] This demonstrates that King's theodical approach to nonviolence did not preclude the proper use of law enforcement to maintain order. The proper implementation of law enforcement is the means that King would advocate to prepare the way for non-violent methods. So long as this lawful use of force restores the just rule of law and order, it does in fact support the aims of redemptive suffering. This is partly why King pushed for legislative reforms, because the law provided the kinds of protections that set the stage for the moral forces to bring transformation. Part of the beauty of redemptive suffering is that it remains effective in non-ideal circumstances. Even in borderline situations like the epidemic of gang-violence in the black community, King would likely advocate nonviolence with a healthy appreciation for the proper role of law enforcement in helping to create the orderly climate for redemptive suffering to be properly appreciated.

This position raises certain difficulties—especially in the post-Michael Brown, Tamir Rice, Eric Garner era. How might black communities appreciate the "proper" place of law enforcement in helping to protect and promote the dignity of blacks when law enforcement abuses appear to be especially rampant in black and Hispanic communities? In her article, "Black Criminal Stereoptypes and Racial Profiling," Kelly Welch says, "throughout American history, blacks have been consistently stereotyped as criminals." She goes on to explain that since the 1970s the popular caricature of young black males has evolved from petty thief or potential rapist to ominous criminal predator. These widely held perceptions have, in part, led to the general acceptance of discriminatory law enforcement practices such as racial profiling and excessive force against blacks. In light of this, the relationship between the certain police precincts and the black communities they serve is especially strained. In order to help ensure the kinds of orderly conditions King deemed necessary to apply redemptive suffering, I suggest that minimally black communities and churches have open and constructive dialogue with law enforcement agents about these issues with a view toward implementing legislation to address discriminatory police practices.[49]

Principle #4: Cruci-centric Hope

Fourth, King's theodicy calls us to *hope*. King's theodical vision is anchored in the hope that with God's help even the most acute suffering can be redemptively engaged, that agapic love can transform the worst ethical emergencies into a "glowing daybreak of freedom and justice."[50] This message is unique to the church because only the cross and resurrection of Jesus Christ provides the definitive revelation of redemptive suffering. As we have seen, King's ideas about the prevailing power of God and the moral foundations of the universe were also deeply rooted within the Christian faith and black church tradition. Although King welcomed people of varying faiths to join the freedom movement, he unapologetically

CONCLUSION

insisted upon the uniqueness of Jesus Christ and his cross and resurrection as the definitive revelation of agapic love and the hope that love will prove triumphant. For him, the cross is *the* answer to the question of theodicy.[51] Therefore, though King's theodical vision is universal in its scope, it is uniquely cruci-centric in its substance.

In order to fully apply King's theodicy to suffering, the church must *lead* with its foundational beliefs about the cross and resurrection of Jesus Christ and the omnipotent personal God who grounded the very creation with a just moral order and, consistent with that moral order "can make a way out of no way." As King's kitchen experience powerfully illustrates, this hope in God is essential to maintaining a proper commitment to the cause of nonviolence. When King could not summon the strength to carry on in the fight for freedom, he drew upon hope in the God his father preached about during his youth at Ebenezer Baptist Church. King's foundational Christian beliefs guided and empowered his commitment to the cause during his most trying times, and it was this faith that he commended to others as the motivation to continue in the movement.[52] King noted that even Gandhi's commitment to the way of nonviolence was inspired by reading the Sermon on the Mount.[53] Through reading Jesus' words to "turn the other cheek," "resist evil with good," and "blessed are the meek for they shall inherit the earth," King said Gandhi was "inspired to no end."[54] Inspired by the words of Jesus Christ, King says Gandhi fought for Indian independence armed with nothing but the love of God. As we consider the life and theodical legacy of Martin Luther King, we must never forget that he was fundamentally a black Baptist pastor. He took up this vocation because he believed in the transformative power of the gospel and indeed preaching was the form of ministry that occupied the bulk of his time and attention.

The gospel preached in word and sacraments are the most powerful means through which the theodical message of the cross can bring the hope of redemption.[55] As the church seeks to see its neighbors transformed and the beloved community become a reality, it must never forsake or downplay the most fundamental means by which this comes about. By the Spirit of God, the bread and the wine become powerful means by which we are continually sanctified by the hope of redemptive suffering. As the bread is broken and the wine poured, we are transformed by Christ's redemptive suffering that brings us healing and we are spiritually nourished to live in his strength. As we observe the sacrament of baptism, we are renewed by the purifying power of Christ's sacrifice. The sacraments are a kind of divinely ordained redemptive drama, a transformative means by which God renews us with the theodical message of redemptive suffering.

CONCLUSION

This final chapter highlighted the continued relevance of King's redemptive suffering theodicy as a powerful and practical resource for agapic engagement with suffering. King's activities during the Chicago campaign proved that his theodicy had traction beyond the institutional black church of the segregated south. King also contextualized redemptive suffering to meet some of the widespread systemic and cultural challenges of poor blacks in the urban North. Based upon King's theodicy, I offered four practical principles for redemptive engagement with contemporary suffering. As the black community and church seeks to address the suffering in its midst, it must 1) critically and empathetically analyze the systemic and personal dynamics behind oppression in order to guide creative interventions, safeguard against destructive interventions, and promote agapic rather than sentimental reactions to suffering 2) see the indestructible dignity inherent in God's free and responsible image bearers which keeps them from being solely defined by their victimization and emphasizes their responsibility to engage their suffering creatively 3) act creatively, dramatically, and redemptively, to creatively engage oppression in a way that cannot be easily ignored, highlighting the courage of the resisters, rather than merely the sufferings of the oppressed, and 4) hope in God's power through the gospel proclaimed in word and sacrament.

This dissertation has examined the roots and implications of Martin Luther King Jr.'s redemptive suffering theodicy, reconsidering its continued relevance to contemporary discussions of the problem of evil among black theologians and within the black church. I have demonstrated that King's theodicy, a unique synthesis of redemptive suffering themes from the black church tradition and twentieth-century Protestant liberalism, successfully answers black humanist and womanist critiques that accuse it of undermining social liberation and prioritizing concern for evildoers at the expense of concern for victims of injustice. With a view towards the cross and the omnipotent personal God's good purposes in the world,

CONCLUSION

King held that persons have the freedom and responsibility to creatively engage their suffering in order to bring personal and social transformation.

The first three chapters examined the roots of King's theodicy. There, we found that King's formulation represents the apex of a 250-year-old theodical tradition handed down through the black church tradition and figures like David Walker, Alexander Crummel, and W.E.B. Du Bois, who articulated widespread cultural understandings of the black experience in America. King also inherited a tradition of ministerial reflection upon black suffering from his maternal great-grandfather Willis Williams, grandfather A.D. Williams and his father Daddy King, who learned his fundamental theodical outlook from his mother Delia Lindsay King. Under the tutelage of George Kelsey and Benjamin Mays, King learned to critically appropriate the tools of protestant liberalism to the social situation of blacks in America. George Kelsey introduced King to liberalism as an intellectually satisfying and socially relevant framework to enhance the homespun faith he embraced at Ebenezer. However, Kelsey modeled and King accepted a critical approach to liberalism which rejected elements that did not fit with black experience and religious sensibilities. At Crozer and Boston University, King went on to advance a personalist approach to theodicy, engaging and ultimately rejecting Brightman's theistic finitism as out-of-step with his basic theodical outlook. King's view ultimately resembled the absolutism of Borden Bowne and Harold DeWolf—versions of personalism which affirmed divine omnipotence in ways which engender unqualified trust in God's incomprehensible purposes for oppressed people. Therefore King's years at Crozer and Morehouse only served to hone the theodicy that he inherited from his black church and cultural roots. King wrestled with the same basic communal and religious contexts as his modern black humanist and womanist critics. His theodicy is fit to speak to their issues and concerns in their language and engaging their sources.

The final three chapters examined the implications of King's theodicy. First, we discovered that King's theodicy successfully avoids the pitfall of quietism alleged by black humanists William R. Jones and Anthony Pinn. Rather than induce social resignation, King's theodicy summons the oppressed to liberative action through its emphasis on the moral responsibility of free agents to engage suffering with the promise that the omnipotent God works alongside the oppressed to bring about God's redemptive purposes. King's theodicy also resists a similar charge by Womanists Delores Williams and Jacquelyn Grant. While avoiding the language of surrogacy that Williams decries, King's theodicy promotes true liberation for black women through emphasizing a moral influence approach to the cross which calls them to learn from and resist experiences of oppression as empowered moral agents. By identifying them with Christ, King's theodicy also casts black women who suffered while resisting oppression as empowered witnesses, rather than as mere victims. King's theodicy also successfully avoids the servanthood language that Grant decries. Rather than subordinate black women as servants to their oppressor's salvation, King's theodicy calls for serving humanity through helping to create the beloved community in which love, justice, and mutual dignity are realized in practical ways.

This led me to the final chapter in which I offered some of the practical ways King's theodicy guides us going forward, the most important of which is offering the hope held out in the gospel. Through his cross, Christ has revealed the redemptive power of creative suffering, and as we hear the gospel and take the sacraments, we are reminded that we can trust the Lord with our tears. As it thinks about suffering, the church must proclaim the good news that painful circumstances are not accidental or meaningless but meaningful opportunities to serve God and neighbor. In fact, Christian disciples have been called and empowered by God to engage suffering in a redemptive way, looking to Christ and his cross as their chief example in view of the beloved community that he is creating. Therefore, the most effective means the church has of conveying the message of redemptive suffering is through consistently proclaiming the gospel itself and its ethical requirement to love God and neighbor agapically.[56]

NOTES

1. Cheryl A. Kirk-Duggan, *Refiner's Fire: A Religious Engagement with Violence* (Minneapolis, MN: Fortress Press, 2001), 76. Although Kirk-Duggan speaks explicitly about King's non-violent strategy rather than his redemptive suffering theodicy, in her minds the two are essentially connected. Speaking of King's nonviolence, Kirk-Duggan notes, "He tied redemptive suffering to nonviolent direct action, and his "no pain no gain," was no suffering no true liberation. . . . Nonviolence would allow one to exercise the virtues of altruism, civic

CONCLUSION

spirit, and friendliness, which required that one first be open to such a message or have a conversion experience that would create an environment where grace, divine loving activity, and love manifested among humanity might occur." Ibid., 80. Therefore, when Kirk-Duggan criticizes King's non-violent direct action strategy, she is also criticizing the redemptive suffering theodicy which undergirded it.

2. Kirk-Duggan, *Refiner's Fire*, 76.
3. Ibid.
4. Ibid. Delores Williams also mentions some of the dynamics that Cheryl Kirk-Duggan says led King to lose confidence in redemptive suffering as an effective message in the North. She notes, "Today, when the African-American issues are white supremacy, black genocide through drugs, white privilege and the need for a redistribution of economic resources in this country moral suasion as a civil rights strategy is about as effective as a cup of water on a forest fire." Delores Williams, *Sisters in the Wilderness: The Challenge of Womanist God-Talk* (Maryknoll, N.Y.: Orbis Books, 1993), 273–274.
5. Kirk-Duggan, *Refiner's Fire*, 80.
6. Ibid.
7. Ibid., 86.
8. Ibid., 81. Overall, Kirk-Duggan strikes an ambivalent tone towards King's approach. At times, she calls his non-violent approach problematic. Following William R Jones, she wonders whether non-violent direct action remains effective in concrete instances of violence created by violent oppressive systems. Ibid., 81–82. At other times, she admits that King's tactics worked, even conceding that they were a powerful means to halting the violence in East Germany prior to the fall of the Berlin Wall. Cheryl A. Kirk-Duggan, *Misbegotten Anguish: A Theology and Ethics of Violence* (St. Louis, Mo: Chalice Press, 2001), 87.
9. Kirk-Duggan, *Refiner's Fire*, 80.
10. Ibid., 81.
11. Ibid., 77.
12. Kirk-Duggan's chapter on King is very insightful, effectively describing large themes in King's ministry in a short space. However, she makes some sweeping assessments of King's approach that do not hold up under scrutiny. For instance, Kirk-Duggan suggests that King retreated back to the South in order to address race and class issues rather than the socio-economic issues plaguing the North. Ibid., 76. While King did return to the South aware that the same sorts of demonstrations and marches were not as effective in the northern ghettos than the south, this did not amount to a repudiation of redemptive suffering or a shift away from economic issues back to racial issues. Rather, King explicitly looked for ways to apply redemptive suffering to the economic issues that he saw typ-

ified in the North. Stephen B. Oates, *Let the Trumpet Sound: A Life of Martin Luther King, Jr.*, Reprint (New York: Harper Perennial, 1994), 416, 448.

13. Quoted in Oates, *Let the Trumpet Sound*, 414.

14. Ibid., 415. Some critics disagreed, suggesting that the Summit Agreement didn't provide enough concrete practical changes to the hardships blacks faced in the urban ghettos. Ibid., 416.

15. Oates, *Let the Trumpet Sound*, 416.

16. Ibid., 447–448.

17. Ibid., 448.

18. King also maintained that redemptive suffering could address the complex socio-economic injustices that persisted on the global stage. Martin Luther King, Jr., "Nonviolence and Social Change," in *The Trumpet of Conscience* (San Francisco: Harper and Row, 1968), 53–64.

19. Oates, *Let the Trumpet Sound*, 392.

20. Ibid.

21. James Gardner Clark (1922–2007) served as the sheriff of Dallas County, Alabama from 1955 to 1967. Clark was noted for his fierce opposition to the freedom movement. On March 7, 1965, the showdown between Clark and the civil rights workers came to a head when Clark and his men brutally attacked civil rights demonstrators seeking to march from Selma to Montgomery. King viewed Jim Clark's tenure as sheriff as a symbol the racial injustices in Selma. In a 1965 interview for New York Times King noted, "Until Sheriff Clark is removed, the evils of Selma will not be removed." Clark's failed reelection bid as county sheriff to Selma's public safety director marked a significant milestone for the freedom movement in Selma. Quoted in John Herbers, "Dr. King Urges Selma Negroes to Wage a More Militant Drive," *New York Times*, February 18, 1965; Clayborne Carson, Tenisha H. Armstrong, and Susan Englander, *The Martin Luther King, Jr., Encyclopedia*, ed. Susan A. Carson and Erin K. Cook (London: Greenwood Press, 2008), 57–58.

22. Oates, *Let the Trumpet Sound*, 393.

23. According to Kirk-Duggan, the success of King's redemptive suffering message and his non-violent direct action as a civil rights strategy actually depended upon provoking violence. She explains that "violence played a part in King's non-violent strategy as his main triumphs happened when protestors experienced violent reactions, which generated public support. Ironically, the strategy often failed when the threat of violence was not apparent." Kirk-Duggan, *Refiner's Fire*, 78. This may reflect a misunderstanding of King's approach. King's strategy did not depend upon provoking violence. It depended upon effectively unmasking the latent violence and suffering that was already present.

24. Oates, *Let the Trumpet Sound*, 448.

25. Rufus Burrow, Jr., "What Martin Might Say about Intracommunity Violence and Homicide among Young African American Males: An Extreme Emergency," in *The Domestication of Martin Luther King Jr.: Clarence B. Jones, Right-Wing Conservatism, and the Manipulation of the King Legacy* (Cascade Books, 2013), 271.

26. Cornel West, "The Crisis in Contemporary American Religion," in *The Cornel West Reader*, (New York, NY: Basic Civitas Books, 2000), 358.

27. John M. Perkins, *With Justice for All: A Strategy for Community Development*, Revised Edition (Grand Rapids: Baker Books, 2011), 60.

28. Christian Community Development Association, "Relocation," accessed February 9, 2015, http://www.ccda.org/about/ccd-philosophy/relocation.

29. Julie Bosman, Monica Davey, and Mitch Smith, "As Water Problems Grew, Officials Belittled Complaints from Flint," *New York Times*, January 20, 2016.

30. Garth Baker-Fletcher, *Somebodyness: Martin Luther King, Jr. and the Theory of Dignity* (Minneapolis: Fortress Press, 1993), 166–167.

31. Kelly Welch, "Black Criminal Stereotypes and Racial Profiling," *Journal of Contemporary Criminal Justice* 23, no. 3 (August 1, 2007): 276–277; William J. Drummond, "About Face: From Alliance to Alienation. Blacks and the News Media," *The American Enterprise* 1, no. 4 (January 1990): 22–29.

32. King's non-violent direct action would be particularly helpful in guiding responses to the deaths of Trayvon Martin and Michael Brown. Some Black responses have fallen into the categories of passivity or violence. However, the majority response has been in keeping with the redemptive suffering tradition that stands in line with King. The "Black Lives Matter" and "Hands Up United" campaigns are interesting examples of this.

33. This point often goes underappreciated by critics of redemptive suffering. For instance, William Jones described two phases in King's protest tactics. He suggests that "if rational and moral persuasion fails, then the non-violent resister shifts gears to a radically different level of activity." He maintains that this second phase of non-violent protest involves using masses of people to cripple the processes of unjust institutions. Jones continues "In phase 2 the goal is to force the oppressor to admit that his resources are inadequate to maintain his unjust institutions and repressive practices. Here the concern is to create an inexorable pressure that forces the oppressor to acknowledge his impotence—not his irrationality of immorality." While Jones rightly notes that mass protests were aimed at creating economic pressure, he wrongly assumes that this phase of King's protest ministry was not also aimed at moral persuasion. William R. Jones, "Liberation Strategies in Black Theology: Mao, Martin, or Malcolm?" *The Chicago Theological Seminary Register* 73 (Winter 1983): 43.

34. King often anticipated the presence of immediate violence in order to dramatize the injustices and suffering that was already latent in an oppressive situation. Sometimes, anticipating their strategy, law enforcement agents refrained from immediate violence precisely so that they could avoid the exposure that this drama would bring to the daily brutality of segregation. Even the proponents of segregation recognized the exposing power of dramatizing suffering.

35. Frank James, "Martin Luther King Jr. in Chicago," *Chicago Tribune*, accessed February 10, 2015, http://www.chicagotribune.com/news/nationworld/politics/chi-chicagodays-martinlutherking-story-story.html.

36. West, "The Crisis in Contemporary American Religion," 294; Cornel West and Christa Buschendorf, *Black Prophetic Fire* (Boston: Beacon Press, 2014), 66; James H. Cone, "The Vocation of a Black Intellectual," in *Cornel West: A Critical Reader*, ed. George Yancy, First edition (Malden, Mass: Wiley-Blackwell, 2001), 108.

37. James H. Cone, *The Spirituals and the Blues: An Interpretation*, Second ed. (Maryknoll: Seabury Press, 1972), 62.

38. This does not mean that James Cone completely subscribes to a Kingian version of redemptive suffering. First, Cone admits that after encountering Reinhold Niebuhr's Christian realism, he lost confidence that moral suasion was sufficient to achieve justice in a racist society. According to Cone, the demands of black power were also necessary. James H. Cone, *The Cross and the Lynching Tree* (Maryknoll: Orbis Books, 2011), 55. Although he has confidence in the persuasive power of redemption to a point, he does not hold to it consistently in a Kingian way. Additionally, Cone notes that he was hesitant to accept any belief that ascribed positive value to suffering. However, as we have seen, King never actually ascribed positive value to suffering *per se*. Instead, he ascribed positive value to redemptive engagement with suffering.

39. Ibid., 166.

40. Ibid., 154.

41. James H. Cone, "Introduction," in *The Cross and the Lynching Tree*, Reprint edition (Maryknoll, N.Y.: Orbis Books, 2013), xiii.

42. Cone does mention Charles Johnston who powerfully preached his own funeral sermon, calling for the crowd to kneel, pray, and sing before they hanged him. Cone, *The Cross and the Lynching Tree*, 26. King Scholar Lewis Baldwin alerted me about this oversight in Cone's book during a personal conversation.

43. Jones, "Liberation Strategies in Black Theology: Mao, Martin, or Malcolm?" 44–45. For instance, William R. Jones complains that King's approach is impractical because does not account for individuals whose hearts are completely calloused to black suffering. He concedes that redemptive suffering could work if the conditions were right. However, he insists that in a racist society, blacks are dehumanized beyond the point of white empathy. This, he says, makes

black suffering all too sufferable and therefore ineffective at compelling redemptive transformation.

44. Burrow, Jr., "What Martin Might Say about Intracommunity Violence and Homicide among Young African American Males: An Extreme Emergency," 273–274. Borderline situations are extraordinary circumstances beyond the regulation of law; they are ethical emergencies that require "extreme measures," to rectify, for the oppressed to do wrong "in order to eradicate or prevent a graver wrong." Ibid., 267. I am unsure whether King would admit there is ever a circumstance where justice requires ethical wrongdoing. As I go on to assert, I think he would recognize the need for restraining force in such circumstances. As long as this restraint was administered wisely and justly, I don't think King would call such force unethical.

45. Burrow, Jr., "What Martin Might Say about Intracommunity Violence and Homicide among Young African American Males: An Extreme Emergency," 267.

46. Strictly speaking, the situation in Little Rock was an ethical emergency, rather than a borderline situation. President Eisenhower's decision was fairly straightforward and federal troops were easily able to bring order to the situation. By definition, borderline situations are beyond the rule of law.

47. Martin Luther King, Jr., "To Dwight D. Eisenhower," in *The Papers of Martin Luther King, Jr., Volume IV: Symbol of the Movement, January 1957–December 1958*, ed. Clayborne Carson et al., 2nd Ed edition (Berkeley: University of California Press, 2000), 278.

48. Martin Luther King, Jr., "Dr. King Asks Non-Violence in Little Rock School Crisis," in *The Papers of Martin Luther King, Jr., Volume IV: Symbol of the Movement, January 1957–December 1958*, ed. Clayborne Carson et al., 2nd Ed edition (Berkeley: University of California Press, 2000), 279.

49. Welch, "Black Criminal Stereotypes and Racial Profiling," 276.

50. Ibid.

51. Martin Luther King, Jr., "Religion's Answer to the Problem of Evil," in *The Papers of Martin Luther King, Jr.: Volume I: Called to Serve, January 1929–June 1951*, First, vol. 1, The Papers of Martin Luther King, Jr. (Berkeley: University of California Press, 1992), 432–433.

52. Martin Luther King, Jr., "Palm Sunday Sermon on Mohandas K. Ghandi," in *The Papers of Martin Luther King, Jr.: Volume V: Threshold of a New Decade: January 1959–December 1960*, ed. Tenisha Armstrong and Clayborne Carson (Berkeley, California: University of California Press, 2005), 148–149.

53. Matthew 5–7.

54. King, Jr., "Palm Sunday Sermon on Mohandas K. Ghandi," 149.

55. Heidelberg Catechism Q&A 66 beautifully captures this sentiment. "Q. What are sacraments? A. Sacraments are visible, holy signs and seals. They were

instituted by God so that by our use of them he might make us understand more clearly the promise of the gospel, and seal that promise. And this is God's gospel promise: to grant us forgiveness of sins and eternal life by grace because of Christ's one sacrifice accomplished on the cross."

56. Rufus Burrow Jr, *Extremist for Love: Martin Luther King Jr., Man of Ideas and Nonviolent Social Action* (Minneapolis: Fortress Press, 2014), 223.

BIBLIOGRAPHY

"America's Gandhi: Rev. Martin Luther King Jr." *Time*, January 3, 1964.
Anderson, Paul N. "The Suffering Servant of Isaiah in Cognitive Critical Perspective: Logotherapy and the Bible." In *Psychological Hermeneutics for Biblical Themes and Texts: A Festschrift in Honour of Wayne G. Rollins*, edited by Harold J. Ellens. New York: T&T Clark International, 2012.
Anderson, Victor. "Faith on Earth." In *Creative Exchange: A Constructive Theology of African American Religious Experience*. Minneapolis: Fortress Press, 2008.
Ansbro, John J. *Martin Luther King, Jr.: The Making of a Mind*. Maryknoll, N.Y.: Orbis Books, 1984.
Atlanta Chamber of Commerce. *Annual Report*. Atlanta, 1907.
Baker-Fletcher, Garth. *Somebodyness: Martin Luther King, Jr. and the Theory of Dignity*. Minneapolis: Fortress Press, 1993.
Baker-Fletcher, Karen, and Garth Baker-Fletcher. *My Sister, My Brother: Womanist and Xodus God Talk*. Maryknoll: Orbis, 1997.
Baldwin, Lewis V. "Family, Church, and the Black Experience: The Shaping of Martin Luther King, Jr." *AME Zion Quarterly Review*, January 1978, 2–10.
———. "Martin Luther King, Jr, the Black Church, and the Black Messianic Vision." *Journal of the Interdenominational Theological Center* 12, no. 1–2 (1985): 93–108.
———. *Never to Leave Us Alone: The Prayer Life of Martin Luther King, Jr.* Minneapolis, MN: Fortress Press, 2010.
———. "Revisioning the Church: Martin Luther King, Jr. as a Model for Reflection." *Theology Today* 65, no. 1 (April 1, 2008): 26–40.
———. *There Is a Balm in Gilead: The Cultural Roots of Martin Luther King, Jr.* Minneapolis: Fortress Press, 1991.
———. *The Voice of Conscience: The Church in the Mind of Martin Luther King, Jr.* Oxford: Oxford University Press, 2010.
———. *To Make the Wounded Whole*. Minneapolis: Fortress Press, 1992.
———. "Understanding Martin Luther King, Jr. within the Context of Southern Black Religious History." *Journal of Religious Studies* 13, no. 2 (1987): 1–26.
Baldwin, Lewis V., and Amiri YaSin Al-Hadid. *Between Cross and Crescent: Christian and Muslim Perspectives on Malcolm and Martin*. Gainesville: University Press of Florida, 2002.
Bauerlein, Mark. *Negrophobia: A Race Riot in Atlanta, 1906*. San Francisco: Encounter Books, 2002.
Bridges, Hal. *American Mysticism, From William James to Zen*. New York: Harper and Row, 1970.

Brightman, Edgar S. *A Philosophy of Religion*. Reprint. Westport: Greenwood Press, 1940.
———. "The Essence of Christianity." *Crozer Quarterly* 18 (April 1941).
———. *The Finding of God*. New York: The Abingdon Press, 1931.
———. "The Given and Its Critics." *Religion in Life* 1, no. 1 (December 1, 1932): 134–45.
———. *The Problem of God*. New York: Abingdon Press, 1930.
Brown, Joanne Carlson, and Carole R. Bohn, eds. *Christianity, Patriarchy, and Abuse: A Feminist Critique*. New York: Pilgrim Press, 1989.
Brown, Joanne Carlson, and Rebecca Parker. "For God So Loved the World?" In *Christianity, Patriarchy, and Abuse: A Feminist Critique*, edited by Joanne Carlson Brown and Carole R. Bohn. Pilgrim Press, 1989.
Broyles, Craig C., and Craig A. Evans. *Writing and Reading the Scroll of Isaiah: Studies of an Intepretive Tradition*. Brill, 1997.
Bryant, William Cullen. "The Battle-Field." In *Yale Book of American Verse*, edited by Thomas Raynesford Lounsbury. New Haven: Yale University Press, 1912.
Burns, Stewart. *To the Mountaintop: Martin Luther King Jr.'s Mission to Save America: 1955–1968*. Reprint. HarperOne, 2005.
Burrow, Jr., Rufus. "Afrikan American Contributions to Personalism." *Encounter* 60, no. 2 (March 1, 1999): 145–67.
———. "Comments on Edmondson Dissertation Chapter 5," March 2014.
———. *Extremist for Love: Martin Luther King Jr., Man of Ideas and Nonviolent Social Action*. Minneapolis: Fortress Press, 2014.
———. *God and Human Dignity: The Personalism, Theology, and Ethics of Martin Luther King, Jr.* Notre Dame: University of Notre Dame Press, 2006.
———. *God and Human Responsibility: David Walker and Ethical Prophecy*. First Edition. Macon, Ga: Mercer University Press, 2004.
———. *Martin Luther King, Jr. for Armchair Theologians*. Louisville: Westminster John Knox Press, 2009.
———. *Personalism: A Critical Introduction*. St. Louis, Mo.: Chalice Press, 1999.
———. "Personalism and Afrikan Traditional Thought." *Encounter* 61, no. 3 (June 1, 2000): 321–48.
———. "Personalism, the Objective Moral Order, and Moral Law in the Work of Martin Luther King, Jr." In *The Legacy of Martin Luther King, Jr.: The Boundaries of Law, Politics, and Religion*, edited by Lewis V Baldwin. Notre Dame, IN: University of Notre Dame Press, 2002.
———. "The Beloved Community: Martin Luther King, Jr., and Josiah Royce." *Encounter* 73, no. 1 (Fall 2012): 37–64.
———. "The Doctrine of Unearned Suffering." *Encounter* 63, no. 1–2 (December 1, 2002): 65–76.
———. "The Personalistic Theism of Edgar S Brightman." *Encounter* 53, no. 2 (March 1, 1992): 165–82.
———. "What Martin Might Say about Intracommunity Violence and Homicide among Young African American Males: An Extreme Emergency." In *The Domestication of Martin Luther King Jr.: Clarence B. Jones, Right-Wing Conservatism, and the Manipulation of the King Legacy*. Cascade Books, 2013.
Camus, Albert. *The Plague*. Translated by Stuart Gilbert. New York: Vintage Books, 1991.
———. *The Rebel: An Essay on Man in Revolt*. Translated by Alfred A. Knopf. New York: Vintage Books, 1991.
Cannon, Katie G. *Black Womanist Ethics*. Eugene, OR: Wipf & Stock, 2006.
Carlyle, Thomas. *The French Revolution: A History*. The Modern Library, 1934.
Carson, Clayborne. "Introduction." In *The Papers of Martin Luther King, Jr.: Volume I: Called to Serve, January 1929–June 1951*, First Edition., 1:359–63. The Papers of Martin Luther King, Jr. Berkeley: University of California Press, 1992.
———. "Introduction." In *The Papers of Martin Luther King, Jr.: Volume 2: Rediscovering Precious Values July 1951–November 1955*, edited by Peter Holloran, Ralph Luker, and Penny A Russell, Vol. 2. Berkeley: University of California Press, 1992.

BIBLIOGRAPHY

Carson, Clayborne, Tenisha H. Armstrong, and Susan Englander. *The Martin Luther King, Jr., Encyclopedia*. Edited by Susan A. Carson and Erin K. Cook. London: Greenwood Press, 2008.
Carter, Harold A. *The Prayer Tradition of Black People*. Reprint. Valley Forge, PA: Judson Press, 2002.
Christian Community Development Association. "Relocation." Accessed February 9, 2015. http://www.ccda.org/about/ccd-philosophy/relocation.
Chung, Hyun Kyung. *Struggle to Be the Sun Again: Introducing Asian Women's Theology*. Maryknoll, N.Y: Orbis Books, 1990.
Cone, James H. "Introduction." In *The Cross and the Lynching Tree*, Reprint edition. Maryknoll, N.Y.: Orbis Books, 2013.
———. "Martin Luther King, Jr, Black Theology-Black Church." *Theology Today* 40, no. 4 (January 1, 1984): 409–20.
———. "Martin Luther King, Jr : Sixty-Fifth Anniversary Overview and Assessment." *Journal of the Interdenominational Theological Center* 21, no. 1–2 (September 1, 1993): 1–9.
———. "Martin Luther King : The Source for His Courage to Face Death." In *Martyrdom Today*, 74–79. New York, NY: Seabury Press, 1983.
———. *Martin & Malcolm & America: A Dream or a Nightmare*. Maryknoll: Orbis, 2001.
———. *The Cross and the Lynching Tree*. Maryknoll: Orbis Books, 2011.
———. *The Spirituals and the Blues: An Interpretation*. 2nd ed. Maryknoll: Seabury Press, 1972.
———. "The Theology of Martin Luther King, Jr." *Union Seminary Quarterly Review* 40, no. 4 (1986): 21–39.
———. "The Vocation of a Black Intellectual." In *Cornel West: A Critical Reader*, edited by George Yancy, First Edition. Malden, Mass: Wiley-Blackwell, 2001.
Courlander, Harold. *Negro Folk Music U.S.A.* New York: Dover, 1992.
Crummell, Alexander. "Hope for Africa." In *The Future of Africa: Being Addresses, Sermons, Etc., Etc., Delivered in the Republic of Liberia*. 1862: Charles Scribner, 1862.
———. "The Destined Superiority of the Negro." In *The Greatness of Christ: And Other Sermons*. New York: Thomas Whittaker, 1882.
Davis, George Washington. "God and History." *The Crozer Quarterly* 20, no. 1 (January 1943).
———. "Some Theological Continuities in the Crisis Theology." *Crozer Quarterly* 27, no. 3 (July 1946).
DeWolf, L. Harold. *Theology of the Living Church*. Revised Edition. New York: Harper and Row, 1953.
Drummond, William J. "About Face: From Alliance to Alienation. Blacks and the News Media." *The American Enterprise* 1, no. 4 (January 1990): 22–29.
Du Bois, W. E. B. "Of Alexander Crummell." In *The Souls of Black Folk*. CreateSpace Independent Publishing Platform, 2013.
———. "Of the Dawn of Freedom." In *The Souls of Black Folk*. New York: Dover, 1994.
———. *The Conservation of Races*. Washington, D.C.: American Negro Academy, 1897.
———. *The Negro*. New York: Oxford University Press, 1970.
———. "The Souls of Black Folk." In *Three Negro Classics*, edited by John Hope Franklin. New York: Avon Books, 1965.
Ellington, G.S. "A Short Sketch of the Life and Work of Rev. A.D. Williams of Ebenezer Baptist Church." In *Programme of the Thirtieth Anniversary of the Pastorate of Rev. A.D. Williams of Ebenezer Baptist Church*. Atlanta, 1924.
"Face to Face: John Freeman of B.B.C. Interviews Martin Luther King, Jr." UK, London: BBC, October 29, 1961. The Archives of Martin Luther King, Jr., Center for Nonviolent Social Change, Inc., Atlanta, GA.
Farris, Christine King. "The Young Martin: From Childhood Through College." *Ebony*, January 1986.
———. *Through It All: Reflections on My Life, My Family, and My Faith*. First. New York: Atria Books, 2010.
Fluker, Walter E. *They Looked for a City*. University Press of America, 1989.

Frank James. "Martin Luther King Jr. in Chicago." *Chicago Tribune.* Accessed February 10, 2015. http://www.chicagotribune.com/news/nationworld/politics/chi-chicagodays-martinlutherking-story-story.html.

Frazier, E. Franklin. *The Negro Family in the United States.* Chicago: The University of Chicago Press, 1968.

Gandhi, M.K. *Non-Violent Resistance (Satyagraha).* Mineola, NY: Dover, 2001.

Garrow, David J. *Bearing the Cross: Martin Luther King, Jr., and the Southern Christian Leadership Conference.* New York: Perennial Classics, 2004.

Gilbert, Olive. *Narrative of Sojourner Truth.* New York: Arno Press, 1968.

Grant, Jacquelyn. "The Sin of Servanthood." In *A Troubling in My Soul: Womanist Perspectives on Evil and Suffering,* edited by Emilie Maureen Townes. Maryknoll, NY: Orbis Books, 1993.

Guth, Karen V. "Reconstructing Nonviolence: The Political Theology of Martin Luther King Jr. after Feminism and Womanism." *Journal of the Society of Christian Ethics* 32, no. 1 (March 1, 2012): 75–92.

Heraclitus. "Heraclitus." In *The Presocratics,* edited by Philip Ellis Wheelwright. New York: The Odyssey Press, 1966.

Herbers, John. "Dr. King Urges Selma Negroes to Wage a More Militant Drive." *New York Times,* February 18, 1965.

Hocking, William E. *The Meaning of God in Human Experience.* New Haven: Yale University Press, 1912.

Hopkins, Dwight N. "Why Lord?: Suffering and Evil in Black Theology." *African American Review* 31, no. 3 (1997): 514. doi:10.2307/3042581.

Hume, David. "Concerning Natural Religion." In *The English Philosophers from Bacon to Hill,* edited by Edwin A. Burtt. New York: Random House, 1967.

Johnson, James Weldon, and J. Rosamond Johnson, eds. *The Books of the American Negro Spirituals.* New York: Da Capo Press, 2002.

Jones, E. Stanley. *Mahatma Gandhi: An Interpretation.* New York: Abington-Cokesbury Press, 1948.

Jones, William R. *Is God a White Racist?: A Preamble to Black Theology.* Garden City, NY: Doubleday, 1973.

———. "Liberation Strategies in Black Theology: Mao, Martin, or Malcolm?" *The Chicago Theological Seminary Register* 73 (Winter 1983): 38–48.

Kane, Brian M. "The Influence of Boston Personalism on the Thought of Dr. Martin Luther King, Jr." Thesis (M.T.S.), Boston University, 1985.

Kelsey, George D. "Protestantism and Democratic Intergroup Living." *Phylon* 8, no. 1 (1947): 77.

———. *Racism and the Christian Understanding of Man.* First Edition. New York: Scribner, 1965.

King: A Filmed Record . . . from Montgomery to Memphis. New York: Kino Lorber, 2013.

King, Coretta Scott. *My Life with Martin Luther King, Jr.* Revised. New York: Puffin, 1994.

King, Jr., Martin Luther. "A Christmas Sermon on Peace." In *A Testament of Hope: The Essential Writings and Speeches of Martin Luther King, Jr.*, edited by James M. Washington, Reprint edition. San Francisco: HarperOne, 2003.

———. "A Comparison and Evaluation of the Philosophical Views Set Forth in J.M.E. McTaggart's *Some Dogmas of Religion,* and William E. Hocking's *The Meaning of God in Human Experience* with Those Set Forth in Edgar Brightman's Course on 'Philosophy of Religion.'" In *The Papers of Martin Luther King, Jr.: Volume 2: Rediscovering Precious Values July 1951–November 1955,* edited by Clayborne Carson, Peter Holloran, Ralph Luker, and Penny A Russell. Berkeley: University of California Press, 1992.

———. "A Comparison of The Conception of God in the Thinking of Henry Nelson Wieman and Paul Tillich." In *The Papers of Martin Luther King, Jr.: Volume 2: Rediscovering Precious Values July 1951–November 1955.* Berkeley, California: University of California Press, 1992.

———. "A Comparison of the Theology of Luther with that of Calvin." In *The Papers of Martin Luther King, Jr. Volume II: Rediscovering Precious Values July 1951–November*

BIBLIOGRAPHY

1955, edited by Peter H. Holloran and Clayborne Carson. Berkeley: University of California Press, 1994.

———. "A Conception and Impression of Religion Drawn from Dr. Brightman's Book Entitled A Philosophy of Religion." In *The Papers of Martin Luther King, Jr.: Volume I: Called to Serve, January 1929–June 1951*, edited by Clayborne Carson, Ralph Luker, and Penny A Russell. Berkeley, California: University of California Press, 1992.

———. "Address to the Initial Mass Meeting of the Montgomery Improvement Association," December 5, 1955. The King Center Archives.

———. *A Knock at Midnight*. Mt. Zion Baptist Church, Cincinnati: Nashboro, n.d.

———. "A Knock at Midnight (1958)." In *The Papers of Martin Luther King, Jr.: Volume VI: Advocate of the Social Gospel, September 1948–March 1963*, edited by Clayborne Carson and Susan Carson. Berkeley: University of California Press, 2007.

———. "An Autobiography of Religious Development." In *The Papers of Martin Luther King, Jr.: Volume I: Called to Serve, January 1929–June 1951*, First Edition., 1:359–63. The Papers of Martin Luther King, Jr. Berkeley: University of California Press, 1992.

———. "An Experiment in Love." In *A Testament of Hope: The Essential Writings and Speeches of Martin Luther King, Jr.*, edited by James M. Washington, Reprint edition. San Francisco: HarperOne, 2003.

———. "Application for Admission to Crozer Theological Seminary." In *The Papers of Martin Luther King, Jr.: Volume I: Called to Serve, January 1929–June 1951*, edited by Clayborne Carson and Ralph E. Luker. Berkeley, California: University of California Press, 1992.

———. "A Prayer for Chicago." *Chicago Defender*. April 16, 1966.

———. *A Testament of Hope: The Essential Writings and Speeches of Martin Luther King, Jr.* Edited by James Melvin Washington. San Francisco: Harper SanFrancisco, 1991.

———. "A View of the Cross Possessing Biblical and Spiritual Justification." In *The Papers of Martin Luther King, Jr.: Volume I: Called to Serve, January 1929–June 1951*, edited by Clayborne Carson, Ralph Luker, and Penny A Russell. Berkeley, California: University of California Press, 1992.

———. "Contemporary Continental Theology." In *The Papers of Martin Luther King, Jr.: Rediscovering Precious Values, July 1951–1955*, edited by Clayborne Carson, Peter Holloran, Ralph Luker, and Penny A Russell, Vol. 2. Berkeley: University of California Press, 1992.

———. "Dr. King Asks Non-Violence in Little Rock School Crisis." In *The Papers of Martin Luther King, Jr., Volume IV: Symbol of the Movement, January 1957–December 1958*, edited by Clayborne Carson, Susan Carson, Adrienne Clay, Virginia Shadron, and Kieran Taylor, Second edition. Berkeley: University of California Press, 2000.

———. "Eulogy for the Martyred Children." In *A Testament of Hope: The Essential Writings and Speeches of Martin Luther King, Jr.* New York, NY: HarperCollins, 1991.

———. "Facing the Challenge of a New Age." In *The Papers of Martin Luther King, Jr.:Birth of a New Age, December 1955-December 1956*, edited by Carson Clayborne, Stewart Burns, Susan Carson, Peter Holloran, and Dana Powell. Berkeley, California: University of California Press, 1997.

———. "Final Examination Answers, Personalism." In *The Papers of Martin Luther King, Jr.: Volume 2: Rediscovering Precious Values July 1951–November 1955*, edited by Clayborne Carson, Peter Holloran, Ralph Luker, and Penny A Russell. Berkeley: University of California Press, 1992.

———. "Final Examination Answers, Philosophy of Religion." In *The Papers of Martin Luther King, Jr.: Volume 2: Rediscovering Precious Values July 1951–November 1955*, edited by Clayborne Carson, Peter Holloran, Ralph Luker, and Penny A Russell. Berkeley: University of California Press, 1992.

———. "Final Examination Answers, Philosophy of Religion." In *The Papers of Martin Luther King, Jr.: Rediscovering Precious Values July 1951-November 1955*, edited by Clayborne Carson and Peter H. Holloran. Berkeley: University of California Press, 1994.

———. "Final Examination Answers, Religious Teachings of the Old Testament." In *The Papers of Martin Luther King Jr., Rediscovering Precious Values: July 1951–November*

1955, edited by Clayborne Carson and Ralph E Luker. Berkeley, California: University of California Press, 1994.

———. "Honoring Dr. Du Bois." *Freedomways* 8, no. 2 (Spring 1968).

———. "How Believe in a Good God in the Midst of Glaring Evil." In *The Papers of Martin Luther King, Jr.: Volume VI: Advocate of the Social Gospel, September 1948–March 1963*, edited by Susan Englander and Troy Jackson, First Edition. University of California Press, 2007.

———. "How Modern Christians Should Think of Man." In *The Papers of Martin Luther King, Jr.: Volume I: Called to Serve, January 1929–June 1951*, First Edition., 1:359–63. The Papers of Martin Luther King, Jr. Berkeley: University of California Press, 1992.

———. "I Have a Dream (1963)." In *A Testament of Hope: The Essential Writings and Speeches of Martin Luther King, Jr.* San Francisco: Harper SanFrancisco, 1991.

———. "Interview on World Peace." *Redbook Magazine*, November 1964.

———. "Karl Barth." In *The Papers of Martin Luther King, Jr.: Volume VI: Advocate of the Social Gospel, September 1948–March 1963*, edited by Susan Englander and Troy Jackson, First Edition. Berkeley: University of California Press, 2007.

———. "Karl Barth's Conception of God." In *The Papers of Martin Luther King, Jr.: Volume 2: Rediscovering Precious Values July 1951–November 1955*, edited by Clayborne Carson, Penny A Russell, Peter Holloran, and Ralph Luker. Berkeley: University of California Press, 1992.

———. "Looking Beyond Your Circumstances." In *The Papers of Martin Luther King, Jr.: Volume VI: Advocate of the Social Gospel, September 1948–March 1963*, edited by Susan Englander and Troy Jackson, First Edition. Berkeley: University of California Press, 2007.

———. "Love in Action." In *The Papers of Martin Luther King, Jr.: Volume VI: Advocate of the Social Gospel, September 1948–March 1963*, edited by Clayborne Carson, Peter Holloran, Ralph Luker, and Penny A Russell. Berkeley, California: University of California Press, 1992.

———. "Love, Law, and Civil Disobedience." In *A Testament of Hope: The Essential Writings and Speeches of Martin Luther King, Jr.*, edited by James M. Washington. San Francisco: Harper and Row, 1986.

———. "Loving Your Enemies." In *A Knock at Midnight: Inspiration from the Great Sermons of Reverend Martin Luther King, Jr.*, edited by Clayborne Carson and Peter Holloran. New York: Warner Books, 1998.

———. "My Call to the Ministry." In *The Papers of Martin Luther King, Jr.: Vol. VI: Advocate of the Social Gospel: September 1948 - March 1963*, edited by Clayborne Carson and Susan Carson. Berkeley: University of California Press, 2007.

———. "Nonviolence and Social Change." In *The Trumpet of Conscience*. San Francisco: Harper and Row, 1968.

———. "On Being a Good Neighbor." In *The Papers of Martin Luther King, Jr., Volume VI: Advocate of the Social Gospel, September 1948–March 1963*, edited by Clayborne Carson, Susan Englander, Tenisha Armstrong, Troy Jackson, and Gerald L. Smith. Berkeley: University of California Press, 2007.

———. "Our God Is Able." In *Strength to Love*. New York: Harper and Row, 1963.

———. "Our God Is Able." In *The Papers of Martin Luther King, Jr.: Volume VI: Advocate of the Social Gospel, September 1948–March 1963*, edited by Susan Englander and Troy Jackson, First Edition. Berkeley: University of California Press, 2007.

———. "Palm Sunday Sermon on Mohandas K. Ghandi." In *The Papers of Martin Luther King, Jr.: Volume V: Threshold of a New Decade: January 1959–December 1960*, edited by Tenisha Armstrong and Clayborne Carson. Berkeley, California: University of California Press, 2005.

———. "Pilgrimage to Nonviolence." In *Stride Toward Freedom: The Montgomery Story*. San Francisco: HarperCollins, 1987.

———. "Playboy Interview With Martin Luther King, Jr." In *A Testament of Hope: The Essential Writings and Speeches of Martin Luther King, Jr.* New York, NY: HarperCollins, 1991.

———. "Preaching Ministry." In *The Papers of Martin Luther King, Jr.: Volume VI: Advocate of the Social Gospel, September 1948–March 1963*, edited by Susan Englander and Troy Jackson, First Edition. Berkeley: University of California Press, 2007.

———. "Qualifying Examination Answers: Theology of the Bible." In *The Papers of Martin Luther King, Jr.: Volume 2: Rediscovering Precious Values July 1951–November 1955*, edited by Clayborne Carson, Peter Holloran, Ralph Luker, and Penny A Russell. Berkeley: University of California Press, 1992.

———. "Questions That Easter Answers." In *The Papers of Martin Luther King, Jr.: Vol. VI: Advocate of the Social Gospel: September 1948–March 1963*, edited by Clayborne Carson, Peter Holloran, Ralph Luker, and Penny A Russell. Berkeley, California: University of California Press, 1992.

———. "Rediscovering Lost Values." In *A Knock at Midnight: Inspiration from the Great Sermons of Reverend Martin Luther King, Jr.*, edited by Clayborne Carson and Peter Holloran. New York: Warner Books, 1998.

———. "Religion's Answer to the Problem of Evil." In *The Papers of Martin Luther King, Jr.: Volume I: Called to Serve, January 1929–June 1951*, First., 1:416–32. The Papers of Martin Luther King, Jr. Berkeley: University of California Press, 1992.

———. "Remaining Awake Through a Great Revolution." In *A Testament of Hope: The Essential Writings and Speeches of Martin Luther King, Jr.*, edited by James M. Washington, Reprint. HarperOne, 1990.

———. "Ritual." In *The Papers of Martin Luther King, Jr.: Volume I: Called to Serve, January 1929–June 1951*, edited by Clayborne Carson and Ralph E. Luker, Vol. 1. Berkeley, California: University of California Press, 1992.

———. "Shattered Dreams." In *The Papers of Martin Luther King, Jr., Volume VI: Advocate of the Social Gospel, September 1948–March 1963*, edited by Clayborne Carson, Susan Englander, Tenisha Armstrong, Troy Jackson, and Gerald L. Smith. Berkeley: University of California Press, 2007.

———. "Some Things We Must Do." In *The Papers of Martin Luther King, Jr.: Symbol of the Movement January 1957–December 1958*, edited by Carson Clayborne, Susan Carson, Adrienne Clay, Virginia Shadron, and Kieran Taylor. Berkeley: University of California Press, 2000.

———. "Statement to the Press Regarding Nobel Trip," December 4, 1964. The Archives of Martin Luther King, Jr., Center for Nonviolent Social Change, Inc., Atlanta, GA.

———. *Strength to Love*. New York: Harper and Row, 1963.

———. "Strength to Love." In *The Papers of Martin Luther King, Jr., Volume VI: Advocate of the Social Gospel, September 1948–March 1963*, edited by Tenisha Hart Armstrong, Clayborne Carson, Susan Englander, Susan Carson, Troy Jackson, and Gerald L. Smith, First edition. Berkeley: University of California Press, 2007.

———. *Stride Toward Freedom: The Montgomery Story*. Harpercollins, 1987.

———. "Suffering and Faith." *Christian Century* 101, no. 77 (April 1960): 510.

———. "The Answer to a Perplexing Question." In *The Papers of Martin Luther King, Jr., Volume VI: Advocate of the Social Gospel, September 1948–March 1963*, edited by Clayborne Carson, Gerald L. Smith, and Tenisha Armstrong. Berkeley: University of California Press, 2007.

———. "The Death of Evil upon the Seashore." In *The Papers of Martin Luther King, Jr.: Volume III: Birth of a New Age, December 1955–December 1956*, edited by Clayborne Carson, Stewart Burns, and Peter Holloran. Berkeley: University of California Press, 1997.

———. "The Death of Evil upon the Seashore." In *The Papers of Martin Luther King, Jr.: Volume VI: Advocate of the Social Gospel, September 1948–March 1963*, edited by Clayborne Carson, Susan Englander, and Troy Jackson. University of California Press, 2007.

———. "The Ethical Demands for Integration." In *A Testament of Hope: The Essential Writings and Speeches of Martin Luther King, Jr.*, edited by James M. Washington, Reprint edition. San Francisco: HarperOne, 2003.

———. "The Ethics of Late Judaism as Evidenced in the Testaments of the Twelve Patriarchs." In *The Papers of Martin Luther King, Jr.: Volume I: Called to Serve, January 1929–June 1951*. Berkeley, California: University of California Press, 1992.

———. "The Meaning of Forgiveness." In *The Papers of Martin Luther King, Jr.: Volume VI: Advocate of the Social Gospel, September 1948–March 1963*, edited by Susan Englander, Susan Carson, Troy Jackson, and Gerald L. Smith, Vol. VI. Berkeley: University of California Press, 1992.

———. "The Personalism of J.M.E. McTaggart Under Criticism." In *The Papers of Martin Luther King, Jr.: Volume 2: Rediscovering Precious Values July 1951–November 1955*, edited by Clayborne Carson, Peter Holloran, Ralph Luker, and Penny A Russell. Berkeley: University of California Press, 1992.

———. "The Power of Nonviolence." In *A Testament of Hope: The Essential Writings and Speeches of Martin Luther King, Jr.*, edited by James Melvin Washington. San Francisco: Harper San Francisco, 1991.

———. "The Purpose of Education." In *The Papers of Martin Luther King, Jr.: Volume I: Called to Serve, January 1929–June 1951*, edited by Clayborne Carson and Ralph E. Luker. Berkeley, California: University of California Press, 1992.

———. "The Significant Contributions of Jeremiah to Religious Thought." In *The Papers of Martin Luther King, Jr.: Volume I: Called to Serve, January 1929–June 1951*. Berkeley, California: University of California Press, 1992.

———. "The Weakness of Liberal Theology I." In *The Papers of Martin Luther King, Jr.: Vol. VI: Advocate of the Social Gospel: September 1948–March 1963*, edited by Clayborne Carson, Peter Holloran, Ralph Luker, and Penny A Russell. Berkeley: University of California Press, 1992.

———. "The Weakness of Liberal Theology II." In *The Papers of Martin Luther King, Jr.: Vol. VI: Advocate of the Social Gospel: September 1948–March 1963*, edited by Clayborne Carson, Peter Holloran, Ralph Luker, and Penny A Russell. Berkeley: University of California Press, 1992.

———. *"Thou, Dear God": Prayers That Open Hearts and Spirits*. Edited by Lewis V. Baldwin. Boston: Beacon Press, 2012.

———. "To Dwight D. Eisenhower." In *The Papers of Martin Luther King, Jr., Volume IV: Symbol of the Movement, January 1957–December 1958*, edited by Clayborne Carson, Susan Carson, Adrienne Clay, Virginia Shadron, and Kieran Taylor, 2nd Ed edition. Berkeley: University of California Press, 2000.

———. "Untitled Montgomery Improvement Association Address." Boston University, 1959. Box 2, I–XI, Folder 2. King Collection.

———. *Where Do We Go from Here: Chaos or Community?*. Boston: Beacon Press, 1968.

———. *Why We Can't Wait*. New York: Harper and Row, 1964.

King, Sr., Martin Luther. *Daddy King: An Autobiography*. First Edition. New York: William Morrow & Co, 1980.

Kirby, Jimmy L., and Rufus Burrow. "Conceptions of God in the Thinking of Martin Luther King, Jr and Edgar S Brightman." *Encounter* 60, no. 3 (June 1, 1999): 283–305.

Kirk-Duggan, Cheryl A. *Misbegotten Anguish: A Theology and Ethics of Violence*. St. Louis, Mo: Chalice Press, 2001.

———. *Refiner's Fire: A Religious Engagement with Violence*. Minneapolis, MN: Fortress Press, 2001.

Knudson, Albert C. "A Vew of Atonement for the Modern World." *Crozer Quarterly* 23 (January 1946): 52–56.

———. *Basic Issues in Christian Thought*. New York: Abington-Cokesbury Press, 1950.

Ling, Peter J. *Martin Luther King Jr*. First Edition. Routledge, 2002.

Lovell, John. *Black Song: The Forge and the Flame; the Story of How the Afro-American Spiritual Was Hammered Out*. First Printing. New York: Macmillan Pub Co, 1972.

Lovell, John Jr. *Black Song: The Forge and the Flame the Story of How the Afro-American Spiritual*. New York: MacMillan, n.d.

Lowell, James Russell. "The Present Crisis." In *English Poetry III: From Tennyson to Whitman*, Vol. 42. The Harvard Classics. New York: P.F. Collier & Son, 1909.

Malcolm X. *Untitled Speech Delivered at Boston University*. Boston, 1960.

BIBLIOGRAPHY

Mays, Benjamin E. *The Negro's God as Reflected in His Literature.* New York: Russel & Russel, 1938.
McTaggart, J.M.E. "An Ontological Idealism." In *Contemporary British Philosophy*, edited by J.H. Muirhead. New York: Macmillan, 1924.
———. *Some Dogmas of Religion.* London: Edward Arnold, 1906.
Melugin, Roy F. "The Book of Isaiah and the Construction of Meaning." In *Writing and Reading the Scroll of Isaiah: Studies of an Interpretative Tradition*, edited by Craig C. Broyles and Craig A. Evans. Leiden: Die Deutsche Bibliothek, 1997.
Mieder, Wolfgang. *"Making a Way Out of No Way": Martin Luther King's Sermonic Proverbial Rhetoric.* New York: Peter Lang, 2010.
Montague, William Pepperell. *Belief Unbound: A Promethian Religion For The Modern World.* New Haven: Yale University Press, 1931.
Moses, Wilson Jeremiah. *Alexander Crummell: A Study of Civilization and Discontent.* New York: Oxford University Press, 1989.
———. *Classical Black Nationalism: From the American Revolution to Marcus Garvey.* New York: New York University Press, 1996.
Muers, Rachel. "Bonhoeffer, King, and Feminism: Problems and Possibilities." In *Bonhoeffer and King: Their Legacies and Import for Christian Social Thought*, edited by Willis Jenkins and Jennifer M. McBride. Minneapolis: Fortress Press, 2010.
Nygren, Anders. *Agape and Eros: A Study of the Christian Idea of Love.* 2 vols. London: Society for Promoting Christian Knowledge, 1932.
Oates, Stephen B. *Let the Trumpet Sound: A Life of Martin Luther King, Jr.* Reprint. New York: Harper Perennial, 1994.
Perkins, John M. *With Justice for All: A Strategy for Community Development.* Rev Upd edition. Place of publication not identified: Baker Books, 2011.
Phillips, Donald T. *Martin Luther King, Jr., on Leadership: Inspiration and Wisdom for Challenging Times.* Reissue edition. New York: Business Plus, 2000.
Pinn, Anthony B. "Introduction." In *Moral Evil and Redemptive Suffering: A History of Theodicy in African-American Religious Thought.* Gainesville, FL: University Press of Florida, 2002.
———. "I Wonder as I Wander: An Examination of the Problem of Evil in African American Religious Thought." Thesis (Ph.D.), Harvard University, 1994.
———. "Martin Luther King Jr.'s God, Humanist Sensibilities, and Moral Evil." *Theology Today* 65, no. 1 (April 1, 2008): 57–66.
———. *Understanding & Transforming the Black Church.* Eugene, OR: Cascade Books, 2010.
———. *Varieties of African American Religious Experience.* Minneapolis, MN: Fortress Press, 1998.
———. *Why, Lord?: Suffering and Evil in Black Theology.* New York: Continuum, 1995.
Ragsdale, Bartow Davis. *Story of Georgia Baptists.* Atlanta: Foote and Davies, 1938.
Rall, Harris Franklin. *Christianity: An Inquiry into Its Nature and Truth.* New York: Charles Scribner's Sons, 1940.
Raper, Arthur F. *Preface to Peasantry: A Tale of Two Black Belt Counties.* Chapel Hill: University of North Carolina Press, 1936.
Reddick, Lawrence Dunbar. *Crusader Without Violence;: A Biography of Martin Luther King, Jr.* First Edition. New York: Harper and Brothers Publishers, 1959.
Richardson, Alan. *Creeds In The Making.* Student Christian Movement Press, n.d.
Richardson, Sara V. Private Interview with Sara V. Richardson. Interview by Lewis V. Baldwin, May 29, 1987.
Ridgeway, Benjamin C. *Atlanta's Ebenezer Baptist Church.* Charleston, SC: Arcadia Publishing, 2009.
Shelton, Robert. "Songs A Weapon in Rights Battle." *New York Times*, August 20, 1962.
Skinner, John. *Prophecy and Religion: Studies in the Life of Jeremiah.* Cambridge: The University Press, 1922.
Smith, Ervin. *The Ethics of Martin Luther King, Jr.* New York: Edwin Mellen Press, 1981.

Smith, Kenneth L., and Ira G. Zepp. "Preface to the Third Printing." In *Search for the Beloved Community: The Thinking of Martin Luther King, Jr.* Valley Forge, Pa.: Judson Press, 1998.
———. *Search for the Beloved Community: The Thinking of Martin Luther King Jr.* Valley Forge: Judson Press, 1998.
Stewart, Maria. "Religion and the Pure Principles of Morality, the Sure Foundation on Which We Must Build." In *Maria W. Stewart, America's First Black Woman Political Writer: Essays and Speeches*, 4th Printing. Bloomington: Indiana University Press, 1987.
Sweet, Leonard I. *Black Images of America, 1784–1870*. First Edition. Norton, 1976.
Terrell, JoAnne Marie. *Power in the Blood?*. Maryknoll, N.Y.: Orbis, 1998.
Thurman, Howard. "Deep River." In *Deep River and the Negro Spiritual Speaks of Life and Death*. Richmond, Indiana: Friends United Press, 1975.
———. *Mysticism and the Experience of Love*. Wallingford, PA: Pendle Hill, 1961.
———. "The Negro Spiritual Speaks of Life and Death." In *Deep River and the Negro Spiritual Speaks of Life and Death*. Richmond, Indiana: Friends United Press, 1975.
Townes, Emilie, ed. *A Troubling in My Soul: Womanist Perspectives on Evil and Suffering*. Orbis Books, 1993.
———. "Notes on Appropriation and Reciprocity: Prompts from Bonhoeffer and King's Communitarian Ethic." In *Bonhoeffer and King: Their Legacies and Import for Christian Social Thought*, edited by Willis Jenkins and Jennifer M. McBride. Minneapolis: Fortress Press, 2010.
Townsend, A. M., ed. *The Baptist Standard Hymnal with Responsive Readings: A New Book for All Services*. Nashville, TN: Sunday School Publishing Board, 1924.
Towsend, Wilma, J.D. Bushell, Lucie Campbell, and E.W.D. Isaac, eds. *Gospel Pearls*. Nashville, TN: Sunday School Publishing Board, 1921.
Wagner, Clarence M. *Profiles of Black Georgia Baptist*. Atlanta: Bennett Brothers, 1980.
Walker, Alice. *In Search of Our Mothers' Gardens: Womanist Prose*. Orlando: Harcourt, 2004.
Walker, David. *David Walker's Appeal, in Four Articles, Together with a Preamble, to the Coloured Citizens of the World, but in Particular, and Very Expressly, to Those of the United States of America*. Edited by Charles M. Wiltse. New York: Hill and Wang, 1965.
Washington, Joseph. *The Politics of God: The Future of the Black Churches*. Boston: Beacon Press, 1967.
Watley, William D. *Roots of Resistance: The Nonviolent Ethic of Martin Luther King, Jr.* Valley Forge: Judson Press, 1985.
Welch, Kelly. "Black Criminal Stereotypes and Racial Profiling." *Journal of Contemporary Criminal Justice* 23, no. 3 (August 1, 2007): 276–88. doi:10.1177/1043986207306870.
Wentz, Cynthia Carsten. "Martin Luther King, Jr, and the American Mystical Tradition." *Sewanee Theological Review* 38, no. 2 (January 1, 1995): 105–13.
West, Cornel. *Prophesy Deliverance: An Afro-American Revolutionary Christianity*. Philadelphia: Westminster Press, 1982.
———. "Prophetic Christian as Organic Intellectual: Martin Luther King, Jr." In *The Cornel West Reader*, 425–34. New York: Basic Civitas Books, 2000.
———. "The Crisis in Contemporary American Religion." In *The Cornel West Reader*. New York, NY: Basic Civitas Books, 2000.
West, Cornel, and Christa Buschendorf. *Black Prophetic Fire*. Boston: Beacon Press, 2014.
Williams, Delores. "A Crucifixion Double Cross? The Violence of Our Images May Do More Harm Than Good." *Other Side* 29, no. 5 (September 1, 1993): 25–27.
———. "A Womanist Perspective on Sin." In *A Troubling in My Soul: Womanist Perspectives on Evil and Suffering*, edited by Emilie Maureen Townes. Maryknoll, N.Y.: Orbis Books, 1993.
———. "Black Women's Surrogacy Experience and the Christian Notion of Redemption." In *After Patriarchy: Feminist Transformations of the World Religions*, edited by Paula M Cooey, William R. Eakin, and Jay B. McDaniel. Maryknoll, N.Y.: Orbis Books, 1991.
———. *Sisters in the Wilderness: The Challenge of Womanist God-Talk*. Maryknoll, N.Y.: Orbis Books, 1993.

Wills, Richard W. *Martin Luther King, Jr., and the Image of God*. Oxford University Press, 2009.

Woodson, Carter G. *Negro Orators and Their Orations*. Washington, D.C.: The Associated Publishers, 1925.

———. *The History of the Negro Church*. Washington, D.C.: The Associated Publishers, 1921.

Zepp, Ira G. "The Intellectual Sources of the Ethical Thought of Martin Luther King, Jr., as Traced in His Writings with Special Reference to the Beloved Community,." Baltimore, 1971.

INDEX

agape, 12, 71, 71–72, 88n57, 91n104, 152, 160, 165, 170, 171, 178n50, 195
Asian women and redemptive suffering See Chung Hyung Kyung
atheist: atheistic humanism of Anthony Pinn, 126–131
atonement, 69–74, 82, 151–173. *See also* Cross

Baker, Ella, 152
Baker-Fletcher, Karen, xvi, 168
Baker-Fletcher, Garth, 171
Baldwin, Lewis, xiv, 10, 16, 17n2, 39, 55n103, 178n48, 182n92, 210n42
beloved community, 4, 14, 16, 135, 141, 142, 143, 152–153, 170, 171, 172, 185, 187, 203, 205–206
Birmingham Campaign of 1963, 42, 133–134, 143, 189; strong type black humanism. *See* Anthony Pinn; weak type black humanism; William R Jones
black-on-black crime, 191, 200–201
Black Theology, 198. *See also* James Cone
Bowne, Borden Parker, 94, 97, 106, 112, 130, 205
boycotts. *See also* Civil Disobedience: Montgomery Bus Boycott, xi, 10–11, 39, 44, 110, 140, 142; Georgian Newspaper, 27
Brightman, Edgar Sheffield, 3, 4, 6, 8, 12, 40–41, 45–48, 57n114, 57n117, 57n120, 59, 76–79, 82, 89n78, 91n100, 93, 95, 97–104, 105, 106–107, 112, 116n24, 129, 147n37, 205
Brown, Joanne Carlson, xv, 151, 154–155
Brown, Michael, 202, 209n32
Brown V Board of Education, 43, 55n99
Burrow Jr., Rufus, xiv, 46, 77, 102–103, 106, 111, 200–202

Carlyle, Thomas, 101
Cannon, Katie Geneva, xvi, 152, 165, 171–172, 173
civil disobedience, xiii, 138
Cone, James, xiii, 72–73, 198–199
Connor, Eugene "Bull", 133–134, 148n50, 149n57
Chivers, Walter, 16, 105
Chicago Campaign of 1965, 42–43, 188–190, 192, 193–194, 196, 198, 204
Cross, xi–xv, xvi, 104, 109, 113, 139, 187, 190, 197, 198–199, 202–203. *See also* atonement
Crummell, Alexander, 13–14, 15, 16, 112

Davis, George Washington, 6, 72, 74
DeWolf L. Harold, xii, xvi, 12, 93–94, 106–108, 112, 130, 139
DuBois, W.E.B, 16, 27, 38, 75, 112, 205

Ebenezer Baptist Church, 61, 72–73, 82, 93, 111, 113, 203, 205

225

Eros, 71

Flint water crisis, 194
fundamentalism, 7, 48, 61

Gandhi, Mohondas K, xiii–xiv, 41, 132, 138, 179n63, 203

Hegel, Georg Friedrich, 97, 105, 112

Johnson, Mordecai Wyatt, 132
Jones, William R., xiv, 124–125, 126, 127, 130, 131, 134, 143, 169, 205

King Sr., Martin "Daddy" Luther, 28–30, 31, 32, 40, 61, 67, 73, 78, 79, 81, 85n29, 109, 112–113, 205
King, Alberta Williams, 28, 51n46, 67
King, Alfred Daniel, 7
King, James Albert, 9
King, Delia Lindsay, 9, 12, 16, 28, 67, 112, 205
King, Coretta Scott, 93
King Jr., Martin Luther: King's black messianic vision, xiv, 9–11, 13–15, 17, 169, 196; King and creative suffering, 4–5, 12, 37, 38, 41–43, 66, 68, 68–69, 72, 80, 103, 132, 133, 136–137, 143, 152, 154, 158, 161, 162, 165, 166, 171, 175n14, 179n63, 185, 190, 192, 194, 195, 197–202. *See also* agape; non-violence; King's doctrine of divine omnipotence, 43, 46–47, 78, 95–96, 100, 101, 104, 106, 112, 128, 129–130, 139, 140, 141, 142–143; King's doctrine of non-violence, xiv, 4, 11, 12, 16, 42, 42–43, 67, 68, 69, 72, 93, 105, 131, 132, 134–135, 136, 138, 142–143, 143, 162; agape; creative suffering; King's earliest theodical crisis, 7–8; King's humor and theodicy, 55n103; King's outreach to gang members in Chicago, 190; King's kitchen vision, 39–41, 110, 111, 113, 203; King's personal trials, xii, 136–137, 140, 198; bloody Sunday; King's kitchen vision; King's rejection of theistic finitism, 78–79, 82, 89n78, 91n100, 94, 97–98; King's rejection of divine retribution, 8, 78, 81; King's sexist attitudes, 152; King's skepticsm in college, 32
Kirk-Duggan, Cheryl, 185, 186–188, 189–191
Knudson, A.C., 59, 69, 79, 82, 97, 157
Ku Klux Klan, 14
Kyung, Chung Hyun, 153, 178n53

Malcolm X, 11
mass incarceration, 191, 196
Matchless Power of God, xv, 40, 45, 46, 47, 91n100, 129, 141, 142. *See also* divine omnipotence
Mays, Benjamin, 32, 59, 61, 63, 81, 113, 123, 144n2, 205
Morehouse College, 32, 50n37, 51n49, 59–65, 75, 84n6, 85n17, 85n29

negro spirituals, xi, 3, 13, 33–38, 113
Niebuhr, Reinhold, xii, xiv, 60, 61, 63, 84n9, 166, 178n50, 210n38
Nygren, Anders, 59, 70, 71, 72, 82, 87n56

Personalism definition of, 76
Perkins, John, 194. *See also* CCDA
Pinn, Anthony, xiv, 126–131, 134, 139, 143, 205; classic formulation of the problem of evil, xi, 44
police brutality, xi, 69, 191, 196

quietism, 124, 125, 126, 130, 131, 132–143

Rall, Harris Franklin, 60, 74–80, 82, 97
Rauschenbusch, Walter, 3, 6, 64
Ray, Sandy, 73, 88n64
Royce, Josiah, 97

segregation, xi, 10, 42, 43, 44–45, 46, 55n99, 73, 135, 138, 162, 170, 185, 197, 210n34
Shiloh Baptist Church, 26
Southern Christian Leadership Conference (SCLC), 14, 32, 152, 190
Stewart, Maria, 14

Washington, Booker T., 27
Walker, David, 13–14, 16, 112
West, Cornel, 21n44, 192, 198
Wieman, Henry Nelson, 94, 107, 129

INDEX

Williams, Adam Daniel (A.D.), 27–29, 30, 31, 32, 205
Williams, Jennie Celeste Parks, 7–8, 12, 28, 30, 78, 79, 81
Williams, Willis, 26–27, 30, 113, 205
Williams, Delores, xv, 151, 153, 153–161, 172, 205
Womanism. *See* Delores Williams; Jacquelyn Grant; Joanne Marie Terrell; Katie Cannon

ABOUT THE AUTHOR

Mika Edmondson is the pastor of New City Fellowship, a cross-cultural church plant in Southeast Grand Rapids. He earned a PhD in systematic theology from Calvin Seminary, where he studied Martin Luther King Jr.'s theology of suffering. He enjoys writing and speaking about how King's ideas inform our understandings of the gospel. He is happily married to Dr. Christina Edmondson and has two beautiful daughters, Zoe and Shiloh.